Praying
Each Day
of the Year

Nicholas Hutchinson FSC

Matthew James Publishing Ltd

Also available:

   1 898 366 30 6   Praying Each Day of the Year - volume 1: (January - April)
   1 898 366 31 4   Praying Each Day of the Year - volume 2: (May - August)

First published 1998 by:
Matthew James Publishing Ltd,
19 Wellington Close, Chelmsford, Essex CM1 2EE

© 1998 Nicholas Hutchinson FSC

ISBN: 1 898366 32 2

Cover design by Jez Coan
Printed by J W Arrowsmith Ltd., Bristol

*Dedicated
to the memory of
Brother Damian Lundy, FSC
(1944-1996)
who shared the Good News with many
and bore sickness bravely.*

Contents

Foreword

A warm welcome to all who have taken up this book, including teachers, individuals using the book for personal prayer, parish leaders accompanying RCIA and other groups, priests and deacons who are keen to incorporate into their homilies an appropriate story, and those who are sick or housebound whose prayer for others is much valued.

You are reading the third of three volumes that together offer for every day of the year a reflection and a prayer. The reflection is a "picture-story" - either a story itself or, more often, details of a specific event whose anniversary it is on that day. The accompanying prayer has been written around the theme. The book illustrates very practically how we can reflect on daily life and experiences and, living in God's Presence, can bring everything to him in prayer. It is hoped that the material may be of help in promoting a sense of reflection and prayerfulness that can pervade the day.

In 1997 a draft version of the book was used in different ways across the country in various schools, homes and parishes, but the book is written in the first instance for use by teachers in secondary schools. Teachers have "tried and tested" much of the material, and I have been very grateful for their comments and suggestions, as also those of various individuals who have used the draft version of the book for their personal reflection and prayer each day, especially several people who are seriously ill. Someone has remarked that "the reflective and prayerful approach of the book clearly proclaims that Jesus is the Way, the Truth and the Life".

Produced after much research, the book is offered in the first instance to busy Form Tutors who don't normally have much time or access to good resources to be producing more than a prayer as the *"daily act of collective worship"* for their own class at the start of each day. Teachers have commented already that this book offers ready-to-use quality material that helps to promote a sense of awareness, wonder and appreciation, that can contribute to the personal and spiritual development of individuals.

May all who use this book find help in reflecting and praying and walking in God's presence each day.

Introduction

The value of "picture-stories"

The most famous of all photographs of the Vietnam War was the horrific scene of several children suffering from the effects of napalm, pictured as they were running along a road, towards the camera. It is recognised that the photograph, taken in August 1972 and seen by millions throughout the world, was instrumental in bringing the war to an end. How powerful a picture can be! For hundreds of years, stained-glass windows presented picture-images mainly to those who could not read the Bible. Through her TV programmes and her books, Sister Wendy Becket has helped many people to *"really see"* and understand various meanings in paintings, illustrating the insight of D.H.Lawrence that *"the sense of wonder is the sixth sense, and it is the natural religious sense."* Saint Augustine has said that *"our whole business in this life is to restore to health the eye of the heart by which God may be seen"*, and we acknowledge that Christian education should promote in people *"a way of seeing"* (Evelyn Underhill), developing what William Blake calls *"the inward eye".*

Stories, too, can be "pictures" that convey a profound message, bringing it all alive. Aesop's fables have remained popular for 2,600 years. The Brothers Grimm recorded such stories as 'Little Red Riding Hood', teaching in a subtle way the need for personal safety. "Picture-stories" can also serve as "hooks" on which to "hang" what may be significant to an individual. Jesus told stories as a means of conveying the deep - yet simple - message of the Good News. That great story-writer, Charles Dickens, remarked that *"the Parable of the Prodigal Son is the best short story in the English language"* - not simply because of the poetry of the words, but because it is a timeless story that can reveal more each time it is heard. Some of Dickens' own stories portrayed a "hidden message" of the need for social change.

Some of the best stories are those that leave questions for the individual to ponder, and so can be more powerful in conveying a message than can an 'explanation' that attempts to summarise the message, just as adverts that leave something to the imagination are the most effective. It has been said that *"Jesus told stories and asked questions; we tend to moralise and give answers!"* It is hoped that each day's reflection and prayer will leave people with questions to ask of themselves in looking upon life critically and creatively, as well as leading them in ways of praying. The material in the book focuses on the specific rather than on what is general, and may encourage people to be reflective and prayerful based on the "here and now" of their daily lives. Some have commented that they have gained insights into how items from the news and newspapers can readily be turned to reflection and prayer.

Growing in awareness of the Presence of God

As the mind wanders during the day, it is likely that a recent "picture-story" is thought of again, encouraging the individual to reflect further. This thoughtfulness can, in turn, become part of a growing sense of being in the Presence of God. *"Prayer is about awakening to the Presence of God within us"* (Laurence Freeman), and *"the more we find Christ within, the more we become aware of Christ without"* (Bede Griffiths). As our young people are encouraged to acknowledge and recognise God's presence in themselves and in others, their lives and the lives of those around them will be enriched. It is true to say that the more we place ourselves in God's Presence, the more likely we are to have the same attitude and actions as Jesus: *"In his Presence we are bound to love"* (Evelyn Underhill).

The witness of reflection and prayer

Occasionally we experience or read about how an individual praying in great sincerity has a profound effect on others, and we can recall Pope Paul VI's memorable words:

People *"today listen more willingly to witnesses than to teachers, and if they do listen to teachers, it is because they are witnesses."*

(Evangelii Nuntiandi, 41)

Twice in his weekly articles in *'The Tablet'*, John Harriot reflected on Brother Alphonsus, a De La Salle Brother who had taught him. Harriot wrote of: *"the effect of seeing him pray and how he seemed to make God visible. Unobtrusively, unselfconsciously, the faith that inspired him was woven in and out of all he did. He was not given to pious exhortations. His pulpit was himself. Above all he was the kindest and gentlest of men."* (*'The Tablet'*: 14/4/90). He went on to write about how Alphonsus was one of many who quietly and perseveringly lived his faith and made it real to all who came under his influence.

The crime-writer, Agatha Christie, wrote in her autobiography:

I can picture one teacher there - I can't recall her name.
She was short and spare, and I remember her eager jutting chin.
Quite unexpectedly one day
(in the middle, I think, of an arithmetic lesson)
she suddenly launched forth on a speech on life and religion.
"All of you," she said,
"every one of you, will pass through a time when you will face despair.

If you never face despair,
you will never have faced, or become, a Christian, or known a Christian life.
To be a Christian
you must face and accept the life that Christ faced and lived:
you must enjoy things as he enjoyed things,
be as happy as he was at the marriage at Cana,
know the peace and happiness that it means
to be in harmony with God and with God's will.
But you must also know, as he did,
what it means to be alone in the Garden of Gethsemane,
to feel that all your friends have forsaken you,
that those you love and trust have turned away from you,
and that God himself has forsaken you.
Hold on then to the belief that that is not the end.
If you love, you will suffer,
and if you do not love, you do not know the meaning of a Christian life."
She then returned to the problems of compound interest
with her usual vigour,
but it is odd that those few words,
more than any sermon I ever heard, remained with me
and, years later, they were to come back to me and give me hope
at a time when despair had me in its grip.
*She was a dynamic figure and also, I think, a **fine** teacher;*
I wish I could have been taught by her longer.

[Agatha Christie: 'An Autobiography'
(William Collins, 1977) page 150]

Both examples are of teachers who reflected on their personal experiences, and shared insights with the young people entrusted to their care - reflections that would bear fruit in years to come.

Good schools promote and cultivate goodness, and we are invited to fill our minds and share with others those things that are *"noble and good, praiseworthy and right, honourable and inspiring"* (Phil 4^{4-9}). This book offers in a clear form many insights from our heritage that can be shared and passed on to others - insights that may be of lasting value to our students as they face the challenge to review their priorities. The reflections are presented in ways that attempt to engage interest and imagination during our *"daily act of collective worship"* in school (The Education Reform Act, 1988, s.6).

Some teachers will be of other than the Catholic faith, and some may choose to involve the students fully in the giving of the reflection and prayer. In time to come, the practice of reflecting and praying may develop in such a way that members of the school community from the youngest to the oldest may be able to share with others the fruits and insights of their own reflection and reading and life-experience and, in God's Presence, bring everything together in prayer. The following words of Pope Paul VI refer to people of all ages:

> *Above all, the Gospel must be proclaimed by witness.*
> *Take a Christian, or a handful of Christians*
> *who, in the midst of their own community,*
> *show their capacity for understanding and acceptance,*
> *their sharing of life and destiny with other people,*
> *their solidarity with the efforts of all*
> *for whatever is noble and good.*
> *Let us suppose that, in addition,*
> *they radiate in an altogether simple and unaffected way*
> *their faith in values that go beyond current values,*
> *and their hope in something that is not seen*
> *and that one would not dare to imagine.*
> *Through this wordless witness,*
> *these Christians stir up irresistible questions*
> *in the hearts of those who see how they live:*
> *Why are they like this?*
> *Why do they live in this way?*
> *What or who is it that inspires them?*
> *Why are they in our midst?*
> *Such a witness is already*
> *a silent proclamation of the Good News,*
> *and a very powerful and effective one.*

(Evangelii Nuntiandi, 21)

Young people need an experience of reflection and prayer.

In today's society with vast knowledge at our fingertips, we need to be careful to avoid "information overload". Peter Walker, a former Secretary of State for Wales, remarked that the hour he set aside every morning simply to reflect and "think his thoughts", with no distractions around him, enabled him to keep everything in perspective and be creative. That extraordinary man, Nelson Mandela, said: *"Although it was a tragedy to spend twenty-seven years in prison, one of the advantages was the ability to sit down and think. This is one of the things I miss most."*

The Book of Proverbs tells us that, *"Where there is no vision, the people perish"* (29[18]), reminding us of Plato's words that *"the unreflected life is not worth living."* Jesus *"offered reflections on every aspect of daily life"*, Pope John Paul remarked during his visit to Scotland (1/6/82). The book illustrates how we can reflect on daily life. Reflections can then be brought together in prayer in the same way as the "collecting" of thoughts and intentions in the prayer that was once called the "Collect" in the Eucharist. The material in this book offers the all-important perspective of unity of life and human experience, seeking to integrate daily life rather than fragment and compartmentalise into "sacred" and "secular". Reflecting and praying may help to clarify our vision, review our priorities, and gain insights into how to learn from our experiences, as well as growing in Christ.

'Praying Each Day of the Year' may help in introducing some students to a spiritual life. Respecting the autonomy of each person, use of this book offers an experience of reflection and prayer in which some of the young people will participate fully. Some students may find it interesting or helpful to 'observe' people praying. Others may, in time, *"pray in their inner room"* (Mt 6[6]) and *"seek first the kingdom of God"* (Mt 6[33]). Some may take away "seeds" that may come to fruition only in the Lord's good time - not necessarily in ours!

The sharing of a reflection and prayer can be one of the means of Christian formation and a powerful means for people to grow. This particular sharing is an aspect of one of the key elements in pastoral care - wanting to *"be with"* the young people and hoping to *"touch (or win) their hearts"*, offering an opportunity and an invitation to grow. The quality of a teacher's *"being with"* reflects the beliefs that the teacher has for the students, and has an impact on what the young people think of themselves. Indeed, one expression of *"invitational teaching"* is for the teacher to give his or her students *"a vision of their own greatness"* (Pullias).

"You send strange invitations, Sir," says Beauty in 'Beauty and the Beast'. Reflecting and praying with others can be a means of extending "invitations":

- invitations to grow in respect and appreciation of self and others;
- invitations to grow in responsibility, and serve those in need;
- invitations to grow in awareness and wonder, in understanding and wisdom (*"Wonder is the seed of knowledge"* remarked Francis Bacon);
- invitations to gain insights into what is of real value, and be life-affirming;
- invitations to discover *"the kingdom within"*, seeking *"life in all its fullness"* as Jesus promised, becoming *"fully alive"* for the glory of God (cf. St Irenaeus).

Indeed, we read in *"The Common Good"* (of the Bishops' Conference of England and Wales, 1996 [37]) that

> *"it is the destiny and duty of each human being*
> *to become more fully human."*

Teaching itself is a way of *"being with"* people, and can include a mutual accompanying on the journey of growing in faith (cf. Emmaus: Lk 24[13-35]). Sometimes we have responded inadequately to young people's thirst for religious experience, yet *"it is necessary that the young know Christ who walks.... alongside each person as a friend"* (Pope John Paul II: 'Crossing the Threshold, p126). Use of this book offers an opportunity for people to walk in God's Presence.

Use in school

Many teachers will attest to the value of praying briefly **for** the students before praying **with** them - whether taking a moment to pray for them on the way to school or whilst walking to class, being conscious that *"if the Lord does not build the house, it is in vain that the builders labour."* (Ps 127[1]). We place our trust in the Lord to whom one of his friends said: *"Lord, teach us to pray"* (Lk 11[1]).

"The daily acts of collective worship" are part of the shared mission of the whole school community, whether they take place as class assemblies or larger group assemblies. As with various pastoral initiatives in secondary schools, if the sharing of a reflection and prayer is started as Year 7 arrive, they will assume it is the usual practice, and so will accept it as the norm for future years.

It is necessary to read through the material at least a day in advance. You may reflect on it personally yourself, and then have other ideas to contribute, so that it will become a personal reflection on your part. On days when it is decided to use the material in the format given, the numbering of each paragraph lends itself to the active participation of several people. If others are to be involved in the sharing of the reflection and prayer, you will want to encourage their preparation of the material in advance. Sometimes teachers take it for granted that readings will be presented clearly, with sufficient volume, and slowly enough! Do alert readers to any unusual words. The fact that students lead or present part of the reflection and prayer may also become one of the means for their growth in self-confidence and self-esteem.

If the prayer to be used is short, it is advisable for it to be written in advance on the board or for use with the overhead projector (prepared in either case before the students are in the room). A sense of involvement and participation and "ownership" is increased if everyone is invited to make such vocal prayer together, and we know that what is visual (in this case, the written word) is understood and retained much longer than what is simply heard. Such a visual stimulus encourages recall and further reflection later in the day.

Many of us have tended to limit ourselves to use only two or three 'formal' prayers as public prayer. Profound as those prayers are, the young people will not necessarily experience that prayer can be 'worded' in a way that is specific to situations in their daily lives. Prayer can be informal and familiar, and Carlo Carretto reminds us that *"prayer takes place in the heart, rather than in the head."* Deliberately the prayers here have not been written in formal or polished English, but generally in the style of spoken English. It is hoped that the style of the prayers will help promote the "speaking from the heart" that prayer is. Having read and used some of the prayers in this book, prayer-leaders may well feel encouraged to extemporise prayer in public, or write down words in advance that will be used as prayer.

On some days a quote or "punchline" may be repeated after the prayer - all the more effective if the prayer-leader avoids making an additional comment, thereby tending to elicit a personal response from some when recalled later in the day. To attempt to "preach" what kind of response there "should" be is likely to put people off and limit the action of the Holy Spirit!

Not all teachers fully appreciate that all the positive elements of a reflection and prayer can be negated by the attitude of one of the prayer-leaders or by the delivery or manner of delivery of comments or notices that might follow.

For those who wish (and have the time) to use the material more extensively (whether for a longer time in class, or for a year or school assembly), additional background information and some biblical references are included at the end of most days (✍). These details may help both teachers and students to introduce further ideas, and the cross-referring between some days may be of help. The additional background information is also there to help promote the thirst for knowledge, wisdom and understanding in the young people who themselves read the material, possibly following up by using CD-ROM encyclopedias, etc.

Teachers will find that materials set out for weekends and for holiday times - particularly the month of August - will provide further resource material for use on school days!

For year or school assemblies, some hymns are listed to offer a ready choice, suitable to the theme of the day (𝄞). Occasionally reference is made to a poem. Such poems are the more commonly known and, for convenience, all are to be found in *"The Nation's Favourite Poems"* (BBC Books 0-563-38782-3), being a compilation of the nation's top 100 favourite poems, according to a Radio 4 nationwide poll in 1995.

'Praying Each Day of the Year' is printed in three conveniently-sized volumes. At the back of the appropriate volume appear materials for such "moveable feasts" as Ash Wednesday, the days of Holy Week, Pentecost, Christ the King and Family Fast Days. The book's comprehensive index should help to locate themes, people, and particular passages, especially if you recall only a few key words of a familiar passage.

Many will find very useful a resource that is printed at the back of Volume 1 -*"Locating passages in the Bible"*, with references to some 600 key events and writings from both the Old and the New Testaments, listed in a very clear and user-friendly way. Too often we have thought of a passage but have been unable to locate it! Many of the prayers in the book have drawn their inspiration from scripture.

Volume 2 has an Appendix of 70 prayers for use on special occasions. This volume concludes with an Appendix of 60 prayers based on Gospel passages. These prayers may be of help each day in recalling that we are in the Presence of God.

As you take up this book each day, it will be in the spirit of all that is presented here if, briefly, you think and pray for all others in different schools and situations who will be using the same material as you. Do pray that we may all become more reflective and prayerful and *"fully alive"* because we have shared an experience of something of God's love. And so may all of us who use this book - fellow pilgrims on the road to Emmaus - each be able to share our own story of what happens to us on our journey through life, and how we recognise Jesus in our midst.

Brother Nicholas Hutchinson, FSC
De La Salle House,
83 Carr Lane East,
Liverpool L11 4SF

Praying
Each Day
of the Year

1 SEPTEMBER

1 In the southern United States, Helen Keller lost her sight and hearing through illness when she was only 2-years old. Annie Sullivan, who had herself been blind, taught the teenage Helen how to speak and how to read Braille writing.

2 On this day in 1904 the deaf and blind Helen Keller graduated with honours from Radcliffe College in Cambridge, Massachusetts. Helen wrote the following words about using well whatever senses we have:

3 *"We differ, blind and seeing,*
one from another
- not in our senses,
but in the use we make of them,
in the imagination and courage
with which we seek wisdom
beyond our senses...

4 *"I have walked with people*
whose eyes are full of light,
but who see nothing
in wood, sea or sky,
nothing in the city streets,
nothing in books.

5 *"What a witless masquerade is this seeing!*
It were better far
to sail for ever in the night of blindness,
with sense and feeling and mind,
than to be thus content
with the mere act of seeing.

6 *"They have the sunset, the morning skies,*
the purple of distant hills
- yet their souls voyage
through this enchanted world
with a barren stare."

7 *Let us pray:*

Lord,
we pray that we may live
in such a way
that we value all that is good in our lives
and never take anyone or anything
for granted.
Amen.

🖎 *Some sighted people use their vision to make distinctions between people for the purposes of prejudice e.g. based on what they can see of others' clothes, appearance, colour, etc. It could be argued that those sighted people would not be prejudiced if, in fact, they were blind on meeting people, because they would never physically see what otherwise would lead them to choose to be prejudiced.*

🖎 *Helen Keller: 1880-1968 - see also 2 January and 1, 3 June and 27 December. For an alternative prayer, see 16 September, emphasising each sense.*

🖎 *See 2 January for Braille writing.*

🎼 Christ is our king; God's Spirit is in my heart; I give my hands; I saw the grass, I saw the trees; Lay your hands

1 The comedian, Roy Castle, was a popular entertainer and presented the programme *"Record-breakers"*. He developed lung cancer, thought to be from passive smoking. Before his death from lung cancer in 1994, Roy was asked what had been the best day of his life. A committed Christian, he said - with his characteristic smile - *"My best day is yet to come!"*

2 *We'll pray using the words of a Muslim prayer:*

**"Lord, may the end of my life
be the best part of my life.
May my closing acts
be my best acts,
and may the best of my days
be the day when I shall meet you."**

3 Always very cheerful, Roy Castle died on this day in 1994, still fund-raising for lung cancer research shortly before he died. His 'International Centre for Lung Cancer Research' was opened in Liverpool four years after his death.

✍ *The great poet and sculptor, Leonardo da Vinci, remarked:*
"Whilst I thought I was learning to live, I have been learning how to die."

✍ *Roy Castle, OBE: 31/8/1932-2/9/94*

✍ *Roy attributed the lung cancer to passive smoking on inhaling smoke-filled air in clubs where he played the trumpet as a young man. He acted in one of the* 'Doctor Who' *films, and presented* 'Record-breakers', *associated with* 'The Guinness Book of Records'.

✍ *The Roy Castle Lung Cancer Foundation was built from money donated. The building was formally opened by Roy's wife, Fiona, and Sir Cliff Richard. Its address is:*
*The International Centre
for Lung Cancer Research,
200 London Road,
Liverpool L3 9TA*

✍ *Shown a draft copy of today's material, Fiona Castle read out the prayer at the opening of a Flower Festival in Liverpool, 13/5/98.*

✍ *For similar thoughts, see 15 November.*

♪ All that I am; Do not worry *("go do your best today")*; Father, I place into your hands; Follow me; Here I am, Lord; I give my hands; Sing a simple song

3 SEPTEMBER

1 *Let us pray:*

Lord, isn't your creation wasteful?
Fruits never equal
    the seedling's abundance;
    springs scatter water;
    the sun gives out enormous light.

2 May your bounty
    teach me greatness of heart.
May your magnificence
    stop me being mean.

3 Seeing you
    a prodigal and open-handed giver,
    may I give unstintingly
    like a king's son
    - like your own Son. Amen.

This is a prayer by Archbishop Helder Camara (born 1909) of Rio de Janeiro, Brazil.

Morning has broken; O Lord my God, the Father of creation; Thank you for fathers

1 Although they know that sleep is very important, some Christians get up a little earlier than they need to, so that they can pray. They see their relationship with God to be even more important than sleep.

2 Although nourishment from food is very important, some Christians delay eating for a few seconds so that they can pray, giving thanks for the food before them. It is a way of reminding themselves that their relationship with God is even more important. It is also a reminder to give thanks for all good things that have come to them.

3 Albert Schweitzer was a missionary doctor. In Africa he set up a hospital and a leper-colony for the very poor. Before sitting down to eat a meal, Albert Schweitzer was always heard to quote from one of the psalms of the Bible: *"We thank the Lord for he is good, and his loving kindness lasts forever."*

4 **Let's pause to express thanks for the good things in our lives: - for people who have given us love and friendship, encouragement and support...**

5 **- for our talents and health, and for the opportunities that come to us...**

6 **- for the beauty that we see, and the inspiration we receive...**

7 Albert Schweitzer died on this day in 1965.

> *"We thank the Lord for he is good, and his loving kindness lasts forever."*
>
> Ps (135) 136[1]

There can be a pause after each of the 3 phrases of the prayer.

Albert Schweitzer was born on 14/1/1875 in Alsace, formerly French territory which then became part of Germany. He died on 4/9/1965. See 14 January.

Praying before or after meals is sometimes called "the grace".

Do not worry; Father, I place into your hands; Lord of all hopefulness; My Lord, my master; Thank you for fathers; Thank you for giving me

5 SEPTEMBER

1 Mother Teresa worked with the poorest of the poor in Calcutta, India. She said that

"being unwanted
is the most terrible disease
a human being can experience."

2 On this day in 1997 she died. She wrote this about dying:

"When you die,
the Lord will not ask you
how much you have done with your life,
*but how much **love***
you have put into the doing."

3 *Let us pray:*

God our Father,
  may all of life's experiences
  lead us to grow
  as people who always put love
  into all that we do.
May we live in such a way
  that our attitude
  and words and actions
  reflect to all people
  their own value, dignity
  and self-worth,
  helping people
  to feel wanted and appreciated
  for who they are.
Amen.

✍ *Mother Teresa: 27/8/10 - 5/9/97. See also 9 Feb; 4 March; 13 June; 13 July; 27 Aug; 12,20 September.*

♪ All that I am; Father, I place into your hands; Take my hands; There is a world

1 On this day in 1997, the funeral of Diana, the young Princess of Wales, was held in Westminster Abbey. The following words were sung, and they can be our words of commitment today:

2 *I would be true*
   - for there are those who trust me.
   I would be pure
   - for there are those who care.
   I would be strong
   - for there is much to suffer.
   I would be brave
   - for there is much to dare.

3 *I would be friend of all,*
   the foe, the friendless.
   I would be giving,
   and forget the gift.
   I would be humble,
   for I know my weakness.
   I would look up,
   laugh, love and live.

The words, "I would be true" , were sung at the funeral to "The Derry Air" (often also called "Danny Boy"). The Biblical passage of 1 Cor 13 on "love" was read at the service by the Prime Minister, Tony Blair.

See also 31 August. 31 million people in Britain watched Diana's funeral on TV, with 2 billion around the world. 10,000 tonnes of flowers were left outside St James' Palace, Kensington Palace, and Buckingham Palace.

Elton John's tribute to Diana, and sung at her funeral - "Candle in the Wind '97" - was declared by the 'Guinness Book of Records' to be the biggest-selling single ever. In October 1997 it overtook Bing Crosby's 'White Christmas' of some 30 million sales worldwide. The difference was that Crosby's sales took place over 55 years, while "Candle in the Wind '97" took only 37 days to pass Crosby's total.

The national expressions of grief at the death of Diana have been compared with events at the early death in 1503 of the young Queen Elizabeth (Elizabeth of York) who was the wife of King Henry VII, the first Tudor king. Henry VII's symbol - called the "Tudor rose" - incorporated the red and the white roses of the rival dynastic houses of Lancaster and York, as their marriage brought to an end at last the 30-year-long "Wars of the Roses". Elizabeth was called the "White Rose" of the House of York, and she gave birth to the "Rosebush of England", Prince Arthur, whose early death left the throne to his younger brother who became King Henry VIII. Whilst Princess Diana was called "England's Rose" in Elton John's song, and had been referred to as the "Queen of Hearts", the image of the same name on playing cards is reputed to be that of Elizabeth of York.

Make me a channel *(which was sung this day at the funeral)*; Lord, make me a means

7 SEPTEMBER

1 From 1664, London suffered for 3 years from the Great Plague - a name given to the deadly bubonic plague. On this day in 1665 a parcel of cloth from London arrived at the house of a tailor in the Derbyshire village of Eyam. The pieces of cloth were damp, and so were spread out in the house to dry. A few days later, George Vickers (the tailor) became very ill and died. Soon the other members of his family died, and the infection began to spread through the village, killing others.

2 William Mompesson (the vicar) gathered the people together. He urged them not to leave the village, as that would only spread the deadly plague and would kill thousands. With great courage, the villagers decided to stay. They put up notices on the roads to warn others to keep away. They arranged for people in other villages to leave food at certain places, paid for by money left in running water or in bowls of vinegar.

3 Month by month, families buried relatives killed by the bubonic plague. One day the vicar's wife, Catherine, mentioned that the air had a sweet smell - but the vicar was horrified: that was one of the first signs of having the plague. She was one of 259 to die of plague in the small village of 350 people - 74% of them died. We can only begin to imagine the experiences of the villagers in those 13 months after the plague arrived in that bundle of cloth from London.

4 *Let us pray:*

Lord Jesus,
the bravery and courage
and self-sacrifice
of the villagers of Eyam
remind us of your words
that there is no greater love
than for someone
    to lay down their life
    for their friends. *Jn 15¹²*
We pray for courage
when difficult times come upon us.
We pray, too, for the generosity
to think of others before ourselves.
Amen.

📖 *For the Great Plague, see also 26 Feb and 21 Aug. The timing of the Great Plague of London (1664-6) should not be confused with the Black Death (also bubonic plague) which raged throughout Europe in the mid 1300s.*

📖 *After their long 13 months, the surviving villagers made a huge bonfire of all their clothes and bedding and furniture, and they fumigated their houses - all to make sure that nothing of the disease remained. 11th October 1666 saw the last death from bubonic plague in the village. Every year since then, a religious service has been held in Eyam on that date in thanksgiving for the courage and self-sacrifice of the villagers.*

📖 *Why did the villagers of Eyam leave their money in vinegar or running water? Why did some people think that the Great Fire of London in 1666 was a blessing in disguise?*

📖 *A nursery rhyme tells of some symptoms of the bubonic plague:*
"Ring-a-ring o' rosies, A pocket full of posies, A-tishoo! A-tishoo! We all fall down."
Marked rings on the skin that resembled roses were a sign of the plague, along with repeated sneezing. The custom of saying "Bless you" after someone has sneezed, stems from when sneezing was observed as one of the early symptoms of the plague. "A pocket full of posies" *may refer either to another symptom (the victim seeming to detect a sweet smell in the air) or the practice of carrying posies of scented flowers (or a pomander of fruit and cloves) thought to ward off illness or at least any unpleasant smells. The symptoms led on to death:* "We all fall down", *says the nursery rhyme.*

🎵 Christ be beside me; Lay your hands

1 Off the coast of Northumberland in the North East, storms in the North Sea can be very strong. Yesterday, 7th September, marks the day in 1838 when rough storms brought out a response of great bravery.

2 Observing the storm was Grace Darling, the daughter of a lighthouse-keeper. The steamer *'Forfarshire'* with 63 people on board had run aground on an island. Grace could see 9 survivors clinging to a rock. Although she was small and her health was poor, the 22-year old Grace launched the small wooden rowing boat with her father, William. Together they rowed the mile to the survivors, across huge waves at the height of the storm.

3 When they set off from the lighthouse, they knew they would not be able to row back to land unless some of the survivors were fit enough to help. They rescued 4 men and a woman. William and two of the survivors rowed back to the wreck for the others.

4 Grace Darling was awarded a medal for her courage and bravery. She became a national heroine and, after many requests for a lock of her hair, she joked that she was going bald! Grace died of tuberculosis (T.B.) only 4 years later, aged 26.

5 *Let us pray:*

Lord, we know that each of us
  will experience difficulties
  of various kinds
  at different times in our lives.
We pray for courage at those times,
  but we also pray
  for courage and strength
  to join others
  and be of support
  when *they* are in difficulty.
Amen.

✍ *Grace Darling: 1815-20/10/1842*

✍ *"There is no greater love than for someone to lay down their life for their friends" - Jn 15[12]*

🎶 Christ be beside me; I will be with you *("stormy waters")*; Walk with me, O my Lord *("the storms that threaten me")*

9 · SEPTEMBER

1 If someone asked
what happened exactly a year ago today,
would we remember?

2 If someone was to ask
what happened in Britain
on this day in 1752,
the answer would be "nothing"!

3 There **was** no 9th September
in Britain in 1752.
The day after the 2nd September
became the 14th.
11 days were "lost"!
Why was this?

4 The arrangement of days in the year
- the calendar -
had been worked out in Roman times,
but the Romans
had made a slight miscalculation
for the length of the year
(being the exact time
that the earth goes round the sun,
giving us the different seasons.)

5 And so, by 1752, nature's seasons
were getting more out of line:
the calendar was 11 days out,
resulting in Spring, for example,
gradually occurring sooner
as a date in the calendar.
In the same way, the dates associated
with planting and harvesting
were changing.

6 The government realised
that they had better alter the calendar,
as many other countries had already done.
And so it was decided
that 11 days should be "lost".

7 It seems funny to us,
but some people thought
that they were being "cheated"
out of 11 days,
and that they would die 11 days sooner!

There were riots in parts of the country
as some people demanded
that the government
give them back their "stolen" 11 days!

8 *Let us pray,*
**thinking of those who look back
and wish they had an extra day
or more time:**
- **those who have too little time
for what they are expected to do;**
- **those who have lost
a sense of balance and proportion
in their lives;**
- **those who feel
that they have made a mess
of everything
and would like to be able
to start again.**

9 We pray, too,
for those who might wish for less time:
- **those who are worried
about what might happen;**
- **those who are in despair;**
- **those who suffer
hours of pain and illness;**
- **those who are in prison
or being tortured;**
- **those who wish to die.**

10 **On all these people, Lord,
we ask your blessing.**

longer than the "solar year", gaining a whole day every 128 years. By 1582, the "vernal equinox" (the date - in March - when day and night are equal in length) took place a fortnight earlier than in Caesar's time, affecting the timing of religious holidays (such as Easter, being the first Sunday after the full moon following the vernal equinox), and the dates associated with planting and harvesting. Pope Gregory XIII decreed that the date after 4th October 1582 should be 15th October, eliminating the 10 days by which the calendar had become "out of season" with the solar year and nature. Accuracy would be maintained by removing 3 days every 400 years - and so leap years now occur every 4 years except if the century year cannot be divided by 400.

✍ Britain, a Protestant nation, decided not to accept the Pope's ruling. It was only in 1752 (as mentioned in today's reflection) that Britain and its Colonies abandoned the Julian Calendar and adopted the Gregorian Calendar (by which time the calendar was not 10 but 11 days out). Britain's late change-over explains why reference books in countries other than Britain record, for example, the birth of Sir Isaac Newton as 4/1/1643 (Gregorian Calendar), whilst British texts record 25/12/1642 (according to the Julian - or "Old Style" Calendar by which England was still living at the time).

✍ The Soviet Union adopted the Gregorian - or "New Style" - Calendar in 1918, which explains why their "October Revolution" (Oct 24th/25th in the Julian Calendar) is now marked in the month of November (6th/7th Nov, Gregorian Calendar). Some countries linked with the Greek churches hold religious feastdays according to the Julian Calendar, celebrating Christmas some 13 days after other countries.

✍ "Carpe diem - Seize the present day, trusting the morrow as little as may be."
(Horace, 65-8 BC;
quoted in the film, 'Dead Poet's Society')

✍ Or could use the prayer from 23 March.

✍ Could use this material on any day from 3rd-13th September inclusive, adapting the date in the first line of the third paragraph above, accordingly. It can be used to good effect with new members of a school in the month of September - possibly then using or adapting one of the prayers from 9 Feb, 6 April, 6 May, 2 June, 13 July, 20 Aug.

✍ It was Pope Gregory XIII (the 13th) who proposed the new "Gregorian Calendar" which we now follow. Before that time, the "Julian Calendar" (based on the "Julian Year" established by Julius Caesar in 46 B.C.) was followed, but the "calendar year" was 11 minutes and 14 seconds

🎵 Lord of all hopefulness; This day God gives me; This is the day

1 The highest mountain in Wales is Snowdon. Nearby lies the village of Beddgelert. *"Bedd"* is the Welsh for *"grave"*, so *"Beddgelert"* means *"the Grave of Gelert"*. This is the story of how the village got its name.

2 A chieftain called Llewellyn had a faithful dog called Gelert. At home the dog was gentle, but was fierce in the hunting pack. One evening, Llewellyn rode back towards his castle, having missed his dog during the day. He heard his barking, but could tell that something was wrong. The dog did not bound forward to greet him, but lay low on the ground, licking his lips. As Llewellyn got off his horse, he could see in the dim light that Gelert's coat and face had blood on them.

3 Llewellyn ran into the castle, and found a trail of blood and signs of a struggle. He rushed upstairs and saw more blood. Behind him came his dog, limping slowly. Llewellyn's eyes were drawn to his baby's cot where his son should have been lying. The sheets were torn and covered with blood and, now, at his side, stood his blood-covered dog, Gelert. Llewellyn could think of only one thing, and cursed his dog: *"You have betrayed my trust and killed my child"* - and he plunged his sword into the dog.

4 No sooner had the dog died, than Llewellyn heard his baby son cry in the next room. He rushed in. There, next to his child, was the torn and mangled body of a huge wolf.

5 His dog had, after all, been faithful and brave, and had been injured in defending his master's child from the wolf. Happy as Llewellyn was that his child was alive, he knew that he had drawn the wrong conclusion from what he had seen. He had not relied on his past experience of his faithful dog. But nothing could be changed. He buried his dog with great sadness. There, beneath a mound of stones, Gelert's grave can still be seen today in the village called *"Gelert's Grave"* - Beddgelert in North Wales.

6 *Let us pray:*

God our Father,
 the Bible reminds us
 that your love for each of us is great
 and that you are faithful for ever,
 never letting us down.
Inspire us
 to value friendship and loyalty,
 and grow in faithfulness
 to those who love and trust us.
 Amen.

 If God is for us; In you, my God

1 One of the world's worst environmental disasters started in September 1997 in the Far East. Fires were lit by landowners in Indonesia, wanting to clear the jungles for quick-cash crops.

2 Fires on the Indonesian islands of Sumatra and Borneo left a blanket of smoke over a vast region. The extensive fires burned for several months, disrupting transport and industry, and causing health problems in several countries - Indonesia, Malaysia, Brunei, the Philippines and Thailand. The smoke is thought to have contributed to at least 3 collisions of ships, and an air crash in which 234 people were killed.

3 Some plantation companies blamed the long drought and the weather-system called 'El Nino', but it was proved that many of the fires were started deliberately by people wanting to make "quick money" by clearing the land of the natural vegetation and habitat of the jungle.

4 In March 1998, similar fires were set in Brazil where, for decades, the practice has been to use fire to clear the land of trees and jungle, ready to farm huge areas of land with fast money-making crops or wood.

5 This process has been shown to produce only short-term financial gain. Much soil - previously protected by the root systems of the jungle vegetation - is later washed away by the heavy tropical rains, leaving barren land. The process has other serious and even global implications, such as reducing significantly the number of trees that absorb carbon dioxide, one of the gases that produce the 'greenhouse effect'.

6 *Let us pray:*

God our Father,
   we give you thanks
   for the talents you have given
   to mankind,
   and for the blessings received
   through those who use their gifts well.

7 We think of the beauty of the world
   which you proclaimed to be good,
   but we are also conscious of our misuse
   of what you have given to us:
   - from the ore in the ground
      we fashion bullets and weapons;
   - from the oil under the sea
      we derive explosives;
   - we damage and pollute
      our own environment
      for short-term gains;
   - from the atoms of existence
      we produce bombs of mass destruction.

8 Our governments spend money
   in our name
   maintaining "butter mountains"
   and "wine lakes",
   and we subsidise farmers
   to "set aside" land
   so that less food is produced,
   even though our brothers and sisters
   die each day from hunger.

9 On our paper money
   we print the images of famous people,
   yet often do not treasure and uphold
   the dignity of all who are made
   in your image and likeness.

10 Open our hearts
   to be influenced for good,
   and inspire us
   to touch the hearts of others.
   Enable us to change
   the things that contradict your love,
   and may all your people
   work and grow together
   as brothers and sisters,
   building up your kingdom on earth.
   Amen.

Laudato sii; Morning has broken; Thank you for fathers

12 SEPTEMBER

1 Mother Teresa, who died a week ago today in 1997, worked with the poorest of
the poor in Calcutta, in north-eastern
India. She talked of what inspired her:

2 *"What is the Good News, the Gospel?*
It is that God loves you,
that God carries you
tattooed on the palms of his hands,
that even if a mother
should forget her own child,
God will not forget you."

Is 49$^{15-16}$

3 On this day in 1997, a 9-year old Romanian boy received a letter from Mother
Teresa, posted just before her death. In
that letter, Mother Teresa wrote:

4 *"I pray for you, Patreascu,*
that you may become
more and more like Jesus,
and be the sunshine of his love
to everyone."

5 *Let us pray:*

God our Father,
for each individual
it is as though
his or her name
is written on the palm of your hand.
Lead us to grow in the faith
that your love for each person
is without limit or condition.
Inspire us to live in such a way
that the light of Christ
may shine through us,
bringing love and warmth
and happiness
to those who share our lives.
Amen.

📖 *Mother Teresa: 27/8/10 - 5/9/97. See also 9 Feb;*
4 March; 13 June; 13 July; 27 Aug; 5 Septem-
ber.

📖 *The Romanian boy had been saved from one*
of the terrible state orphanages of the former
Ceaucescu regime, and became adopted by a
British lady working with Mother Teresa's Sis-
ters, the Missionaries of Charity.

🎵 I will never forget you *(being the Isaiah*
text); Shine, Jesus, shine; The light of
Christ; Though the mountains may fall
(incorporating the Isaiah text)

1 Tomorrow, the 14th, marks the death in 1851 of Arthur Wellesley, the Duke of Wellington, a famous soldier and prime minister.

2 When Wellington died, Prime Minister William Gladstone wrote to one of the Duke's sons. In the letter he said that Wellington had been outstanding - not because of his talents, which were fairly ordinary ones - but because of the extraordinary use that he had made of those ordinary talents.

3 *Let us pray:*

Lord, as I offer you
all that is ordinary and everyday
in my life,
I ask you
to give me the power of your Spirit
that I may do the ordinary things of life
in an extraordinary way.
Amen.

✍ *See also 17 January and 18 June. An alternative prayer would be that for 9 January.*

✍ *"Make your lives extraordinary" - words addressed to his students by the teacher, Mr Keating (Robin Williams), in the film* "Dead Poets' Society".

♪ All that I am; Do not worry; I give my hands; Take my hands

14 SEPTEMBER

1 In 1997 a TV programme interviewed Jason Robinson, a member of the Wigan Warriors Rugby League team. He mentioned that being a Christian touched every part of his life, and he was convinced that he should use his talents well.

2 As he gets changed to play a match, he applies bandages to his legs to help give strength and protection where there is weakness. With his thumb he then makes the sign of the cross on those bandages, as a sign that he is committed to Christ in all that he does, as well as praying for Christ's strength through his weaknesses.

3 *Let us pray:*

Lord Jesus,
   by loving to the extent
   that you were wounded,   *Is 53*
   we are healed.   *1 Pet 2[24]*
By loving to the point of death
   and by rising from the dead
   you have set us free.
You remind us
   that it is when we are weak *1 Cor 1[27]*
   that we can be strong   *2 Cor 12[10]*
   because of your love
   and the power of your Spirit.
Enable us
   to take up our cross each day, *Lk 9[23]*
   share the burdens of others,
   and follow you faithfully.
Amen.

I sign my ears with the sign of your cross
that I may listen and really hear
the communication that comes to me
in different ways
- from you
and from the people
you place into my life.

I sign my shoulders, Lord, with your cross,
knowing that you call me
to carry my own cross each day
and support others
in the burdens and difficulties
that they have.

All that I do today
I set out to do
in the name of the Father (+)
and of the Son
and of the Holy Spirit.
Amen.

📖 *The practice of making the 'Sign of the Cross' - touching one's forehead, chest and shoulders - certainly took place as early as the 5th Century. In the 13th Century, Pope Innocent III (1198-1216) decreed that the Sign was to be made with three fingers from forehead to chest and then from the right to the left shoulders (sic). It was later that the whole hand was used for the Sign, and the direction changed from left to right, as is the present practice except in the Eastern Churches.*

📖 *Today is the Feast of 'The Triumph of the Cross'. It was formerly called 'The Exaltation of the Cross', recalling the miraculous appearance of a cross in the year 312 to the Emperor Constantine, who was told: "In this sign, conquer." We read that 14 years later his mother, St Helen, recovered the cross on which Jesus had been crucified.*

📖 *Mk 8^{34}; 1 Cor 1^{18}; Gal 2^{19}-3$^{7,13-14}$,6^{14}; Phil 2^{8}; 1 Pet 2^{24}*

𝄞 Abide with me *("hold thou thy cross")*; All that I am; Come, come, follow me; Follow me *("take my cross")*; I give my hands; Lay your hands; Take my hands

♦♦♦♦♦♦♦♦♦♦♦♦♦♦♦♦♦♦♦♦♦

📖 *The early Christian theologian, Tertullian (c.160 - c.220 A.D.), mentions the practice of tracing a cross on objects and on the forehead of people:* "At every step and movement, when we go in or out, when we dress or put on our shoes, at the bath, at the table, when lights are brought, when we go to bed, when we sit down - whatever it is which occupies us, we mark the forehead with the sign of the cross."

📖 *A prayer of commitment for personal use:*

Lord Jesus,
I sign my heart with the sign of the cross,
reminding myself
of your love for each person.
I ask that I may grow in faithfulness
as your friend.

I sign my lips with the sign of the cross,
that I may speak as you would speak.

I sign my hands with the sign of the cross
asking that you enable me
to do your work,
and be your hands
in our world which you love so much.

I sign my eyes with the sign of your cross
that I may really see, Lord,
and be aware
of all that is around me.

1 In 1939 several nations were at war with Hitler, to try to prevent him taking over other countries. By the summer of 1940, only the English Channel stopped the Germans invading Britain. Hitler's invasion plans (called *"Operation Sealion"*) were put into effect, and men and boats were assembled, ready to invade.

2 The British Royal Air Force would, first of all, have to be destroyed. Germany's Air Force (led by Hermann Goering) had over 2,600 planes. The R.A.F. under Air Chief Marshal Sir Hugh Dowding, had less than a quarter of that number - no more than 650 planes. Britain's radar early-warning stations were a very great help.

3 The first heavy attack took place on 10th July 1940, and then wave after wave of fighter-escorted bombers attacked the ships and the harbours of the south coast, as well as the airfields. The Battle of Britain had begun - the first battle to take place only in the skies.

4 One night, a single German bomber lost its way and jettisoned its bombs - they landed on London, which had not previously been hit. In retaliation, British bombers attacked Berlin the following night. Hitler was so outraged at the attack on his capital city, that he switched the Luftwaffe's bombing away from the English airfields to London itself. Although this was a tragedy for London, it gave an opportunity for the R.A.F. to build themselves up again and then destroy many more German planes on their way to London.

5 The British had been very close to defeat, and Winston Churchill, the war-time Prime Minister, said of the Royal Air Force: *"Never in the field of human conflict was so much owed by so many to so few."* This was the first battle that Hitler lost.

6 Today is called *'Battle of Britain Day'*, acknowledging that Britain would have been invaded sooner or later if it had not been for the courage and skill and sacrifice of the R.A.F. pilots.

7 *Let us pray:*

Lord Jesus,
we can understand your feelings
when your friends abandoned you
and left you alone
when times were difficult.
We ask that we, too,
may have strength and courage
in the difficult times that we will face.
Inspire us to live in such a way
that we are prepared
to be one of only a few,
willing to make sacrifices
and stand up for what is right.
Lead us to work well with others
and help bring out the best
in one another,
and readily thank those
who contribute to our lives. Amen.

📖 Poem: *'High Flight'* by John Gillespie Magee, killed as a Second World War pilot, aged 19 - see 28 January.

📖 It is recognised that, although Germany's planes far outnumbered those of Britain, the latter's 'Spitfires' and 'Hurricanes' were better planes. Radar not only gave advance information but avoided the need for constant patrolling of the skies, which would have worn down the British pilots even more. It is also the case that, whilst British fighters could refuel in their own country, the German planes had to travel back to France to refuel.

🎼 Amazing grace; Happy the man; I am with you forever; Walk with me, O my Lord; Yahweh, I know you are near *("if I fly to the sunrise")*; You shall cross the barren desert

1 On this day in 1987, 70 countries signed up to an agreement to curb the production of industrial gases that are damaging the ozone layer, 10-15 miles above the Earth in the upper atmosphere. Ozone - O_3 - is formed from three oxygen atoms linking together, instead of the usual two that make the oxygen that we need to breathe - O_2.

2 The ozone layer absorbs ultra-violet radiation from the sun. Otherwise, ultra-violet light would increase skin cancer and also cause further changes in the earth's weather.

3 In 1984 scientists discovered a large "hole" in the ozone layer above the Antarctic. It is thought that this destruction is caused by our use of chlorofluorocarbons (CFCs) which rise into the atmosphere and then react with the ozone, so letting through the dangerous rays from the sun. CFCs have been used until recently as the cooling gas (such as Freon) in refrigerator piping, and as the propellant gas in aerosol sprays.

4 *Let us pray, giving thanks for the goodness of creation:*

God our Father,
we thank you for this earth, our home;
for the wide sky and the blessed sun,
for the salt, earth and the running water,
for the everlasting hills
and the never-resting winds,
for trees
and the common grass underfoot.

5 We thank you for our senses
by which we *hear* the songs of birds,
and *see* the splendour
of the summer fields,
and *taste* of the autumn fruits,
and rejoice in the *feel* of the snow,
and *smell* the breath of the spring.

6 Grant us hearts that are wide open
to all this beauty;
and save us from being so blind
that we pass unseeing
when even the common thornbush
is aflame with your glory,
O God, our Creator. Amen.

✍ *The source is unknown of the prayer which is by Walter Rauschenbusch (1861-1918). In the second verse of that prayer, the naming of each of the senses should be emphasised. For an alternative prayer, see 16 March.*

✍ *Genesis 1^1-2^4; Psalm 8 (7 Aug); Psalm 104 (26 Oct). "The common thornbush aflame" refers to the encounter of Moses with God - Exodus 3^{1-6}. On that same passage Elizabeth Barrett Browning (1806-61) shares the profound thought that:*

> "Earth is crammed with heaven,
> and every common bush
> is afire with God.
> But only he who sees
> takes off his shoes;
> the rest sit around
> and pluck blackberries."

✍ *Does my concern for the environment include my immediate surroundings? What is my practice regarding litter? Do I help to improve the locality - home, school, garden, neighbourhood? Do I consider cigarette smoke and noise as forms of pollution? Do I buy aerosol cans that are marked "CFC-free"?*

✍ *The Antarctic is around the South Pole; the Arctic is around the North Pole.*

♪ Laudato sii; Look at the sky; Sing all creation; Thank you for fathers; This day God gives me; Oh the love of my Lord

17 SEPTEMBER

1 Tomorrow, the 18th, marks the anniversary in 1709, of the birth of the English writer called Doctor Johnson, who often wrote short passages on different topics. For example, he wrote about friendship:

"I look upon every day to be lost
in which I do not make
a new acquaintance.

2 On friendship, he also said:
"A man, Sir, should keep his friendship
in constant repair."

3 Saint Paul wrote a famous passage about love, which is often used at weddings. We can reflect on those words, but mentioning *"friends"* instead of *"love"*:

4 **Friends are patient and kind;**
they are not jealous or boastful;
they are not arrogant or rude.

5 **Friends do not insist**
on having their own way.
They are not touchy or resentful.
They don't take pleasure
when things go wrong for others,
but they are pleased
with what is good and right.

6 **Friends are always ready to excuse,**
to believe the other person,
to have hope,
and to stand beside their friend
in bad times as well as good.
True friendship never ends.

✍ *Dr Samuel Johnson: 18/9/1709-13/12/1784*

✍ *The "friends" passage is adapted from 1 Corinthians 13, by St Paul. How do I match up to this description of a friend, line by line?*

✍ *A French proverb records that* "A faithful friend is an image of God."

🎶 If I am lacking love *(being a setting of 1 Cor 13)*

1 Dag Hammarskjöld was born in Sweden and became the second Secretary General of the United Nations in 1953. He was re-elected to the post, but was killed in a plane crash on this day in 1961. He was trying to resolve problems in the African Republic of the Congo. 3 months later he was posthumously awarded the Nobel Peace Prize for his struggles to promote peace.

2 A reflective and prayerful man, he said:
"We die on the day
when our lives
cease to be illumined
by the steady radiance
- renewed daily -
of a wonder,
the source of which
is beyond reason."

3 *Let us pray:*

Lord God,
may the sight of your creation
- from the vastness
of mighty stars and planets
to the lowliness
of the smallest living creature
that I can see
- inspire me to grow
in wonder and awe,
in reverence for life,
and in appreciation
of the people I meet
and of all that is around me.
Amen.

✍ *Alternative prayers could be those of 8 Jan, 16 Feb, 14 March, 16 September, and Psalm 8 (found on 12 Feb and 1 June).*

✍ *Poem - 'Pied Beauty' by Gerard Manley Hopkins*

✍ *United Nations Secretaries General:*
1946-53: Trygve Lie (Norway)
1953-61: Dag Hammarskjöld (Sweden)
1962-71: U Thant (Burma)
1971-81: Kurt Waldheim (Austria)
1982-92: Javier Pérez de Cuéllar (Peru)
1992-97: Boutros Boutros Ghali (Egypt)
1997- Kofi Annan (Ghana)

✍ *Dag Hammarskjöld (1905-1961) - pronounced* "Hammer-sh-cold". *See 2 and 26 September. He also wrote:*
"The best and most wonderful thing that can happen to you in this life is that you should be silent and let God work and speak."

✍ *He also wrote:*
"Night is drawing nigh.
For all that has been - thanks!
For all that shall be - Yes!"

♩ Do not worry; I watch the sunrise; Laudato sii *("Yes, be praised")*; Oh the love of my Lord

19 SEPTEMBER

1 Today saw the birth of George Cadbury in 1839, renowned for starting to produce the Cadbury's chocolate that we now know.

2 He moved the factory from Birmingham itself to a new site outside the city, which he called 'Bournville'. He is well-remembered for building there a 250-acre village of good, spacious houses for all his workers. Each house had a garden, and the village had wide open spaces - remarkable conditions for workers of the 1800s. George Cadbury sold the houses to the workers at cost price on very reasonable loans.

3 The money spent on such excellent facilities reflected the value that George Cadbury placed in each of his workers and their families. He was a committed Christian, and a member of the 'Society of Friends', more generally known as 'Quakers'.

4 *Let us pray:*

Lord God,
may others respect and value me
as much as I do them.
Amen.

✍ *George Cadbury: 19/9/1839-25/10/1922*

✍ *The villagers of Bournville vote from time to time as to whether or not they should allow the sale of alcohol in the village itself. Being a Quaker foundation, the Bournville Trust generally wishes to conform to the original intentions of the Cadbury founders. Bournville is also the site of the chocolate museum, "Cadbury World".*

✍ *A review in 1998 indicated that the British eat an average of 16 kg (more than 35 lbs) of chocolate and sweets per person each year, followed by the United States at 10 kg, and France at 9 kg.*

✍ *The following list shows the years in which many of the more common items of confectionery were first produced:*

1881 - Rowntree's Fruit Pastilles
1899 - Licorice Allsorts
1910 - Flake
1918 - Jelly Babies
1920 - Cadbury's Creme Egg
1920 - Cadbury's Fruit and Nut
1929 - Crunchie
1932 - Mars
1935 - Chocolate Crisp
      renamed 'Kit-Kat' in 1937
1935 - Aero
1937 - Smarties
1937 - Rolo
1948 - Polo
1948 - Picnic
1967 - Marathon
      renamed 'Snickers' in 1990
1967 - Twix
1976 - Yorkie
1991 - Wispa

✍ *See also 20 August.*

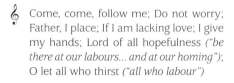
Come, come, follow me; Do not worry; Father, I place; If I am lacking love; I give my hands; Lord of all hopefulness *("be there at our labours... and at our homing")*; O let all who thirst *("all who labour")*

1 From time to time,
   one of Charlie Chaplin's silent films
   is shown on TV.
   He was a small man, with a moustache
   and a hat and walking stick,
   and a funny way of walking!

2 Because he was very popular,
   "Charlie Chaplin
   LOOK-ALIKE COMPETITIONS"
   were held,
   and a few people would line up
   and be judged
   on who looked most like Charlie Chaplin,
   walking like him
   and doing tricks like him.

3 One day, just for the fun of it,
   Charlie Chaplin himself
   entered one of these
   "look-alike" competitions.
   He didn't win - he came third!

4 When God looks at me with love,
   how close might I be
   to the true "look-alike"
   that he calls me to be,
   having been made
   in his own image and likeness?

5 What changes
   do I need to make in my life
   that I may succeed
   in the REAL "look-alike" competition?

6 I am not called to be Charlie Chaplin.
   I am not called to be Mother Teresa.
   God calls me by name
   - that is who I am called to be.

7 Let us pray:

   **Inspire me, Lord,
   so that I may reflect
   your image and likeness
   a little more clearly
   each day.
   Amen.**

Charlie Chaplin: 16/4/1889-25/12/1977. He was knighted by the Queen in 1975, aged 86.

Abba, Father, you are the potter; Do not worry; Father, I place; I give my hands; Lay your hands; Make me a channel; Oh the word of my Lord; Seek ye first

1 About this time, people of the Jewish faith will celebrate the feast of *'Rosh Hashanah'.* The words in Hebrew mean "beginning of the year".

2 On the feast of *'Rosh Hashanah'*, people celebrate God's creation. During a festive meal, pieces of apple dipped in honey are eaten. It is an expression of hope for a sweet and pleasant year ahead.

3 *'Rosh Hashanah'* is also the first day of a ten-day period of reflection, asking God's forgiveness for faults of the past, promising to approach things in a better way in the year ahead. On this day, a ram's horn - called the *'shofar'* - is blown.

4 *Let us pray:*

Blessed are you, Lord,
  God of all creation,
  for having made us all different.
What I don't know about you
  I need to learn from others
  because they reflect
  your image and likeness
  in a different way.
I ask you to lead me
  to seek to understand
  the many people of good will
  who are different from me.

5 Blessed are you, Lord,
  God of all creation.
I am grateful
  for all that is good in my life.
I know that you look on me
  with tender love,
  and invite me
  to assess and renew
  my attitude and direction in life.
Be with me in my determination
  to live in a positive way.
Amen.

✏ *Derived from lengths of time mentioned in the Old Testament, it was once thought that the creation of the world took place in 3761 B.C. - and it is from that date that the Jewish calendar is named. Accordingly, add 3,761 to the year of the Christian Calendar to determine the number of the Jewish year e.g. 2000 is the Jewish year 5761; 2012 is the Jewish year 5773.*

✏ *The Jewish New Year is celebrated on the first and second days of the Jewish month of Tishri (which falls in September or October).*

✏ *Genesis 22 details the episode of Abraham and Isaac, and the sacrifice of a ram. The blowing of the 'shofar', the ram's horn, recalls this incident. The Book of Numbers 29[1-11] mentions the 10 day period of reflection, penitence, and atonement that starts with this feast and concludes with Yom Kippur - see 8 October.*

✏ *The phrase "Blessed are you, Lord, God of all creation" occurs in the prayers of the Jewish Sabbath (see 30 March), and form the basis for the Offertory prayers in the Roman Catholic Eucharist (Mass).*

✏ *For 'New Year', see also 1 and 16 January.*

♩ Blest be the Lord; God forgave my sin; Oh the love of my Lord; O Lord all the world; Seek ye first; The Lord's my shepherd; You shall cross the barren desert

Changed for the better

We spend a moment, Lord,
reminding ourselves
that you are present with us,
knowing that when you are present
people are changed for the better.

(e.g. Lk 19¹⁻⁹)
(see page 183)

1 On this day in 1586, Sir Philip Sydney was mortally wounded in battle. He had been shot in the leg, and collapsed from loss of blood and the setting in of fever. A fellow-officer ran to get some water. Sir Philip, desperate to drink, raised the water to his lips, but then saw an ordinary soldier lying nearby, also seriously wounded. Philip did not drink, but handed the water to the soldier, saying:

"Your need is greater than mine."

2 *Let us pray:*

**Lord our God,
may we grow
as people who think of others
and see their needs
never "passing by
on the other side",**   *Lk 10³¹*
**but being willing to make sacrifices
and be generous
for the good of others.
Amen.**

"Your need is greater than mine."

📖 *Sir Philip Sydney (1554-1586) lived at the time of Queen Elizabeth I. He was a courtier, soldier, scholar and poet. This incident took place in battle against the Spaniards who were holding out in the town of Zutphen in what is now The Netherlands.*

📖 *A fellow-courtier, Lord Brooke, valued so highly his friendship with Sir Philip Sydney, that he left instructions that his gravestone should read: "Here lies the friend of Sir Philip Sydney".*

📖 *We could think of specific instances over the last few days when we made a personal sacrifice - or when we could have, but didn't.*

🎵 I am with you forever; If I am lacking love; Make me a channel; Take my hands

1   Many thought that King James II was not a good king and, for various reasons, he was deposed. In 1688 the throne was offered jointly to his daughter, Mary, and her husband (who was also her cousin), the Dutch prince, William of Orange.

2   Mary's sister, Anne, became the next Queen and, under her rule, the Parliaments of Scotland and England were united, forming (with Wales) the nation of Great Britain.

3   On Anne's death, the next-in-line to the throne for a Protestant Succession was a distant relative - a German prince from Hanover, who became King George I. He could speak little English and so came to rely more and more on his chief minister of the government who, in George's time, became known as the "Prime Minister". It is because the king could speak little English that power began to change hands from that time on from the king to the elected Prime Minister.

4   Yesterday marks the anniversary in 1735 of Number 10 Downing Street becoming the residence for British Prime Ministers.

5   *Let us pray:*

God our Father,
  we pray for all
  who are in positions of leadership
  in our country,
  that they may be inspired
  by the values of the Gospel.
We pray that they may live
  as people of integrity and honesty,
  growing in a sense
  of duty and responsibility,
  always being aware of the needy,
  and ready to be of service to others.
Amen.

✍ *Like Mary II and Anne, George I was a great-grandchild of King James I (who was called King James VI in Scotland).*

✍ *"Great Britain" is Scotland and England and Wales.*

✍ *Number 11 Downing Street is the residence of the Chancellor of the Exchequer. The new Prime Minister from the 1997 General Election was Mr Tony Blair. As the flat above Number 10 Downing Street is very small, it was decided that part of Number 11 be adapted for use by Mr and Mrs Blair and their three children.*

♩   Christ is our king; God's Spirit is in my heart; If I am lacking love; O Lord, all the world

1 Lourdes in France is well-known as a place for pilgrimage. For nearly 500 years, England had its own shrine - Walsingham - a village in Norfolk. There, in the year 1061, a Lady Richeldis had a vision. Our Lady told her to build a church which would include a room resembling Mary's house in Nazareth.

2 Eventually a large church and a priory (a monastery) were built which helped to house some of the many pilgrims. Thousands of people each year walked or rode on pilgrimage to Walsingham, which became known as *"England's Nazareth"*. Almost every king and queen for 300 years made at least one pilgrimage to the Shrine at Walsingham, including King Henry VIII *(the eighth)* who walked the last mile barefoot.

3 In 1534, the monastery and church and pilgrim centre at Walsingham were closed and sold off by King Henry VIII as part of what is called the *"Dissolution of the Monasteries"*. The king gained a lot of money from the sale of all the monasteries.

4 In the 1920s - nearly 400 years after the Shrine's destruction - people started to visit Walsingham again to pray there. Since then, new churches have been built, and the ruins of the monastery church are visited. On their pilgrimage, many people find peace and inner healing and encouragement in difficult times.

5 The original statue of Our Lady of Walsingham had been taken to London and burnt on Henry VIII's orders. 450 years later, a copy of that statue was on display in Wembley Stadium, at the occasion of a Mass celebrated there by Pope John Paul II in 1982.

6 Today is the feastday of Our Lady of Walsingham.

7 *Let us pray:*

Mary, teach us
 how to say "Yes" to the Lord
 every moment of our lives.
Mary, teach us
 how to say "Thank you" to the Lord
 every moment of our lives.

📖 *The prayer is one that is used in the "Fiat Rosary".*

📖 *At the* "Dissolution of the Monasteries", *the fine buildings were pillaged for their stone, which was then often used to build large houses for the new owners who were sometimes merchants who formed a new 'middle class'.*

📖 *A courtier reported that, nearing death, King Henry VIII (possibly regretting some of his actions) was heard to say:* "Our Lady of Walsingham, pray for me."

📖 *In the British Museum is an ancient wax Seal of Walsingham. It was only by looking at the image of the statue depicted on that seal, that contemporary statues of Our Lady of Walsingham have been produced.*

📖 *The present-day Anglican Shrine is built opposite the ruins of the priory church (now in private hands). The Roman Catholic Shrine is built around the "Slipper Chapel" - the last of a series of "station churches" which pilgrims of old would visit on their way to Walsingham. On leaving the Slipper Chapel, many pilgrims would walk the last mile barefoot, as did Henry VIII himself. There is now also an Orthodox Shrine in the village.*

📖 *See also 20 May and 15 August.*

📖 *Poem: T.S.Eliot - Little Gidding*

🎵 Hail Mary *(Carey Landry)*; Holy Virgin, by God's decree; Mary, most holy; Oh Mary, when our God chose you; The angel Gabriel; Where are you bound?

1 There was a standing ovation at the *'Oscar'* ceremonies in 1996 for the wheelchair-bound actor Christopher Reeve, who was born on this day in 1952.

2 The touching tribute was made to Christopher Reeve for his courage, having been paralysed from the neck down since a fall from a horse the year before, when he was aged 43. He is well-known for playing the part of *'Superman'* in various films, and he was a role-model of an active and healthy man.

3 Some months after his disabling accident, Christopher Reeve stated that *"laughter has the power to restore life".* A newspaper commented that he has been determined to set his disability aside and still aim to live life to the full. The newspaper wrote these words:

4 *"Christopher Reeve - Superman -*
will never resume his old role
but, when he shares of himself
as he **now** *is, on a million TV screens,*
then he will be facing
the greatest challenge we can imagine
- and then he really will be a 'super-man'."

5 *Let us pray:*

God our Father,
we bring before you today
those who suffer
from chronic illness or disability
- those for whom sickness or disability
profoundly affects their lives.

6 When they feel diminished,
remind them that you call them by name
and hold them
in the palm of your hand. *Is 43¹*

7 When they feel fragile and broken,
mould them and heal them,
that they may more closely resemble
the image of Jesus,
your Son and our Brother.

8 When they are reminded
of different times in the past,
lead them to grow in the faith
that you love them today, as they are,
in the reality of their lives this day.

9 When they feel uncertain
about the future,
lead them to that perfect love
which casts out all fear. *1 John 4¹⁸*

10 When situations remind them
- not of what they *can* do,
but of what they *cannot* do -
remind them
that "love never fails", *1 Cor 13⁸*
and that, living in your love,
they will bear your fruit in plenty. *Jn 15⁵·⁹*

11 May all of us
- whatever our circumstances -
never be so taken up
with our own concerns
that we do not see or respond to
the needs of others.
May we live with courage
the different challenges
that each of us faces.
Amen.

✍ *Or, for the prayer, could simply take the last paragraph, prefacing with* "God our Father....".

✍ "Laughter has the power to restore life" - *see 17 June for a reflection on sharing a smile.*

✍ *Paraplegia is the paralysis of the lower half of the body; quadriplegia (also called tetraplegia) is the paralysis of all 4 limbs.*

♪ Be still and know I am with you; Father, I place into your hands; Lay your hands; Yahweh, I know you are near

26 SEPTEMBER

1 In parts of Africa, when people have a very heavy burden to carry, they sometimes place it at one end of a pole, and then tie a stone of the same weight on the other end. Then the pole or stick is carried across the shoulders, with one weight or burden balancing the other. Carrying two burdens is easier than carrying one.

2 Dag Hammarskjöld, the second Secretary General of the United Nations (who was killed in a plane-crash in September 1961), expressed the same thing in a different way:

"What makes loneliness and anguish
is not that I have no-one
to share my burden,
but this -
I have only my own burden to bear."

3 *Let us pray:*

Lord, when I am hungry
- lead me to feed others.
When I am thirsty
- give me water
to satisfy others' thirst.
When I am sad
- lead me to bring joy to others.
When burdens weigh upon me
- lay upon my shoulders
the burdens of other people.
Lord, when I am greatly in need
of tenderness and support
- lead me to help someone
in greater need.
Amen.

✍ *Dag Hammarskjöld (1905-1961). See also 18 September.*

✍ *The prayer is based on ideas in a French prayer, source unknown.*

♪ Father I place into your hands; Follow me *("take my cross")*; I am with you forever *("burdens")*; If God is for us; If I am lacking love; I give my hands; In you, my God; O let all who thirst *("all who are laden")*

1 In September 1997 a version of the 7-sided 50 pence coin was introduced in Britain - smaller than the original 50 pence. The larger coin had been introduced in 1973, the year that the United Kingdom joined what was then called the *"European Economic Community"*.

2 One of the versions of the large 7-sided 50 pence piece shows nine hands linked together in unity, representing the then nine members of what is now called the *"European Union"*. The hands shown on the coin were sculpted by David Wynne.

3 In a radio interview, David Wynne told of how the Queen sat for a sculpture of her face. He asked if he might touch her face, and the Queen mentioned that she was surprised that other sculptors had not asked that before. David Wynne said that the Queen went on to remark how important it is for parents to touch and cuddle their young children. "Touch" can convey care and love and support.

4 *Let us pray:*

Lord Jesus,
> you took young children in your arms
> and blessed them.
Many times we find in the Gospel
> that you touched people
> and cured them.
Place your hands on us today
> that we may know
> your healing in our lives.
May we live in such a way
> that we help to bring
> healing and peace and reconciliation
> to those who share our lives each day.
Amen.

David Wynne also designed the Queen Mother's "Lion and Unicorn Gate" in London's Hyde Park. He was Sue Lawley's guest on Desert Island Discs on Radio 4, 11/5/97.

Mark 9$^{33\text{-}37}$: Who is the greatest?
Luke 18$^{15\text{-}17}$: Jesus blesses little children.

The "European Union" is composed (1998) of the following countries:

> *1958 - Belgium, France, Germany, Italy, Luxembourg, The Netherlands.*
> *1973 - Denmark, Ireland, United Kingdom.*
> *1981 - Greece.*
> *1986 - Portugal, Spain.*
> *1995 - Austria, Finland, Sweden*
>
> *- totalling 15 countries.*

 In you, my God; Lay your hands; Oh the love of my Lord

1 In the *"Star Trek"* science fiction series, the Vulcan greeting is sometimes heard from Mr Spock or Ambassador Sarek: *"Live long and prosper."*

2 They are words that can be found in the Old Testament of the Bible. There are other phrases from the Bible that people sometimes use in conversation, such as these:

3 "Sour grapes"   *- Ezek 18²*

4 "The writing's on the wall"   *- Dan 5²⁵*

5 She is "the salt of the earth"   *- Mt 5¹³*

6 "To go the extra mile"   *- Mt 5⁴¹*

7 "Not letting his left hand know what his right hand is doing"   *- Mt 6³*

8 "On the straight and narrow"   *- Mt 7¹⁴*

9 "Fallen by the wayside"   *- Mt 13⁴*

10 "The blind leading the blind"   *- Mt 15¹⁴*

11 "Good Samaritan"
- someone who doesn't "pass by on the other side"   *- Lk 10³¹*

12 "Seeing is believing"   *- Jn 20²⁵*
Doubting Thomas;
I'll believe it when I see it.

13 *Let us pray:*

**Lord, inspire us
in every moment before we speak,
so that our words to others today
may all be positive.
Amen.**

✏ *An alternative prayer would be number 30 in the Appendix of Volume 2 - "Prayers for Use by Teachers".*

✏ *The words referred to as* "the Vulcan Greeting" *may be found in the Bible in Deuteronomy 4⁴⁰:* "The Lord is God indeed in heaven and on earth - he and no other. Keep his laws and commandments that are given to you today, so that you and your children will live long and prosper in the land that God gives you." *This text is part of the Old Testament Reading for Trinity Sunday in Year B of the 3-year cycle of readings.*

✏ *Other biblical passages used in ordinary speech, include:*

"An eye for an eye, and a tooth for a tooth" - Ex 21²³
"Tablets of stone"   *- Ex 34*
"Scapegoat"   *- Lev 16¹⁶*
"To spy out the land"   *- Num 13¹⁶*
"The apple of his eye"   *- Deut 32¹⁰*
"Someone after his own heart"   *- 1 Sam 13¹⁴*
"How the mighty are fallen!"   *- 2 Sam 1²⁷*
"Escaped by the skin of their teeth" - Job 19²⁰
"Pride goes before a fall"   *- Prov 16¹⁸*
"Don't know what tomorrow may bring"- Prov 27¹
"Put your own house in order"   *- Is 38¹*
"No peace for the wicked"   *- Is 48²²*
"Holier-than-thou"   *- Is 65⁵*
"He is found wanting"   *- Dan 5²⁷*
"Don't cast your pearls before swine"   *- Mt 7⁶*
"O ye of little faith"   *- Mt 8²⁶*
"Fallen on stony ground"   *- Mt 13⁵*
"Walking on water"   *- Mt 14²⁵*
*"The first will be last;
the last will be first"*   *- Mt 19³⁰*
"A worker is worthy of his hire"   *- Mk 10⁷*
"The spirit is willing but the flesh is weak"- Mk 14³⁸
"Physician, heal thyself"   *- Lk 4²³*
We have our "cross to bear/carry"   *- Lk 9²³*
*"Once you've put your hand to the plough...
there's no turning back*   *- cf Lk 9⁶²*
"Kept the good wine until last"   *- Jn 2¹⁰*
"A law unto themselves"   *- Rom 2¹⁴*
"The love of money is the root of all evil" - 1 Tim 6¹⁰
"I have fought the good fight"   *- 2 Tim 4⁷*
"He's got the patience of Job"   *- James 5¹¹*
"Streets paved with gold"   *- Rev 21¹*

 Oh the word of my Lord

1 The *'Pink Panther'* comedy films starred Peter Sellers as Inspector Clouseau, with Herbert Lom as Chief Inspector Dreyfus. Clouseau, speaking with an outrageous French accent that leads people to query what he is saying, bungles all that he does and creates trouble for everyone around. Yet he always wins through and captures the criminals who sometimes find him so frustrating that they give themselves up.

2 At the start of the 1976 film, *'The Pink Panther Strikes Again'*, a real-life Frenchman is quoted. Émile Coué had recommended to patients that they recite some words up to 30 times a day, and it is these words that are quoted in the film:
   "Each day and in every way
   I am becoming better and better."

3 Coué's idea was that this would be a way of getting people to realise that, if they are positive about life, they have the potential to be able to help themselves in some ways.

4 In 1922, whilst on a ship approaching New York, a 100-miles-an-hour gale made most people very sea-sick. It was reported that Émile Coué was not sick, but was repeating to himself in his own language:
   "Each day and in every way
   I am becoming better and better."

5 *Let us pray:*

   Lord God,
   keep in me a sense of humour
   and the ability to laugh at myself.
   Lead me always to be positive,
   looking for the best
   in people and in situations.
   Each day and in every way
   may I grow in the love of the Father
   and the presence of the Son,
   and the power of the Holy Spirit.
   Amen.

✍ *The Pink Panther films offer a dry humour - the actors themselves don't laugh.* "Does your dog bite?" *asks Clouseau.* "No, sir," *says the inn-keeper who has a large dog sitting beside him. Clouseau pats the dog on the head and, of course, it bites him.* "I thought you said your dog does not bite?" *stammers Clouseau.* "That is not my dog" *replies the inn-keeper.*

✍ *Peter Sellers (1925-1980) was born in Southsea, Portsmouth. He was well-known for 'The Goon Show' and for comedy films such as 'The Ladykillers', and 'The Pink Panther' films: 'The Pink Panther' - 1963; 'The Return of the Pink Panther' - 1974; 'The Pink Panther Strikes Again' - 1976; 'The Revenge of the Pink Panther' - 1978.*

✍ *Émile Coué (1857-1926) [pronounced* "Ay-meal Coo-ay"*] was a French pharmacist who began to study hypnotism.* "Auto-suggestion" *or* "self-suggestion" *was popular in Britain and the United States at that time. His other phrase to repeat was* "Ça passe, ça passe" - "It will soon be over; it will soon be over".

✍ *See also 22 February for some similar ideas.*

♪ Come, come, follow me; Do not worry; Father, I place into your hands; If God is for us; In you, my God; Lay your hands

30 SEPTEMBER

1   In a speech in Glasgow in September 1963, the Labour leader, Harold Wilson, proposed the setting up of what we now know as *'The Open University'*.

2   It is highly successful in offering teaching and research through TV and radio lectures, course materials, correspondence courses, and computer software. *'The Open University'* emphasises independent learning, and students study at their own time and pace, making progress by gaining credits. *'The OU'* (as it is often called) is for older students who may have missed earlier opportunities, and they normally study part-time. Those who gain degrees include some retired people.

3   No initial educational qualifications are needed to join, but the quality of learning is as high as demanded by other universities, regularly checked by coursework and exams. Summer schools are set up in some subjects. Personal tuition is planned on a regional basis.

4   The idea of such a *"university of the air"* has been copied by many countries, such as China, India, Holland, Portugal, Thailand, and South Korea. Some countries use the same name - *'The Open University'*.

5   *Let us pray:*

God our Father,
  whatever our age,
  may we always have a thirst
  for knowledge and understanding,
  and be ready to learn
  from all of life's experiences.
Inspire us always with a sense of wonder
  and a great reverence for life.
Amen.

Jennie Lee was responsible for establishing the OU on 30 May 1969 under a Royal Charter. The first 25,000 students started their degree courses in January 1971. It is now funded in the same way as other universities.

Do not worry; Father, I place into your hands; God's Spirit is in my heart; Walk with me, O my Lord; Yahweh, I know you are near

Gathered on the lakeside

Lord, by the side of the Sea of Galilee,
there were so many
gathered around you,
that you got into the boat
of Simon Peter the fisherman.
You asked him to push out into the water
so that the people
could see and hear you better.
Years later, we are another group of people
keen to encounter you.
Show us how to see and hear you better
as we pause now
to remind ourselves
that we are in your presence.

(Lk 5¹⁻³)

(see page 178)

OCTOBER

1 St Teresa of Lisieux, in northern France, was a young Carmelite Sister who died at the age of 24. She said: *"I will spend my time in heaven doing good on earth."* Today is her feastday.

2 Teresa was aware that most of us will never achieve anything great or be well-known. Her *"little way"* (as she called it) was to choose to live in a loving way her ordinary daily life, no matter how monotonous it might be.

3 When somebody was annoying her, Teresa set out to think of that person's qualities and good intentions. *"You've always got a smile for me,"* remarked someone who, in fact, always irritated her! *"My vocation, my calling,"* Teresa said *"is to love."* Whatever was frustrating and annoying in daily life she offered to God to be transformed into something good for other people.

4 Teresa said: *"Love can do all things. Our Lord does not look so much at the greatness of our actions - or even at their difficulty - as at the love with which we do them."*

5 She was often ill - and she would die of tuberculosis when she was only 24. She realised that, as quiet and hidden suffering and sacrifice is offered to God, it is transformed into being of help to other people.

6 *"My little way,"* she wrote *"is the way of childhood - the way of trust and absolute self-surrender. In my little way, everything is most ordinary. Jesus will transform us."*

7 *Let us pray:*

Lord Jesus,
   you told your friends
   not to worry about the future. *Mt 6³⁴*
You showed them
   how to have the attitude
   of simple trust *Mk 10¹⁵*
   that young children have,
   so that they could place themselves
   into the caring hands of our Father.
And so
   I ask for the power of your Spirit
   that I may remain positive
   throughout all that is ordinary
   in my daily life.
I know that your touch
   can change people and situations,
   and so I ask you
   to join me in offering to our Father
   not only the good things of this day
   but also the suffering and sacrifices
   that I want to offer
   cheerfully and lovingly,
   and in a quiet and hidden way.
And so I pray that everything
   - including what is not to my liking -
   may be transformed in your presence
   for the benefit of other people.
Amen.

✍ *Although she never left the Convent, Teresa has become known as the Patroness of all who work on the Missions because, whilst alive, she offered her sufferings and her prayer for them, joining her prayer and her life to theirs.*

✍ *Teresa's "Little Way" is the approach lived out by many people who are seriously ill, who offer their pain and suffering and sacrifice as prayer in itself, which God can transform into "doing good" for others - even for people whom the sick person has not met (just as Teresa did not meet the missionaries who benefited from her offering and prayer). Some people find helpful the symbolism of raising hands a little or lifting a saucer or bowl, whilst offering themselves to God in prayer. Even in pain, the slight raising of a hand can symbolise personal offering to be transformed by the Lord for the benefit of others. See also 11 February.*

✍ *Thérèse of Lisieux (often called "The Little Flower") was declared a saint in 1925, only 28 years after her death. On 19/10/97 Pope John Paul II declared her to be a "Doctor of the Church" (joining only 32 others), recognising that her writings have been of inspiration to many people.*

✍ *See also the prayer of 13 July: looking not so much at the achievement, but at the effort put in.*

✍ *"Sacrifice and a long face go ill together"*
- Mahatma Gandhi.

✍ *"Creative suffering is redemptive"*
- Martin Luther King.

🎼 All that I am; Dear Lord and Father of mankind *("in simple trust")*; Do not worry *("trust and pray... leave it in the hands of the Lord")*; If I am lacking love; Lord of all hopefulness *(whose trust ever child-like")*; Lord for tomorrow and its needs; Seek ye first; Sing a simple song

✍ *Teresa was instructed by her Superior in the Convent (who was also her sister) to write her own life-story. 'The Story of a Soul' has sold many copies in different languages.*

2 OCTOBER

1 This is part of a poem and prayer by John Oxenham. about the beauty of the changing season of Autumn. We make his words our prayer today, giving thanks that nature's beauty can inspire us.

2 **We thank thee, Lord...**
For all the rich autumnal glories spread -
The flaming pageant
   of the ripening woods,
The fiery gorse,
   the heather-purpled hills,
The rustling leaves
   that fly before the wind
and lie below the hedgerows
   whispering;
For meadows silver-white
   with hoary dew...
We thank thee, Lord.

William Dunkerley wrote under the pseudonym (pen-name) of John Oxenham. and lived from 1852-1941. A book of his verse is called "Bees in Amber", and this extract is from his poem called "A Little Te Deum of the Common-place" which explores characteristics of each season and then gives thanks to God. The 'Te Deum' itself is a hymn of thanksgiving recited in monasteries and enclosed convents at the 'Office of Readings' (Matins) at a very early hour each morning.

See also 31 October.

Laudato sii; Morning has broken; O Lord my God, the Father of creation; Thank you for fathers

1 Tomorrow, 4th October, marks the anniversary in 1957 of the launching into earth's orbit of the first satellite. The Soviet Union's *"Sputnik 1"* transmitted radio waves that could be picked up on earth as a beeping sound. The satellite was only 58 cm *(23 inches)* in diameter. It orbited the Earth every 96 minutes.

2 Its four antennae sent information back to Earth about the temperature and density of the outer atmosphere. After 3 months in orbit, *"Sputnik"* fell back into the atmosphere, burning up on re-entry.

3 The satellite's name, *"Sputnik"*, is Russian for *"fellow-traveller"*. Its launch in 1957 was a great achievement, having a huge impact throughout the world. Rivalry between the Soviet Union and the United States started the *"Space Race"*, culminating in the landing on the Moon by the United States in July 1969.

4 *Let us pray:*

Creator God,
>   we thank you for the creative skills
>   of all human beings,
>   made as we are
>   in your image and likeness.
> **Inspire us to use our skills**
>   **for the benefit**
>   **of all our brothers and sisters**
>   **- working not in competition**
>   **with others**
>   **but as "fellow-travellers"**
>   **who share the same journey.**
> **Amen.**

📖 *Sputnik's maximum height of orbit was 947 km (587 miles). It weighed 83.6 kg (184.3 lbs), and transmitted results down to Earth until its batteries ran out after 21 days. It made 1400 orbits of the planet.*

📖 *After the Resurrection, Jesus joined two of his disciples as a "fellow-traveller" as they walked along the road to Emmaus - see Lk 24.*

🎵 Morning has broken; My Lord, my master *("Lord of earth and heaven, be my food for the journey)*; O Lord all the world; O Lord my God, the Father of creation; O Lord my God, when I in awesome wonder; Yahweh, I know you are near *("if I climb to the heavens")*

1 It was the year 1205 in the town of Assisi, in northern Italy. Francis was the son of a cloth merchant, and he was thought of as rather "wild", seeming to have more money than was good for him. He had fought in two wars, spent over a year in prison, and almost died of an illness that had lasted for months.

2 Now, trying to sort out his life, he was spending a few moments in quiet prayer in a small stone church with a low curved roof. Suddenly, with no-one else in the very small church, he heard himself being addressed by name. Three times the voice spoke the same words to him, and he was convinced that he heard the words being spoken from the cross itself:

3   *"Francis - go and build up my church which is falling down."*

4 Francis presumed that Jesus meant the run-down church-building in which he was at that moment. In the following days he set about repairing the stonework of that church. He began to realise that to *"build up the Church"* wasn't referring to a building, but to the strengthening of the community of God's people.

5 Deep within himself, Francis was being re-built as a person. The re-formed Francis - now more clearly formed in God's own likeness - was able to help lead people to "open themselves" to God's Spirit working in their lives. It wasn't by force of his own efforts that Francis became a better person, but by "allowing God to **be** God" in his life. Many people followed Francis and returned to the simplicity of the Gospel.

6 One of his most famous prayers is sometimes called *"The Peace Prayer"*. Before we use that prayer we can think of some other words of Francis:

7   *"While you are proclaiming*
     peace with your lips,
     be careful to have it even more fully
     in your heart."

8 *Let us pray:*

Lord, make me an instrument of
your peace:
  where there is hatred, let me sow love;
  where there is injury, pardon;
  where there is doubt, faith;
  where there is despair, hope;
  where there is darkness, light;
  and where there is sadness, joy.
O Divine Master,
  grant that I may not so much seek
  to be consoled, as to console;
  to be understood, as to understand;
  to be loved, as to love.
For it is in giving that we receive,
  it is in pardoning
  that we are pardoned,
  and it is in dying
  that we are born to eternal life.
Amen.

❖❖❖❖❖❖❖❖❖❖❖❖❖❖❖❖❖

✍ *St Francis of Assisi: about 1182-1226.*

✍ The church where Francis heard Jesus speaking to him is called San Damiano (St Damian's), and copies of the very striking and inspiring crucifix (or photographs and cards of it) are readily available in religious bookshops.

✍ *See also 10 October, 23 December, and a footnote of 20 October.*

♪ Lord, make me a means of your peace;
  Make me a channel

1 Sometimes on cars we see a badge of a simple outline of a fish:

2 It is a symbol that was used as a secret sign when Christians were persecuted in the time of the Roman Empire. Greek was one of the languages spoken throughout the Roman Empire, and the Greek word for FISH

ΙΧΘΥΣ

is pronounced "ik-thus". The 5 letters of the Greek word can stand for the first letters of 5 other words:

"Jesus Christ, God's Son (and our) Saviour".

3

I	I	**I**esous	- Jesus
X	CH	**CH**ristos	- Christ
Θ	TH	**TH**eou	- God's
Y	U	**U**ios	- Son
Σ	S	**S**oter	- Saviour

4 Today, the outline of a fish seen on the back of cars means nothing to those who are not Christian, but is a sign of recognition and encouragement to other Christians.

5 *Let us pray:*

God our Father,
 we could never "prove"
 or "justify" ourselves to you.
Instead, your love for us
 is without limit or condition.
It is Good News
 that your love is free
 and can never be "earned"
 by any human achievement.
Jesus your Son was a perfect sign
 of the wealth of your love.
We ask for the power of your Spirit
 in our lives
 that we, in turn,
 may be credible signs of your love
 to the people
 we will meet today. Amen.

📖 *IΧΘΥΣ The five Greek letters in the word for FISH are named: iota, chi (pronounced "k-eye"), theta, upsilon, sigma. The capital form of the Greek letters is used here.*

📖 *The symbol of the fish is found in Christian art from the 2nd Century A.D. as a sign of Christ and the newly-baptised.*

📖 *An early Christian writer, Tertullian (c.160-220A.D.) wrote:*
"Our sacrament of water (baptism) is blessed because it washes away the sin of our previous blindness. We are set free and received into everlasting life. But we, **LITTLE FISHES**, after the example of our **ICHTHUS**, are born in water. Unless we live in that water we will die."

📖 *This secret sign of the fish is used in the film 'Quo Vadis' as a slave draws the sign in spilt wine for another Christian to recognise.*

📖 *X = chi*

 P = rho

are the first two letters in Greek of the word "CHRIST". These two letters are sometimes overlapped and used as another Christian sign which can be seen in some churches and on candles, banners and the clothes a priest wears in church. The sign simply means "Christ".

📖 *See also 1 August, including the prayer.*

🎼 Jesus to the rescue *(referring to the "seven signs" in John's gospel)*; Oh the word of my Lord *("I called to you to be my sign")*; The seed is Christ's *("his the fish")*

6 OCTOBER

1 The following words are from the *"United Nations' Declaration of the Rights of the Child"*. We can think of our own background, and also that of young people in our country and across the world.

2 Children and young people have the right:

"- to affection, love and understanding;
- to adequate nutrition and medical care;

3 *- to free education;*
- to full opportunity for play and recreation;

4 *- to a name and nationality;*
- to special care, if handicapped;

5 *- to be among the first to receive relief*
   in times of disaster;
- to learn to be a useful member of society
   and to develop individual abilities;

6 *- to be brought up in a spirit of peace*
   and universal brotherhood.
To enjoy these rights,
   regardless of race, colour, sex, religion,
   national or social origin."

7 *Let us pray:*

In my own part of the world, Lord,
   I pray today and commit myself
   to be loving and understanding
   in all that I do,
   and to be generous
   in giving of myself
   without expecting anything in return.
I pray and commit myself
   to have an attitude of respect
   for each and every person,
   treating everyone
   as the equals that they are.
All that I am determined to be, Lord,
   I ask for the power of your Spirit
   to enable me to be.
Amen.

✍ *Contrast 7 October.*

✍ *Each line of the quotes should be read slowly.*

✍ *See also 6 December.*

✍ "The secret of education
   is respecting the pupil."
   - Ralph Waldo Emerson

♪ Christ is our king; If I am lacking love; I give my hands; Take my hands; This is what Yahweh

58

1 20 miles outside Pope John Paul's city of Krakow in Poland lie the remains of the Nazi concentration camp of Auschwitz. The terrible place remains as a memorial to the dead, and a warning about the inhumanity that human beings can show to one another.

2 Many people visit Auschwitz and see the careful and systematic planning that went into the murder of 1.5 million people who were sent there during the Second World War.

3 There are many photographs on display in some of the buildings that used to be the concentration camp. Next to a photograph of starving children in Auschwitz is another of healthy, strong and cheerful German children wearing the uniform of the 'Hitler Youth'. Underneath that photo appear these words of Adolf Hitler:

4 *"I freed Germany*
from the stupid and degrading
errors and weaknesses
of conscience and right and wrong.
We will train young people
who will be capable of violence,
who will be domineering, cruel,
unyielding and without pity."

5 *Let us pray:*

God our Father,
it has been said
of many of the world's
worst war-criminals,
just how ordinary they looked.
In the ordinary events
of our daily lives,
inspire us always to be positive
in our attitude and in our decisions.
Deliver us from all that is evil.
Amen.

✍ *"Krakow" is pronounced "crack-ov".*

✍ *Contrast Hitler's words with what Jesus says about children in Luke 9⁴⁶⁻⁴⁸, 10²¹⁻²², 17², 18¹⁵⁻¹⁷. Contrast also 6 October.*

✍ *See 14 August regarding Maximilian Kolbe in Auschwitz.*

♪ If I am lacking love; Lord, make me a means, Make me a channel; Oh the word of my Lord *("you are young, my child")*; O let all who thirst *("bring the children")*

8 OCTOBER

1 People of the Jewish faith celebrate the New Year - 'Rosh Hashanah' - when it is late September or early October. It is the first of 10 days of prayer for forgiveness - 10 "penitential" days: a time when people focus on returning to God, growing closer to him, and realising how they need to grow in kindness to others. The last of the ten days is called 'Yom Kippur', which is considered the most holy of days in the Jewish Calendar. 'Yom Kippur' is sometimes called 'The Day of Atonement' - a word that means becoming "at-one" with God again.

2 Until the Temple in Jerusalem was destroyed by the Romans in 70 A.D., it was on this feastday that the high priest entered what was called "the holy of holies" in the Temple, where God's presence was thought to be focused in a special way. There the high priest would confess his sins and pray for all the people.

3 On the same day, the high priest would place his hands upon a goat as he prayed for God to forgive everyone. The goat - symbolically carrying the sins of the people - was then taken out into the wilderness of the desert. It is from this practice that we have the term "scapegoat" - one who is made to carry the wrongdoing of someone else; someone who can be blamed for the faults of others.

4 In our own times, 'Yom Kippur' remains the most special and prayerful day of the year. People of the Jewish faith spend most of 'Yom Kippur' in prayer and fasting, expressing sorrow for what they have done wrong.

5 In the synagogue, the rabbi and many of the worshippers wear white clothes. These reflect the joy of knowing that God takes away the sin of those who are sorry, and who are genuine in being deter-mined to change their attitude. At the end of the prayer service in the synagogue, the 'shofar' - the ram's horn - is blown, reminding people of the promises they have made to change their lives for the better.

6 *We'll take as our prayer a few words from the Old Testament prophet, Micah:*

7 **Who can compare with the Lord?**
He pardons what we do wrong,
and takes great pleasure
in having mercy.
He treads down our faults,
and he casts our sins
to the very bottom of the sea.

(Micah 7[18-20])

✍ *See 'Rosh Hashanah' - 21 September.*

✍ *The New Testament Letter to the Hebrews is written to Christians who converted from the Jewish faith. That letter, and particularly Hebrews 4[14]-5[10],7[26]-10[25] presents Jesus as the perfect high priest who enters the presence of God the Father, offering the perfect sacrifice of himself that does take all our sin away, making us "at-one" again with God.*

𝄞 Be not afraid; Come into his presence; Do not be afraid; In you, my God; Oh the love of my Lord

1. In 1990, the Hubble Telescope was launched into orbit 373 miles *(600 km)* above the earth's surface. The telescope observes distant space without interference from the atmosphere or light in the sky from cities. Signals beamed down from Hubble show objects far more clearly than seen before, viewing seven times further away than can telescopes on the Earth itself.

2. On this day in 1997, newspapers reported that the Hubble Telescope had detected a star that is brighter than 10 million suns, giving out as much energy in 6 seconds as our sun does in a year. It has been called *"the Pistol Star"* and is in our own galaxy - our own gathering of stars. It is about 25,000 light-years away from us - in other words it takes light 25,000 years to reach us from there. We therefore see it as it was 25,000 years ago.

3. If this star was placed where our sun is, its diameter is so great that it would extend far beyond Earth's orbit, to about that of Mars.

4. *Let us reflect and pray*
   about our ordinary vision,
   and our vision
   through telescopes and microscopes:

5. **God our Father,**
   may the vastness of your creation
   that we can begin to see
   through a telescope,
   remind us of the abundance
   of your love.
   May the lowliness
   of the smallest creatures and cells
   that we can see through a microscope,
   remind us
   of how insignificant - yet special -
   we appear to be.
   May our vision each day
   of the world around us
   remind us that you so loved the world
   that you sent Jesus, your Son,
   to be one of us.
   In all that we observe,
   open our eyes
   so that we may really see
   and grow in wonder and appreciation.
   Amen.

✍ *Light travels at 186,000 miles per second (300,000 km/sec)*

✍ *Our galaxy of stars we call "the Milky Way". It is spiral-shaped and 'flat' like a saucer when viewed sideways and from within. As we are part of that "saucer", we view the rest of our galaxy as a light milky streak or band across the sky in the same way as a saucer held horizontally in front of our eyes appears as a band before us.*

✍ *Sherlock Holmes said to Doctor Watson: "You see, but you don't observe."*

♪ I watch the sunrise; Laudato sii; O Lord my God, the Father of creation; O Lord my God, when I in awesome wonder

10 OCTOBER

1 An inspiring prayer of Saint Francis of Assisi is called *"The Canticle of Creation"*, which we will use as our prayer today:

2 O Most High, all-powerful,
good Lord God,
to you belong praise, glory,
honour and all blessing.

3 Be praised, my Lord,
for all your creation
and especially for our Brother Sun,
who brings us the day and the light;
he is strong and shines magnificently.
O Lord, we think of you
when we look at him.

4 Be praised, my Lord, for Sister Moon,
and for the stars
which you have set shining and lovely
in the heavens.

5 Be praised, my Lord,
for our Brothers Wind and Air
and every kind of weather
by which you, Lord,
uphold life in all your creatures.

6 Be praised, my Lord, for Sister Water,
who is very useful to us,
and humble and precious and pure.

7 Be praised, my Lord, for Brother Fire,
through whom
you give us light in the darkness:
he is bright and lively and strong.

8 Be praised, my Lord,
for Sister Earth, our Mother,
who nourishes us and sustains us,
bringing forth
fruits and vegetables of many kinds
and flowers of many colours.

9 Be praised, my Lord,
for those who forgive for love of you;
and for those
who bear sickness and weakness

in peace and patience
- you will grant them a crown.

10 Be praised, my Lord, for our Sister Death,
whom we must all face.

11 I praise and bless you, Lord,
and I give thanks to you,
and I will serve you in all humility.

✍ *For St Francis, see 4 October and a footnote of 20 October.*

✍ *Daniel 3$^{52-90}$ is the Litany or Song of the Three Young Men in the fiery furnace. The words include thanks expressed to God for all of creation.*

✍ "Joy in looking and comprehending
is nature's most beautiful gift."
- Albert Einstein

✍ *It is from paragraph 9 that the dedication at the front of this book is made.*

🎶 All creatures of our God and King; Laudato sii; Look at the sky, the stars proclaim my glory; *(all of which are wordings of this Canticle of St Francis)*

1 A British nurse called Edith Cavell was invited to become matron of a nurses' training centre in Brussels, Belgium. 7 years later, with the outbreak of the First World War in 1914, the place became a Red Cross hospital. During the German Occupation, she treated German soldiers sent there, and also nursed captured British, French and Belgian soldiers.

2 Meanwhile, over a period of months, Edith gave shelter in her house to some 200 British, French and Belgian soldiers, and then arranged for them to escape from Occupied Belgium. She was found out and arrested by the Germans. On this day in 1915, Nurse Edith Cavell was sentenced to death by the German authorities. She was executed by firing squad at 2.00am the following morning, aged 50.

3 With "patriotism" meaning love of one's country, Edith Cavell said:

> *"I realise that patriotism is not enough. I must have no hatred or bitterness towards anyone."*

4 *Let us pray:*

**Lord our God,
we pray that,
no matter what happens to us,
we may grow
as people who are generous enough
to hold no hatred or bitterness
towards anyone.
Amen.**

✍ *Edith Cavell: 1865-12/10/1915*

✍ *On hearing of Edith Cavell's execution, British Prime Minister Herbert Asquith addressed the House of Commons, saying:*
    "She has taught the bravest men among us the supreme lesson of courage."

🎵 Abide with me; Father, I place *(sung slowly)*; God forgave my sin *("to share his love")*; If I am lacking love

1 In the early 1800s a child could be hanged for stealing. Society's attitude to those committing crimes was very harsh.

2 Elizabeth Fry set out to visit the women in Newgate Prison in London. The governor of the prison told her that the women were wild. He himself never entered except with soldiers to guard him, but she was determined to go to them. There she found 300 women living in filthy conditions, and without heat or light or fresh air. There were no places for washing, and no beds - just straw on the floor. Perhaps worst of all, the women's children lived with them in the prison.

3 *"Together we can make this prison a better place,"* Elizabeth Fry said to the women. *"Let us work together and ask for God's help,"* she said. Others volunteered to visit the prison and help improve conditions there, along with the prisoners themselves. Medicines, clothes and food were brought in. Elizabeth showed the women how to sew and knit, and they began to make clothes for themselves and their children. One of the prisoners became a teacher for the children there.

4 Elizabeth Fry approached Members of Parliament, newspaper editors and other influential people, to help in reforming prison life. *"Prisons are not just places for punishing people,"* she said. *"We must help them to lead better lives. Kindness will do far more than cruelty."*

5 Elizabeth told of the need to provide work materials for the prisoners. She brought about so many changes for the better that she was asked to visit prisons throughout Britain and other European countries.

6 Elizabeth Fry shared with the women her great faith in God's love, and she prayed with them. She died on this day in 1845, having influenced many people to change their attitude towards prisoners.

7 *Let us pray:*

God our Father,
one of the greatest yearnings
of the human spirit
is to be free,
and we know
that there are many kinds
of restriction
that limit and confine us.
Inspire us today to help others
to grow in freedom
through the respect
and understanding
and kindness
that we can offer.
Amen.

✍ *Elizabeth Fry: 21/5/1780-12/10/1845. She was a Quaker.*

✍ *St Augustine said:* "Hate the sin but love the sinner."

✍ "When Christ said 'I was in prison and you visited me', he did not draw a distinction between the guilty and the innocent."
- Pope John Paul II, June 1982

🎼 God's Spirit is in my heart *("prisoners no more")*

Zacchaeus - a changed person

The little man, Zacchaeus,
was the tax-collector
who cheated people
and was isolated by others.
No force of argument could change him,
nor any name-calling
by those he had mis-treated.
It was only in your presence, Lord Jesus,
that he changed
and became a better person.
It was only in your presence
that this little man
learned to walk tall.
Influence us, Lord,
as we now pause to remind ourselves
that you are with us.

(Lk 19$^{1-9}$)
(see page 183)

13 OCTOBER

1 In the 1800s, as European settlers moved further west in the United States of America, attempts were made to restrict the Native Americans to *'Indian Reservations'*. Chief Seattle of the Suquamish Tribe (in what is now the State of Washington) spoke about his people's love of and respect for the land. We'll hear part of *"Chief Seattle's Testimony"*:

2 *"The Great Chief in Washington sends word*
that he wishes to buy our land.
We will consider your offer,
for we know that if we do not sell,
the white man may come with guns
and take our land.

3 *"How can you buy or sell the sky,*
the warmth of the land?
The idea is strange to us.
If we do not own the freshness of the air
and the sparkle of the water,
how can you buy them?

4 *"Every part of this earth*
is sacred to my people.
Every shining pine needle,
every sandy shore,
every mist in the dark woods,
every humming insect is holy
in the memory and experience
of my people.

5 *"The perfumed flowers are our sisters.*
The deer, the horse, the great eagle
- these are our brothers.

6 *"So, when the Great Chief in Washington*
sends word that he wishes to buy our land,
he asks much of us,
for this land is sacred to us.

7 *"The earth is not the white man's brother*
but his enemy,
and when he has conquered it
he moves on.
He kidnaps the earth from his children
and does not care.

He treats his mother, the earth,
and his brother, the sky,
as things to be bought, plundered,
sold like sheep or bright beads.
His appetite will devour the earth
and leave behind only a desert.

8 *"This earth is precious to God,*
and to harm the earth
is to heap contempt on its Creator.
Preserve the land for your children
with all your strength,
with all your mind,
and with all your heart,
and love it - as God loves us all."

9 We'll use as our prayer some words written by a Native American:

10 **Great Spirit,**
whose voice I hear in the winds,
and whose breath
gives life to all the world,
hear me!
I am small and weak;
I need your strength and wisdom.

11 **Let me walk in beauty,**
and may my eyes always see
the red and purple sunset.
May my hands
respect the things that you have made,
and my ears be sharp to hear your voice.

12 **Make me wise**
so that I may understand
the things that you have taught
my people.
Let me learn the lessons
that you have hidden in every leaf
and rock.

13 **Make me always ready to be with you**
with clean hands and straight eyes.
So, when life fades as the fading sunset,
my spirit may come to you
without shame.

✍ "The Great Chief in Washington" *refers to the U.S. President, living in the U.S. capital city of* "Washington D.C." *on the eastern coast, whereas the State of Washington is on the western coast.*

✍ *Chief Seattle died in June 1866. Compare this* 'Testimony of Chief Seattle' *(written in 1854) with the* 'Canticle of Creation' *(10 October) of St Francis of Assisi, and* 'Psalm 104' *(26 October).*

✍ *What might be meant by saying that the white man* "kidnaps the earth from his children" *(paragraph 7 above)?*

✍ *The last lines of paragraph 8 reflect Mt 22³⁶. Chief Seattle (after whom the sea-port is named) became a Christian.*

✍ *The spirit of what we have read today can be observed in the film* 'Dances With Wolves', *starring Kevin Costner.*

𝄞 Laudato sii; Thank you for fathers *(verses 2 & 3)*; This day God gives me

14 OCTOBER

1 On 3 occasions in English history, 3 kings have ruled one after the other in the same year. It happened in 1936 and in 1483 and - most famously - in 1066.

2 King Edward the Confessor died that year. He was succeeded by his cousin, Harold. On this day in 1066, the Battle of Hastings took place. Harold (the last Saxon king) was killed in battle, and another cousin - William of Normandy - became the first Norman King of England. William the Conqueror was crowned king on Christmas Day 1066, in Westminster Abbey. The building of the Abbey by King Edward the Confessor had been finished earlier that year.

3 *Let us pray:*

**There are likely to be some sudden
  and abrupt changes in my life,
but there will be
many more changes
  that are slow in taking place.
When I face difficulties and crisis,
  I ask you, Lord, to help me
to be wise and balanced
  in my decisions,
strong in my friendships,
and faithful to you,
and so be more able
  to live at peace within.
Amen.**

The Saxon King Harold fought the Battle of Stamford Bridge (near York), defeating and killing the powerful Harald Hardrada, King of Norway, who had invaded. The battle-weary English (Saxon) army raced south on hearing the news of William's invasion from Normandy. At the Battle of Hastings (three weeks after the northern battle) King Harold was killed, and the English throne passed to the Normans, to the 38-year old William. The Conqueror claimed that his cousin, Edward, had promised him the throne. Yesterday, 13th October, marks the feastday of St Edward the Confessor.

The events of 1066 were recorded in what is known as the "Bayeux Tapestry" - 79 scenes embroidered on cloth that is 70 metres (230 feet) long. 978 years later, the reverse journey was made on D-Day as the Allies set out from England to invade Normandy (NW France) to defeat Nazi Germany. An equivalent tapestry of that invasion is on display in Portsmouth.

The phrase "It's all part of life's rich tapestry" (sometimes rendered "pageant" or "pattern") was used in the film "A Shot in the Dark" in which Peter Sellers played Inspector Clouseau.

If I was thinking of designing a "tapestry" of my own life, which places and key events (both positive and negative) and which significant people would I include? How might I decorate the margins of the tapestry e.g. with symbols of my talents and interests, and world events that have taken place during my lifetime?

*In **1936** George V died. His son became Edward VIII but abdicated later that year, and Edward's brother became King George VI - he was Queen Elizabeth's father.*

*In **1483** Edward IV died. He was succeeded by his 12-year-old son, Edward V, who was murdered - possibly by his uncle, who became King Richard III.*

♪ Come let us go up; Father, I place; His banner over me is love; In you my God; Lord, make me a means; Make me a channel

1 The persecution of Christians has been severe in Communist countries. Karl Marx was the inspiration behind Communism.

2 The daughter of Karl Marx explained to a friend that she had never been brought up in any religion, and had never been religious in any way. She said that she had just come across a prayer *"which I really wish could be true"*, she said.

3 She was asked about the prayer. Then slowly, the daughter of the founder of Marxism began to say: *"Our Father, who art in heaven, hallowed be thy name..."*

4 Let's remind ourselves for a moment that we are in our Father's presence...

(Pause...)

5 Let's pray those same words - *"the Lord's Prayer"* - joining in spirit with those millions of people down the ages who have suffered and been imprisoned and tortured for their faith:

6 **Our Father, who art in heaven,
hallowed be thy name;
thy kingdom come;
thy will be done on earth
as it is in heaven.
Give us this day our daily bread;
and forgive us our trespasses
as we forgive those
who trespass against us;
and lead us not into temptation,
but deliver us from evil.**

✍ *Dag Hammarskjöld said:*
*"Hallowed be **thy** name*
- not mine.
***Thy** kingdom come*
- not mine."

✍ "In the Lord's prayer we have a summary of the entire Gospel"
— *Tertullian (c.160-220AD)*

✍ *Karl Marx: 5/5/1818-14/3/1883. He died in London and is buried in Highgate Cemetery.*

✍ *Karl Marx's daughter spoke the prayer in her own language of German.*

♪ Abba, Father; Seek ye first; Sing a simple song

1 750 years ago, Leonardo Fibonacci solved a puzzle about the numbers of breeding rabbits that might be produced. Mathematically he worked out that the numbers of pairs of rabbits, month by month, would be:

1, 1, 2, 3, 5, 8, 13, 21, 34, 55....

2 What do we notice about these figures? Each is the sum of the previous two numbers.

3 The numbers 5, 8, and 13 occur in music: an octave (for example 'C' to 'C') covers 8 white notes and 5 black (13 in all) on the piano.

4 This 'Fibonacci Series' of numbers occurs throughout nature. We could look at plants with individual leaves coming out from a single stem. If we count the number of leaves from one leaf to the next that is directly above it, that will be a Fibonacci Number. It is the same with pine cones and a leafed cactus.

5 We can look at plants like the sunflower or the daisy. Counting the clockwise and then the anti-clockwise spirals of seeds or tiny flowers on the head of the plant, they will be consecutive Fibonacci Numbers.

6 Dividing a Fibonacci Number by the previous Fibonacci Number gives a result close to 1.618 . The higher up we go in the Fibonacci Series, the more precise the result becomes. That number (a recurring decimal) is given the Greek letter "phi":

$$\varphi = 1.618034$$

7 Experiments have shown that buildings whose walls are in proportions that are 1 to 1.618 look "just right" to people - aesthetically they are the most pleasing to the eye. The Greeks knew this, and so much Greek art and architecture (such as the Parthenon in Athens) is based on these proportions which are called the *"Golden Ratio"* or *"Golden Mean"*.

8 Artists down the ages have often used the same proportions which they know are naturally appealing to the observer.

9 Within a *"Golden Ratio Rectangle"*, we could make a square that is based on one of the shorter sides. The remaining rectangle is then of exactly the same proportions as the original. That, too, can be divided into a square and rectangle, and that can be repeated, on and on. If diagonally opposite points in the squares are joined up to form a spiral, we get precisely the same spiral as a snail's shell, a nautilus sea-shell, the flower of a rose, and a breaking wave on the sea-shore. The same proportions are seen in the great spiral galaxies of stars in space.

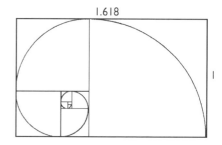

1.618

1

10 *Let us pray:*

**Lord God,
may all that we see and discover
lead us to grow
in wonder and appreciation.
Amen.**

which is much more easily understood if expressed in the form
263 + 38 = 301
in the Arabic-Hindu system that we now use!
Try division or multiplication with Roman numerals!

🖎 Fibonacci had set a question. If a pair of rabbits take a month to mature, and then produce a new pair every month after that, what would be the total number of rabbits each month?

Presuming that each pair is one male and one female and that no rabbits die, the following set of numbers is the result:
1,1,2,3,5,8,13,21,34,55,89,144,233....

🖎 Leonardo da Vinci's drawing ("Vitruvian Man") of a man with outstretched arms and legs within both a circle and a square, demonstrates the same proportions of Φ (phi) in the measurements from head to waist, from waist to feet, and from head to feet. The "Divine Proportion" and the "Golden Section" are other names for the "Golden Mean".

🖎 In Van Gogh's painting, "Mother and Child", Mary's face fits perfectly into a "Golden Rectangle". Use of the same proportions is seen in the work of more recent artists, e.g. with the Impressionist Georges Seuret. The innovative 20th Century architect, Le Corbusier, designed the rooms of multi-storey villas in the proportions of the 'Golden Rectangle'.

🖎 Before Britain joined the international standard for paper sizes (e.g. A4, A5), British Imperial measurements included Foolscap paper, measuring 8 inches by 13 inches - two consecutive Fibonacci Numbers which, as we know, when divided give Φ (the "Golden Ratio") producing that aesthetically pleasing "Golden Rectangle".

🖎 Another curiosity is that
whilst Φ = 1.618
its reciprocal (1 divided by Φ) = 0.618
and its square = 2.618

🖎 Leonardo Fibonacci (pronounced "fib-on-atch-ee"), 1175-1250, was a contemporary of St Francis of Assisi (c. 1182-1226). Fibonacci was one of the first to introduce into Europe the Arabic-Hindu system of numbers that we now use and take for granted:
0, 1, 2, 3, 4, 5, 6, 7, 8, 9
including the all-important concept of zero!
Prior to his time, Roman numerals were still in use e.g.
CCLXIII plus XXXVIII = CCCI

🎼 Oh the love of my Lord ("all the beauty I see")

17 OCTOBER

1 At this time of year, we can see and hear flocks of geese as they fly in V-formation, migrating into Britain from Iceland or Russia.

2 Scientists at California's University of Technology have used computers and flight simulators to show that flocks of geese fly in V-formation because that is the most energy-efficient way to fly.

3 The air turbulence from the lead goose gives uplift to the two geese on either side. In turn, uplift is passed on to the geese further out in the V-formation. Each goose takes its turn to be leader, and then moves to rest on the outer edge of the V-shape. As the geese co-operate with one another, a flock can fly over 70 % further than the same number of geese flying individually.

4 *Let us pray:*

In times of difficulty, Lord,
  we appreciate
  the support and encouragement
  of others.
In better times
  we feel stronger and more secure.
Remind us then
  to co-operate with other people
  and look out
  for the needs of others,
  being ready to offer a smile, a word,
  and other support
  and encouragement.
Amen.

✍ *The newly-introduced Canada Geese do not migrate. Other geese in Britain migrate into the country each October, and return to Iceland or Russia in March. The front cover of this volume shows snow geese in flight.*

✍ *It is also the case that if a goose has to drop out of the flock because of illness or exhaustion, one or two other geese will accompany it and stay with it until strong enough to fly again. St Paul remarks that*
  "we who are strong
  ought to shoulder
  the burdens of the weak"
          - *Romans 14[1]*.

✍ *In Romans 12 (as given on 26 January) we read:* "love each other as much as brothers and sisters should".

✍ *Although a dove is generally accepted as one of the symbols of the Holy Spirit, in Celtic spirituality the Holy Spirit is represented by a Wild Goose.*

♪ Come, come, follow me; Follow me; For to those who love God; This day God gives me

1   When Thomas Edison died on this day in 1931, he had over 1,200 inventions patented to his name. He is perhaps best remembered for his invention of the electric light bulb, which we take so much for granted today.

2   Thomas Edison and his assistants tried various substances as the filament of the bulb, and different gases enclosed within the glass. One of the first bulbs that Edison produced, he handed to a young assistant to carry upstairs to another laboratory. Carefully the young man carried the bulb, step by step up the stairs. Suddenly he dropped it, and all their painstaking work was destroyed.

3   Edison and his team returned to work and spent 24 hours producing another bulb. When it was finished, and again had to be carried upstairs, he handed it to the same young man in a marvellous gesture of trust and confidence.

4   Thomas died on this day in 1931 - 52 years after inventing the light bulb. People throughout the United States were invited to turn off their lights for a minute that night as a sign of respect for Thomas Edison, who had brought such benefits to mankind.

5   *Let us pray,*
    remembering how Edison showed trust
    in giving his light bulb for a second time
    to the young man:

    Lord, may people be as ready
    to give me a chance, a break,
    and let me make a new start,
    as I am ready to be
    as equally generous to others.
    Forgive me my faults
    in the same way
    as I forgive and accept other people.
    Amen.

✍ *Thomas Edison: 11/2/1847-18/10/1931. He once said: "To stop is to rust." See also 19 October.*

✍ *It was in 1879 that Edison finalised his carbon-filament light bulb. He also produced motion picture equipment and discovered thermionic emission which would lead to the production of valves.*

♦ Father, I place into your hands; God forgave my sin; I give my hands; I watch the sunrise; Make me a channel *("where there is darkness, only light")*; The light of Christ

1 Thomas Edison, the great inventor, died on yesterday's date in 1931. He had invented the light bulb, the film projector, and a storage battery. He improved the telephone, the telegraph and the gramophone (record player).

2 Edison had only 3 months of formal schooling. Later in life he said:
> *"I never used to be able to get along.*
> *I used to feel that the teachers*
> *did not sympathise with me,*
> *and that my father*
> *thought I was stupid."*

3 He learned from his mother, and had an inquisitive mind which led him to explore and invent. When someone remarked how easy it must be for him to invent, he said:
> *"Genius is 1% inspiration*
> *and 99% perspiration!"*

4 *Let us pray:*

God our Father,
  may your Spirit be at work in my life
  so that I may transform
  into something positive
  whatever negative experiences
  I will face in life.
If I have been done down
  or treated unfairly,
  lead me to be concerned
  about fairness and justice to others.
If I have felt misunderstood,
  inspire me to listen to others
  and show genuine interest.
If I have been left out of things,
  remind me
  to welcome and include others.
If I have felt
  that I have experienced little support,
  show me how best to encourage others.
If I have not felt really appreciated,
  lead me to be generous
  in valuing and thanking others.

What I pray for today, Father,
  I also commit myself to work at.
Amen.

> *"Genius is 1% inspiration*
> *and 99% perspiration!"*

📖 *See 18 October.*

📖 "If people knew how hard I work to get my mastery, it wouldn't seem so wonderful after all" - *Michelangelo (which is similar to the quote in paragraph 3).*

🎵 Christ be beside me; Do not worry; Father I place; For to those who love God; If God is for us

1 Jesus talked of people - on dying - being faced with the consequences of what they have done (or not done) to others. He talked of how individuals react to those who are hungry or thirsty, strangers or without clothing, sick or imprisoned.

2 Each day we meet people who are - in many different ways - "hungry" or "thirsty" or are "strangers". Let's reflect as though Jesus himself was speaking the following words, knowing that he said that we are brothers and sisters to one another. Jesus added that what we do to them, we do to himself.

3 **I was hungry for a generous word**
- and you smiled and talked warmly.
I was hungry for a gesture of kindness
- and you went beyond
what I had hoped for.
I was hungry
for genuine understanding
- and you heard beyond my words.

4 **I was thirsty for life and vitality**
- and you helped me to grow.
I was thirsty for encouragement
- and you affirmed me and built me up.
I was thirsty for moral support
- and, willingly,
you shared my cup of suffering.

5 **I was a stranger to genuine welcome**
- and you gave me your full attention.
I felt lonely
- and you blessed me
with your presence.
I was a stranger to care and appreciation
- and you treated me
with courtesy and respect.

6 *Let's pause in silence to think how, in such small ways, we can set about to touch the lives of a few people today.*

The reflections today and on the 22nd were inspired by an idea of Flor McCarthy, SDB, based on Mt 25³¹⁻⁴⁶. See 22nd October for the other half of the text - "naked", "sick", "imprisoned".

Maybe it is this kind of attitude and action that St Francis of Assisi was referring to when he said to his followers:
"Go out and preach the Gospel.
If necessary, use words."
The feastday of St Francis is 4th October.

In Matthew 25³¹⁻⁴⁶ we read of Jesus saying that at the Last Judgement the (bad) goats will be placed on hs left hand and the (good) sheep at his right hand, from where the "good" will be called forward: "Come, receive your inheritance!" *This may be the foundation for the tradition in the theatre that "good" normally enters from the right - such as the "good fairy" in a pantomime.*

Christ is our king; God's Spirit is in my heart; If I am lacking love; I give my hands; O let all who thirst; O Lord all the world; Take my hands; Whatsoever you do

1 As primary school children set out to school on this day in 1966, 116 of them would be killed in the South Wales mining town of Aberfan.

2 It was 9.15 in the morning, and the young children were settling down to the first lesson of the day. Suddenly the mountain behind their school - 2 million tons of wet coal slag - began to move as a wall of mud about 20 metres high and 100 metres wide. 10-year-old Ashley Coffey later said:

3 *"We had swopped homework books, and were checking each other's sums. Suddenly the room caved in, and most of us were covered. Our teacher told me to run, but I looked down at my friend, David, and all his face was covered in blood. So I got him out and helped him up and dragged him out. The next thing I remember is being at home, and Grandpa was washing David's blood off me."*

4 Mothers who had seen their children off to school an hour earlier, dug with their hands, sinking waist-deep into the still-moving mud. Many had to be pulled away or they would have been trapped and killed themselves.

5 The collapse of the huge slag-heap was heard at the colliery a mile away. A thousand miners rushed over to dig their way into the school and neighbouring houses that were also engulfed. Every shovelful taken away was soon filled with more slime from the shifting mountain. Rescuers saw hundreds of tons of wet slag still breaking away 250 metres above them - the deadly waste was still moving.

6 Men worked for 3 days and 2 nights, digging for their children. A would-be rescuer said that they had discovered the body of the deputy headteacher, Mr Benyon, *"clutching 5 children in front of him, protecting them. They died holding each other."*

7 144 people were killed that morning at Aberfan, including 116 children aged between 5 and 11. Fewer than half of the students in the school survived.

8 Serious complaints had been made for years about the safety of the coal tip that towered over Aberfan. It had been built over a spring of water, sometimes causing flooding in the main street, and the tip was known to move.

9 At several of the funeral services, Psalm 23 was sung, and we use the words of that prayer from the Bible today:

10 **Lord, you are like a shepherd to me, and so I have all that I need.**

11 **You give me rest
in meadows of green grass,
and you lead me to water
where I gain new life and strength.
You guide me
along the way that is best for me.**

12 **Even when I walk in darkness
and everything around seems like death,
you are there, walking with me,
and the promise
of your love and faithfulness
helps to conquer my fear.**

13 **In the sight of those who do me down,
you invite me
to sit at table with you.
There you offer me
even more than I need,
and you remind me
that I am significant and special.**

14 **You call me to goodness and kindness
every day of my life,
and your house will be my home
my whole life long.**

📖 *Two years earlier thousands of tons of the coal sludge moved to the edge of the farm near the school, and many complaints had been made to the then Coal Board. A local vicar said of the Aberfan disaster:* "Some people are saying that it was an 'Act of God'. This was not so. It was a direct consequence of man's neglect and man's failure to act when every intelligent person must have foreseen a disaster of this kind."

📖 *When young people die suddenly, we are reminded poignantly to cherish the people we still have amongst us, showing them that we love and care for them - and telling them so.*

🎼 Abide with me; The Lord's my shepherd

1 Jesus talked of people - on dying - being faced with the consequences of what they have done (or not done) to others. He talked of how individuals react to those who are hungry or thirsty, strangers or without clothing, sick or imprisoned.

2 Each day we meet people who are - in many different ways - "naked" or "sick" or "imprisoned". Let's reflect as though Jesus himself was speaking the following words, knowing that he said that we are brothers and sisters to one another, and what we do to them we do to Jesus himself:

3 **I was naked**
because my dignity and self-respect
were undermined
- but you remained constant
and faithful.
I was stripped of my good name
through rumours that were untrue
- but you spoke up for me.
I felt diminished and vulnerable
- but you restored my confidence
and faith.

4 **I was sick and tired and downcast**
- but you brought healing into my life.
I was anxious about my future
- but you lifted my spirits,
and your love cast out my fear.
I felt overburdened
- but you shared my difficulties
and helped me to carry my cross.

5 **I felt imprisoned**
by those who judged and sentenced me
- but you accepted me for who I am.
I felt entrapped by circumstances,
- but you showed me
that I have control over my own life.
I was imprisoned
by hurts and anguish
- but you helped to ease the pain.

6 *Let's pause in silence to think how, in such small ways, we can set about to touch the lives of a few people today.*

✍ *The reflection is based on Mt 25$^{31-46}$ See 20 October for the other half of the text: "hungry", "thirsty", "strangers".*

✍ *We may miss some of the elements in the gospel passage of Mt 25$^{31-46}$. For example, we might miss the significance of the **good** people asking sincerely "When was it that...?" It has become second-nature to them to promote goodness and respond to the needs of others.*

✍ "God has imprinted on the soul of every human being the image of the world as he wants it to be."

Hildegard of Bingen

♪ Christ is our king; God's Spirit is in my heart; If I am lacking love; I give my hands; O Lord all the world; Take my hands; Whatsoever you do

1 Tomorrow is the anniversary of the death in 1991 of Gene Roddenberry, the creator of *'Star Trek'*, the science-fiction series.

2 In an episode of *'Star Trek: The Next Generation'*, the people who live on two moons are about to go to war with each other. With the help of the crew of the *'Enterprise'*, an ambassador persuades representatives of each group to trade places for a week, so that they will understand the others' point of view more clearly.

3 Having swopped places, both grow in their understanding of the other group. War is averted and they all live in peace.

4 The Sioux Native Americans had a custom that, before leaving to visit members of another tribe, individuals would raise their hands and pray these words:

5 *"Great Spirit,*
help me never to judge another person
without having first
walked in their moccasins
for two weeks."

6 *Let us pray to be free of prejudices:*

Lord, lead me
  not to be hasty
  in jumping to conclusions
  about people.
Influence me
  not to stereo-type individuals
  or make sweeping generalisations.
Free me from prejudices
  which leave no-one free.
Help me to appreciate
  that there are other ways
  of looking at things,
  realising that others can have
  as equally valid a view
  as mine.

Inspire me
  to grow in the ability
  to understand others
  and think as generously of them
  as I would like them to think
  of me.
Amen.

✍ *The incident from Star Trek is mentioned in the episode* "The Host" *of* 'Star Trek: the Next Generation', *and concerned the two moons of the planet* 'Peliar Zel'.

✍ *'Sioux' is pronounced 'soo'.*

✍ *Gene Roddenberry: 19/8/21-24/10/91*

✍ *'Trading Places' is the name of an amusing film in which Wall Street trader Dan Ackroyd is forced to swop roles with Eddie Murphy who had been walking the streets.*

✍ *"Sympathy" = having a sense of compassion for someone.*

"Empathy" = being involved and so really understanding and experiencing the same feelings as the other. "Empathy is *your* pain in *my* heart" - H.E.Luccock.

✍ *See also 13 July re judging others.*

♪ If I am lacking love; I give my hands; Lord, make me a means; Make me a channel; O Lord my God *("I see the stars")*; O Lord, all the world

24 OCTOBER

1 Today is **"United Nations Day"**, being the day on which the UN was established in 1945, after the world had seen what total war could do.

2 At the inaugural session of the United Nations in 1945 at the end of the Second World War, Britain's Prime Minister - Clement Attlee - stated that

"It is for the peoples of the world
to make their choice
between life and death."

3 We know that "peace" isn't simply the "absence of war", and so the UN seeks to promote good relationships between people and countries. The UN's choices for "life" include working
   - for refugees,
   - in health care,
   - in the growing of food, and
   - in promoting science and culture.

4 A passage in one of the first books of the Bible has God speaking these words about *"choosing life"*:
   "I set before you
   life or death,
   blessing or curse.
   Choose life, then,
   so that you and your descendants
   may live in my love."

   (Deut 30[19-20])

5 *Let us pray about "choosing life"*
in our own daily circumstances:

God our Father,
   peace in our world
   begins with the attitude and actions
   of individual people.
We pray
   that we may live in such a way
   that we are positive in our attitude,
   choosing "life"
   in the small events of this day

- **rather than choosing "death"**
that comes from a negative attitude
of criticism and finding fault,
of doing others down
and being miserable.
In choosing
   "life" rather than "death",
   living positively and cheerfully,
   may we bring life to others.
Amen.

📖 *"Inaugural" - the opening.*

📖 *Clement Attlee was elected British Prime Minister as the Second World War ended in 1945, and remained in office until 1951.*

📖 *For the United Nations, see also 27 Feb, 25 June, and 6 October.*

📖 "Why do you not look at God's love, which could set you free? Why do you not see all the good things that God is doing for you? Why do you not listen when God calls you back from spiritual death? Why do you prefer death to life?"
   Hildegard of Bingen (Scivias 1.4.10)

📖 *See the prayer of 12 October.*

📖 *St Francis of Assisi said:*
   "While you are proclaiming peace with your lips, be careful to have it even more fully in your heart."

🎵 Come let us go up; Lord, make me a means; Make me a channel

1 Margaret Clitherow was a butcher's wife in York during the sad and tragic times of the 16th Century when people were persecuted - some for being Catholic, and some for being Protestant.

2 In Margaret's time, an Act of Parliament had made it high treason to be a Catholic or encourage others to be Catholic. Yet Margaret kept a Catholic teacher for her own children and those of a few neighbours. She had a priest's hiding-place in her house, ready to conceal a visiting Catholic priest if her house was about to be searched.

3 One day, the house **was** searched, and candles and vestments used for Mass were discovered. Margaret was taken to Court and charged with treason. Standing before the Judge, she refused to plead "guilty" or "not guilty" to the charge of treason. By not pleading, she wanted to spare her children and servants and neighbours from having to give evidence. At the same time, she did not want to trouble the consciences of members of a jury.

4 The crime of sheltering or helping a priest was punishable by hanging, but Margaret knew that she faced a worse penalty if she did not plead in court. She was to be lain on the floor and have weights placed onto a door that would lie on top of her. A sharp stone was placed under her back and, on 25th March 1586, Mrs Margaret Clitherow was crushed to death in York, after she had prayed for Queen Elizabeth I.

5 Margaret Clitherow was one of the 40 Martyrs of England and Wales to be canonised - made "saints" - on this day in 1970.

6 In that century - the 1500s - there were also Protestant martyrs. 31 years before Margaret Clitherow's death, two Protestant bishops were burned at the stake in Oxford whilst the Catholic Mary was Queen. Bishop Hugh Latimer spoke to Bishop Nicholas Ridley as the flames were about to be lit:

"Be of good comfort, Master Ridley,
and play the man.
We shall this day light such a candle
by God's grace, in England,
as I trust shall never be put out."

7 *Let us pray:*

Jesus, light of the world,
lead us to be
tolerant and understanding of others,
looking for what unites people
rather than
what might divide and separate.
Inspire us always
to discover the best in one another
and work together
to build up your kingdom
in our world today. Amen.

✍ *Margaret Clitherow's house can still be visited at number 36, The Shambles, York. Her feastday is now 30th August, along with St Anne Line (another married woman) and St Margaret Ward - all martyrs. It was Pope Paul VI who canonised 'The 40 Martyrs of England and Wales' on this day in 1970.*

✍ *See 17 August for prayers of intercession based on themes in the sermon of Pope John Paul II during his visit to York on 31/5/82. The gathering was at Knavesmire Racecourse, York - the site of the gallows of other martyrs. John Paul said: "I deeply appreciate the presence here of many fellow-Christians. I rejoice that we are united in a common Baptism and in our renewed search for full Christian unity."*

✍ *An alternative prayer would be that of 1 August which gives thanks for those down the ages who have passed on the heritage of the faith.*

♪ Father, I place; Follow me *(sung slowly)*; O Lord all the world; Take my hands

1 *We'll use as our prayer today*
   a psalm from the Bible
   in which we give thanks for all of creation,
   knowing that what we see
   can inspire us
   to grow in a sense of wonder:

2 Lord our God, how great you are,
   and I give thanks to you.

3 You stretch out the heavens like a tent,
   with the sun to mark our days of work
   and the moon for our nights of rest.

4 Your fingers created the earth
   and wrapped it with the ocean
   like a cloak.
   There the ships sail,
   and beneath them
   glide the great sea creatures
   that you made to play with.

5 You pour down rain
   which the ground takes up.
   You set springs
   gushing forth in the valleys,
   and streams that flow
   between the mountains,
   giving water to all that lives.

6 You make grass grow for the cattle
   and crops in abundance for our needs.
   You bring goodness to the trees,
   and in their branches
   the birds build their nests.
   Swarms of all living creatures
   are so many
   that they could never be counted.
   What variety you have created, Lord,
   arranging everything so wisely!

7 You send your Spirit,
   and all things have life.
   Fill us with your Spirit, Lord,
   and give us new life,
   and renew the earth that you love.
   Amen.

   (Psalm 104)

📖 *Compare this psalm with St Francis' 'Canticle of Creation' (10 Oct) and 'The Testimony of Chief Seattle' (13 Oct).*

📖 *"A thing of beauty is a joy for ever" - John Keats - see 31 October.*

🎵 Laudato sii; Morning has broken; Thank you for fathers; Though the mountains may fall; Yahweh, I know you are near

1 One of the best-known landmarks in the world is that of the Statue of Liberty on an island in New York Harbour. The famous statue is over 46 metres *(152 feet)* high and is of a woman with a spiked crown, with a book in her left hand, and a torch held high in her outstretched right hand. That light shines as a beacon at night and through mists.

2 At the feet of the statue are broken chains, representing release from oppression, persecution and poverty - left behind by many of the immigrants arriving on ships in New York Harbour.

3 France had helped the United States to gain independence from Britain in 1776. 100 years later, French people raised money to build the Statue of Liberty as a gift to the U.S.A.

4 The people of Paris saw the huge statue rising above the housetops. 32 tons of copper were made into the 'skin' of the statue. Once completed, the statue was taken apart and crated to New York. As intended the copper would eventually corrode, giving the statue a blue-green colour.

5 Tomorrow, the 28th October, is the anniversary of the dedication of the Statue of Liberty by President Cleveland in 1886.

6 Let us pray for all refugees and exiles who are far from their homeland.
Lord, in your mercy - **hear our prayer.**

7 Let us pray for a greater understanding between people, in places where there is civil unrest and war.
Lord, in your mercy - **hear our prayer.**

8 Let us pray for all who are experiencing persecution and oppression.
Lord, in your mercy - **hear our prayer.**

9 Let us pray for all who would like to make a new start in their lives.
Lord, in your mercy - **hear our prayer.**

✍ *Could use the prayer about freedom on 12 October.*

✍ *The sculptor, Frédéric Bartholdi, called on Gustave Eiffel (who built Paris' metal tower) to design the iron support structure around which the figure would be built.*

✍ *The following words are from a poem entitled 'The New Colossus' by Emma Lazarus, and were placed on a plaque by the huge statue in 1903. "The golden door" is a name for New York Harbour.*
   "Give me your tired, your poor,
   Your huddled masses
      yearning to breathe free,
   The wretched refuse
      of your teeming shore.
   Send these, the homeless,
      tempest-tossed to me,
   I lift my lamp beside the golden door!"

✍ *The statue has since become an international symbol of liberty itself. During the pro-democracy demonstrations in Tiananmen Square in Beijing, China, from April to June 1989, a rough copy of the Statue of Liberty was built in the Square beneath the large portrait of Mao-Tse-Tung, China's first Communist leader. That demonstration was crushed ruthlessly with the deaths of hundreds of students on 3rd/4th June 1989.*

✍ *When carbon dioxide (CO_2) dissolves in rain water (H_2O), carbonic acid (H_2CO_3) is produced. This reacts slowly with copper to produce the blue-green copper carbonate that we see on roofs and statues and water fonts etc made of copper itself or brass (copper-zinc alloy) or bronze (copper-tin alloy). Blue-green corrosion products are often called 'patinas' or 'verdigris'.*

🎼 Christ is our king *("freedom is waiting; all one day will be free")*; Follow me; God's Spirit is in my heart *("set the downtrodden free")*; Lay your hands *("sent to free the broken-hearted")*

1 It is in late October or early November that the State Opening of Parliament takes place. Many people crowd the streets of London to watch the Queen's procession to the Palace of Westminster - the Houses of Parliament. Many others watch on TV, and it was on this day in 1958 that the State Opening of Parliament was televised for the first time.

2 The Queen sends her messenger (called "Black Rod") to the House of Commons to summon MPs to join her in the House of Lords. As "Black Rod" approaches the doors to the debating chamber of the House of Commons, the doors are closed on him. With a steel rod he knocks three times. The Commons then invite the Queen's messenger to enter.

3 It was over 300 years ago that King Charles I stormed into the House of Commons, seeking to arrest 5 MPs who opposed him. It was the start of the Civil War. Since then no king or queen has ever set foot in the House of Commons. These days, the closing of the door on "Black Rod" is a reminder that Parliament is the supreme authority in the land, and no leader or king or queen is above the laws set by Parliament.

4 When the MPs arrive in the House of Lords, the Queen reads out words that have been given to her by the government. The Queen's Speech sets out what the government intends to do in the following months. At the end of the Speech, the Queen says:

"My Lords
and Members of the House of Commons,
I pray that the blessing of Almighty God
may rest upon your counsels."

5 *Let us pray:*

Almighty God,
  we pray for all
  who are in positions of leadership
  in our country,
  that they may show
  wisdom and understanding.
We pray that they may live
  as people of integrity and honesty,
  growing in a sense
  of duty and responsibility,
  always being aware of the needy
  and ready to be of service to others.
Amen.

❖❖❖❖❖❖❖❖❖❖❖❖❖❖❖❖❖

✏ *The word "parliament" comes from the French "parler" - to speak. "Counsels" means discussion, recommendations, decisions.*

✏ *See also 5th November.*

✏ *The Queen's grandfather, King George V, was given a draft copy of the Speech that the government wanted him to make at the Opening of Parliament. He returned the Speech with a note: "What about A.G.?" No-one knew what "A.G." meant, and so a secretary asked him. "Almighty God!" the King replied. "There is not a word about him in this Speech!" It is said that George V never made a public speech without some reference to "Almighty God."*

♪ All that I am; Christ is our king; Come let us go up to the Lord; God's Spirit is in my heart; O Lord, all the world; Take my hands

1 In October 1997 some newspapers reported that an investment bank had given all its employees a day off to do charity work. From the secretaries to the chairman there were over 1,250 volunteers from the London office of Goldman Sachs. The scheme was also offered to the 10,000 staff world-wide.

2 The company did not seek publicity, and they acknowledged that some other firms also set aside a day for charity work. They said that they were determined to give something to local communities and, at the same time, help to build up the company's strong team spirit.

3 Some charity work involved being with young people. One group worked in an adventure playground, making as much noise as the children themselves. It was a new experience for some of the children, finding adults who were willing to spend quality time with them and play games with them. One bank employee later said that he was glad of the opportunity: *"My work is quite intense, with long hours and lots of travelling. You lose focus on things like this. It's good to get a proper balance on the real world."*

4 *Let us pray:*

Lord,
   let us never be so tied up or occupied
   only with our own concerns
   that we lose focus on the real world.
Inspire us to live in such a way
   that we live
   balanced and unselfish lives,
   having quality time for others
   in which we are genuine
   in our attention
   and compassion and care,
   knowing that we are all
   brothers and sisters.
Amen.

📖 One group offered sports to children, giving each team-member of the 6 teams a coloured T-shirt with a letter from the word "united" on it. On the back of each was the letter and a word. "U" stood for "understanding",. "N" for nation, "I" for "international", "T" for "trust", "E" for "equal", "D" for "determination". What other words could have been chosen for the 6 letters of "united"? What words other than "united" could have been chosen, and what words could then have matched those letters?

📖 Hebrews 10^{24}: "God is faithful. Let us be concerned for each other, to stir a response in showing love and doing good." *See also James* 2$^{12-26}$ - *faith and good works.*

📖 Some Christians commit themselves to a "tithe" (as did the Jews) - giving a tenth (or another proportion) of their salary to the Church - see Deut 14$^{22-25}$, 2 Chron 31^5, Neh 10^{38}, Tobit 1$^{6-7}$. In a similar way, Muslims give money for the poor - "zakat" is one of the "Five Pillars" of Islam.

🎵 All that I am; If I am lacking love; I give my hands; O Lord all the world; Take my hands; Whatsoever you do

1 In 1938 it was clear to many people that war with Germany and with Japan was fast approaching. Even in the distant United States, many were fearful that their country would be drawn into war.

2 As many people shared that sense of anxiety, it was on this day in 1938 - before the advent of TV - that a broadcast went out on the radio in the United States. The broadcast included the sounds of panicking and attack, with police sirens and explosions and army gunfire.

3 On the radio, people heard the start of this broadcast as a newscaster suddenly stopped some music that was playing, and said: *"We interrupt this programme as we go over live to our reporter at the scene of the landing of the spacecraft from Mars."*

4 All of this was, in fact, a superb radio drama of a science-fiction book called *"The War of the Worlds"* by H.G. Wells. The brilliant 23-year-old director of the play was Orson Welles. The broadcasting of the drama had to be genuinely interrupted because police switchboards were jammed by people phoning in, thinking that the very real-like drama was, in fact, real! Thousands of people in New York and nearby towns panicked, jamming the roads, desperate to escape the destruction brought about by the Martians who were fast approaching them, according to the radio report!

5 Orson Welles went on to become a world-famous film director.

6 *Let us pray:*

Lord God,
when difficulties surround us,
help us to keep a sense of balance,
and stay peaceful within.
Amen.

Their surnames sound identical, but H.G. Wells and Orson Welles were not related.

Lord, make me a means; Make me a channel; Walk with me, O my Lord; Yahweh, I know you are near

1 This day saw the birth in 1795 of the poet, John Keats. We'll listen to the first verse of his poem, *"Ode to Autumn"*:

2 *Season of mists and mellow fruitfulness,*
Close bosom-friend of the maturing sun;
Conspiring with him how to load and bless
With fruit the vines
  that round the thatch-eaves run;
To bend with apples the mossed cottage-trees,
And fill all fruit with ripeness to the core;
To swell the gourd, and plump the hazel shells
With a sweet kernel; to set budding more,
And still more, later flowers for the bees,
Until they think warm days will never cease,
For summer
  has o'er-brimmed their clammy cells.

3 *Let us pray:*

Lord, we give thanks
   for all that the earth has given
   in recent months,
   and we give thanks, too,
   for all the work of human hands.
As the land lies fallow, at rest,
   remind us of our need
   to keep a healthy balance
   in our lives each day.
Amen.

✏ *John Keats: 31/10/1795-23/2/1821. See the foot-note of 26 October.*

✏ *"Gourd" is any fleshy-fruited plant that trails or climbs e.g. cucumber, marrow, pumpkin.*

✏ *In the last 3 lines (which are about bees) we have repetition of "mm" and "ss" - the very sounds of bees. "Onomatopoeia" is the term used for sounds in words that reflect what they are referring to.*

✏ *See also 2 October regarding Autumn.*

✏ *31st October is the eve(ning) before the feast of All Hallows, All Saints - hence "Hallowe'en".*

🎵 Laudato sii; Thank you for fathers *("sing of the autumn")*

1 Today's feastday of 'All Saints' **isn't** about those who are publicly named as saints - each of those has their own feastday. Instead, on the Feast of 'All Saints' we think of many ordinary good people who walked with God in their daily lives, and who are now dead. Today is **their** feastday - the unmentioned saints - who now live in God's presence.

2 In the early Church, "saint" was a name for a person whom today we would call a "committed Christian". In the Bible - after the four gospels - we can find the word "saint" over 60 times. Each reference concerns **living** people who seek to follow Jesus. For example, Paul writes to some Christians:

3 *"If any of the saints are in need,*
you must share with them."   Rom 12[13]

4 *"To all of you in Rome*
whom God loves greatly,
all of you called to be saints:
may God our Father...
send you peace."   Rom 1[7]

5 This feastday of 'All Saints' also reminds us of our own potential, of what (hopefully) we are in the process of becoming. A Christian living 150 years after Jesus, wrote:
"The glory of God
is a person living fully."

6 Paul writes to a group of "saints" - committed Christians - in the Greek city of Ephesus. He starts off that letter with the words:
"To the saints
who are faithful to Christ..."   Eph 1[1]

7 We'll make our prayer today from other words in that same letter.

8 *Let us pray:*

When I think of the greatness
of God's plan,
I fall on my knees
before God the Father.
From his great wealth
may he give us power through his Spirit
that we may grow strong within.
Through faith, may we discover
that Christ has made his home
within each of us.

9 Then, with our roots and foundations
firmly built on God's love,
may we, with all of his saints,
grasp just how wide and long
and high and deep
is Christ's love.
Yes, may we come to experience
for ourselves
the love of Christ
so that we may be filled completely
with God himself.

10 This prayer we ask of God
who can accomplish far more
than we could ever ask for or imagine.
Amen.

(based on Eph 31[14-21])

ment of the concentration camp victim, Corrie Ten Boom:

"There is no pit so deep
that God's love is not deeper still."

✎ Other references in the New Testament to "saints" as living people who are committed Christians, include: 2 Cor 9^{12},13^{12}; Phil 1^1; Col 1^2. See also Colossians 3^{12-17}: "You are God's chosen ones, his saints, and this is how you should live..."

✎ "The glory of God" quote is by St Irenaeus of Lyons, c. 140-202.

✎ The gospel for this feastday is that of the Beatitudes: Matthew 5^{1-12}(see 16 Dec).

✎ The Second Vatican Council was a meeting in Rome of the world's RC bishops between 1962 and 1965. In their document called "The Church" (Lumen Gentium/De Ecclesia) they wrote:
"All Christians in whatever walk of life are called to holiness - the fullness of Christian life which leads to a more fully human way of living.... They should use their Christ-given strength to become holy so that, following in his footsteps and growing in his image, and doing the will of God in everything, they may wholeheartedly devote themselves to the glory of God and to the service of their neighbour. And so the holiness of the Church - the People of God - will grow and bear fruit, as the life of many a saint shows clearly." (#40, paraphrased)

✎ "The saints
are the sinners who keep on trying"
- Robert Louis Stevenson.

✎ The Maastricht Treaty came into force on this day in 1993. 'The European Community' was re-named 'The European Union'.

❖❖❖❖❖❖❖❖❖❖❖❖❖❖❖❖❖❖❖❖

✎ In the prayer, the 4 terms "wide and long and high and deep" are not meant to indicate the 3 spatial dimensions, but are descriptive of the fullness of God's love, as reflected in the state-

𝄞 For all the saints; In him we knew a fullness; This, then, is my prayer ("may you, with all the saints" = Ephesians 3)

2 NOVEMBER

1 Today is often called "All Souls' Day" and it is an opportunity to remember and pray for those we have loved who have died. We'll listen to a short poem about 'dying':

2 *"What is dying?*
The ship sailed away
and I stand watching
till it fades on the horizon,
and someone at my side says: 'The ship is gone.'
Gone where? Gone from my sight, that is all;
the ship is just as large as when I saw it.
As I see the ship grow smaller
and go out of sight,
it is just at that moment
that there are others in a different place
who say:
'Watch; here the ship comes'"
and other voices take up a glad shout:
'You have arrived!'
- and that is what dying is about."

3 *Let us pray:*

We give back to you, Father,
   those whom you first gave to us.
You did not lose them
   in giving them to us
   and so we do not lose them
   in their return to you.

4 Your Son has taught us
   that life is eternal
   and love cannot die.
So death is only an horizon
   - the limits of our sight.

5 Open our eyes
   and lift us up,
   so that we may see more clearly.
Draw us closer to you
   so that we may know
   that we are nearer to our loved ones
   who are with you.

6 **And while you prepare a place for us**
as you have promised,
prepare us also for that happy place,
that where you are, we may be also,
with those we have loved, for ever.
Amen.

📖 *The prayer is based on words variously attributed to William Penn (1644-1718), subsequently adapted by Bede Jarret OP and others. See also 5, 8 April; 25 and 31 August; and prayers 65-67 in the Appendix of Volume 2.*

📖 *The source of the reflection* "What is dying?" *is not known.*

📖 *See also 15 & 27 November re. dying.*

📖 *Jesus said:*
"Blessed are those who mourn", *knowing that only those who love greatly can mourn. Similar emotions and feelings as to the death of a loved one may be faced in other situations. "Mourning" may be an appropriate term to use at times of failing health, the loss of a job, the breakdown of a relationship, no longer being able to do what one used to, divorce, removal of part of the body, loss of reputation or standing, or a radical change in circumstances.*

🎵 Abide with me; Blest be the Lord *(sung slowly)*; For to those who love God; He who would valiant be; If God is for us; My Lord, my master

1 The late 1960s and the 70s saw the start of exploration for oil and gas in the North Sea. It was on this day in 1975 that Queen Elizabeth formally opened the first underwater pipeline to bring North Sea oil ashore. From BP's *'Forties Field'* in the North Sea, the pipe runs 110 miles on the sea bed, and then 130 miles to the oil refinery at Grangemouth on the Firth of Forth, near Edinburgh.

2 We live in a nation of many natural resources - such as coal, oil, gas, metal ores and water - all of which we tend to take for granted. Without such natural resources, Britain could never have started the Industrial Revolution, and our history and our present circumstances would be quite different.

3 *Let us pray:*

God our Father,
  we live in a nation
  of many natural resources.
We pray for wisdom
  that we may use them well
  whilst also caring for our environment.
We pray, too,
  that the many *human* resources
  of all nations
  may develop
  as people respect and value
  the dignity and rights
  and responsibilities
  of each individual.
Amen.

📖 *Over millions of years, oil and gas have formed as tiny sea creatures died and fell to the bottom of the sea where they became subjected to great pressure and heat from sediments forming above them.*

📖 *Today saw the launch by the Soviet Union in 1957 of* 'Sputnik II'. *The spacecraft had a dog on board - called Laika - which was the first living creature to orbit the Earth.*

🎼 Be not afraid *("raging waters in the sea")*; Colours of day; Give me joy *("oil")* in my heart; Morning has broken

4 NOVEMBER

1 Living on the relatively small island of Great Britain, we tend to think in terms of short distances. We may imagine, for example, that Australia and New Zealand are near-neighbours, yet they are 1100 miles apart, with a 2-hour time-difference between New Zealand and the nearest point on the east coast of Australia.

2 We may think our own continent of Europe is big, but Africa is almost 3 times the land area of Europe.

3 We may have the impression that India is teeming with people. Yet, thinking of an area of land in the United Kingdom occupied on average by 100 people, India has 124 people living in the same area of land. Holland is far more heavily populated with 190 to the same area of land.

4 *Let us pray:*

God our Father,
 extend our horizons,
 widen our vision,
 and remind us
 how inter-connected we are
 as your sons and daughters.
Breathe your Spirit into us
 that we may live more truly
 as brothers and sisters
 who care for one another. Amen.

dren - but I have never seen any programme so full of love, the foster families so well-planned, the children so vibrant and healthy."

For more details and leaflets about the wide variety of self-help offered at 'RTU' by Brother James and his colleagues, and for ways in which you might possibly help to sponsor a child (or make a special donation at Christmas or in someone's memory) you are welcome to write to:

> *Mr & Mrs Cassidy, AFSC*
> *11 Ovington Avenue,*
> *Boscombe East*
> *Bournemouth BH7 6SA*

Mr & Mrs Cassidy co-ordinate in Britain the raising of funds for "Reaching the Unreached", *which is Registered Charity No. 362675. All contributions are acknowledged and received with gratitude.*

A full-page advertisement about the work of 'RTU' and Brother James Kimpton appeared in the 'Universe' *on 8/3/98 and the* 'Catholic Times' *on 15/3/98.*

> *Brother James Kimpton, FSC*
> *Reaching the Unreached of Village India,*
> *Ganguvarpatti,*
> *Periyakulam TK*
> *S.India 624203*

📖 *The natural resources in Britain (such as coal, oil, gas, ores, water, good soil) are vastly greater than those of India, and have contributed to a certain quality of life for those who live in Britain.*

In the 6-14 age group, only $^1/_2$ of India's 179 million children attend school.

Over $^1/_2$ of India's primary schools have no drinking water facilities. 85 in every 100 schools have no toilets.

Britain has an average of one doctor for every 600 people. India has one doctor for every 30,000.

❧❧❧❧❧❧❧❧❧❧❧❧❧❧❧❧❧❧❧❧

📖 *India has about 770 people per square mile* (300 per square kilometre), *which is only 1.24 times that of the UK, with about 620 people per square mile* (240 people per square kilometre). *Holland (the Netherlands) is far more densely populated with 1,180 people per square mile* (455 people per square kilometre). *Source for the figures:* 'The Cambridge Factfinder, 1997'.

📖 *Brother James Kimpton, a British De La Salle Brother, has worked in southern India with the poorest of the poor for over 45 years. He has set up* "Reaching the Unreached" (RTU) *as a means of helping the poor to help themselves. For example, in two of the 'RTU' villages, there are young people from babyhood to high school level who have been orphaned or abandoned. 5 or 6 children are placed with a 'mother' who is a widow or who has been deserted by her husband, but who is now paid to look after these children. Each foster mother runs her house independently as a family, and the children quickly learn to be brothers and sisters. 'RTU' arranges for the children's education and health-care. Each house is an integral part of the village community, giving the children cultural roots and a feeling of belonging.*

Visitors to 'RTU' have written: "I am deeply impressed by the beautiful smiles of the children... For years in the U.S. I have worked with abandoned, abused and neglected chil-

🎼 All the nations of the earth; Do not worry; If I am lacking love; O Lord all the world; Thank you for fathers *("and mothers and children")*

5 NOVEMBER

1 On the death of Queen Elizabeth I of England, the throne passed to the son of her cousin, Mary Queen of Scots. King James VI *(the sixth)* of Scotland became King James I of England. Uniting the two thrones would eventually lead to the joining of Scotland, England and Wales to form "Great Britain".

2 King James enforced some harsh anti-Catholic laws. A small group of Catholics conspired together in what is now known as the *"Gunpowder Plot"*. They placed 36 barrels of gunpowder in cellars underneath the House of Lords in the British Parliament. Guy Fawkes was to be the one who would light the fuse. It was intended that the explosion would kill the king and members of the Lords and Commons as they gathered for the State Opening of Parliament.

3 One of the conspirators leaked details of the Plot, and Guy Fawkes was discovered in the cellars. He was arrested, tortured and executed, along with the other conspirators.

4 Parliament decreed that, from then on, bonfires should be lit each year on the 5th of November to celebrate the deliverance from the *"Gunpowder Plot"*. Nowadays a "guy" is often still burnt as a reminder of Guy Fawkes.

5 In our own times, on the night before the State Opening of Parliament, there is a symbolic searching of the cellars of Parliament by the ceremonial *'Yeomen of the Guard'*, bearing lanterns.

6 *Let us pray:*

**God our Father,
  open our eyes
  to whatever may not be just and right
  in our own surroundings
  and in our society.**

**Enable us to be of good influence
  and work in a non-violent way
  to promote understanding
  and better relationships
  that will lead to justice and peace.
Amen.**

❖❖❖❖❖❖❖❖❖❖❖❖❖❖❖❖❖❖

📖 *See also 28 October re the State Opening of Parliament.*

📖 *"Great Britain" = England, Scotland and Wales.*

"The United Kingdom" = Great Britain and Northern Ireland.

📖 *It is this King James who ordered a new translation of the Bible into English in 1611. That "King James Bible" is also called "The Authorised Version".*

 Lord, make me a means; O Lord all the world

1 Dwight Eisenhower was the Supreme Commander of the Allied Force that invaded France on D-Day in 1944, that would lead on a year later to the downfall of Hitler.

2 After the War, Eisenhower went on to be elected President of the United States on the 5th of November in 1952. We'll listen to some words of his (spoken in Washington 5 months after his election), and we can bear in mind his own military background:

3 *"Every gun that is made,*
every warship launched,
every rocket fired
signifies, in the final sense,
*a **theft***
from those who hunger and are not fed,
those who are cold and are not clothed.
This world in arms
is not spending money alone.
It is spending the sweat of its labourers,
the genius of its scientists,
the hopes of its children."

4 **Let us pray for the wise use**
of the talents of our people
and of the wealth
of the natural resources
of our nation.

Lord, in your mercy, *hear our prayer.*

✍ *Dwight D Eisenhower: 14/10/1890-28/3/1969. He was elected President on 5/11/52, and took up office the following year, being President from 1953 to 1961. The speech quoted above was given in Washington on 16/4/1953.*

♪ Christ is our king; Come, let us go up; Lord, make me a means; Make me a channel; O Lord, all the world; There is a world

1 Albert Camus was a French writer and philosopher, reflecting on what life is about. He was born on this day in 1913. He wrote the following words about true friendship, trying to understand how best to be a friend to someone, how best to "be with" a person in difficulty:

2 *"Don't walk in front of me - I may not follow.*
Don't walk behind me - I may not lead.
Just walk beside me - and be my friend."

3 We'll listen to some words from the Bible where the word "love" has been changed to "friends":

4 *Friends are patient and kind;*
they are not jealous or boastful;
they are not arrogant or rude.

5 *Friends do not insist*
on having their own way.
They are not touchy or resentful.
They don't take pleasure
when things go wrong for others,
but they are pleased
with what is good and right.

6 *Friends are always ready to excuse,*
to believe the other person,
to have hope,
and to stand beside their friend
in bad times as well as good.
True friendship never ends.
(1 Cor 13, written by St Paul)

7 **We pray today for the gift of knowing how best to "be with" someone, remaining faithful through good times and bad.**

8 Albert Camus said:

"Don't walk in front of me - I may not follow.
Don't walk behind me - I may not lead.
Just walk beside me - and be my friend."

✍ *It is worth encouraging listeners to tease out what Camus may have meant by his words about not walking ahead or behind, but beside and being a friend.*

✍ *Albert Camus: 7/11/1913-4/1/1960. He won the Nobel Prize for Literature in 1957. He also said:* "In the midst of winter, I finally learned that there was in me an invincible summer."

✍ *Jesus said:* "I call you friends." *- John 15^{15}. For 'friendship' see also 23 April, 17 & 22 September.*

♪ Christ be beside me; Father, in my life I see *("walk with me")*; If I am lacking love; Walk with me, O my Lord

1 In 1987 this day was Remembrance Sunday, and people in the town of Enniskillen in Northern Ireland gathered around their War Memorial to honour those who had died in the two World Wars.

2 At 10.45am a 30-pound bomb exploded. Several people lay under a collapsed wall, including 20-year-old nurse, Marie Wilson. *"I love you,"* were her last words to her father, Gordon, as they held hands under the rubble. Marie was one of 11 killed that day. 63 others were wounded - some seriously.

3 The following day, Marie's 60-year-old father said:
"My wife and I do not bear any grudges. I am very sorry for those who did this, but I bear them no ill-will. I prayed for them last night. I shall pray for those people tonight and every night. May God forgive them."

4 Gordon Wilson's words touched many people throughout the world. Listeners to BBC Radio 4 voted Gordon Wilson as *"Man of the Year"*. In her Christmas Broadcast, Queen Elizabeth remarked that he had *"impressed the whole world by the depth of his forgiveness."*

5 Yet, each day, Gordon has experienced physical and emotional pain, and he and his wife find they can take only one day at a time.

6 *Let us pray:*

God our Father,
  may no-one's negative actions
  ever overpower my determination
  to choose to live in a positive way.
I know that to forgive someone
  can be far from being an easy option,
  and I know that forgiveness
  isn't somehow pretending
  that something wrong
  hasn't happened.

For what I have done wrong, Father,
  forgive me
  to the extent that I am generous
  in forgiving - or hoping to forgive -
  those who have done wrong to me.
Empower me
  to break the cycle
  of any hatred, resentment
  or bitterness,
  always resisting evil
  and conquering it with goodness.
Amen.

✍ *An alternative prayer would be that of 13 May, about influencing for good the people of violence.*

✍ *On the night of a memorial service in Dublin for the victims of Enniskillen, the Republic of Ireland came to a standstill at 6pm for a minute's silence.*

✍ *On Good Friday, 10th April 1998, the film* 'Ben Hur' *was being broadcast on BBC 1. At 5.36pm - as Jesus was shown dying on the cross - words flashed on the TV screen that a Peace Agreement had been reached by all sides at the Peace Talks in Stormont, Northern Ireland.*

✍ "Love means to love that which is unlovable - or it is no virtue at all. Forgiving means to pardon that which is unpardonable - or it is no virtue at all. To hope means hoping when things are hopeless - or it is no virtue at all."
  - G. K. Chesterton

✍ *In 1993, Yitzhak Rabin (the Israeli Prime Minister) before signing an agreement with Yassar Arrafat of the Palestine Liberation Organisation, remarked to U.S. President Bill Clinton:* "You don't make peace with your friends; you make peace and then you make friends".

♪ Come, let us go up to the Lord; God forgave my sin; Lay your hands; Lord, make me means; Make me a channel

9 NOVEMBER

1 For 40 years after the end of the Second World War in 1945, the Western World and the Communist World were hostile to each other. It was called the *"Cold War"*. Germany was still divided into East and West, and so was its former capital, Berlin.

2 In 1961 Communist East Germany had put up a 28-mile wall to stop its own citizens leaving for West Berlin. Some died as they tried to cross the Wall. Then, in 1989, there were mass demonstrations throughout the countries of Eastern Europe, protesting against the lack of freedom in those Communist countries. Their governments began to give way, and parts of the Berlin Wall were opened up to allow free access to the West.

3 On the night of the 9th/10th of November 1989, ordinary people used hammers to begin to demolish parts of the huge Berlin Wall.

4 *Let us pray:*

Lord,
   if I ever "build walls",
   cutting people off
   or isolating myself
   from the needs of others,
   alert me to what I am doing.
Open my eyes
   to see what unites people
   rather than what divides us.
Show me
   how to be inclusive
   and build bridges between people
   instead of being exclusive
   and putting up walls that divide.
Amen.

📖 *See also 13 August re the Berlin Wall.*

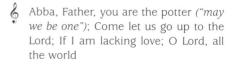 Abba, Father, you are the potter *("may we be one")*; Come let us go up to the Lord; If I am lacking love; O Lord, all the world

1 Robert Louis Stevenson was born in Edinburgh in November 1850. He is known for having written *'Treasure Island'*, *'Kidnapped'* and *'The Strange Case of Dr Jekyll and Mr Hyde'*.

2 We are going to listen to 6 of the 12 points which he called his *"Pattern for Living"*. We'll **pause** for a moment after each one:

3 *"Make up your mind to be happy, and learn to find pleasure in simple things…*

4 *"Make the best of your circumstances. No-one has everything, and everyone has something of sorrow intermingled with the gladness of life. The trick is to make the laughter outweigh the tears…*

5 *"Don't take yourself too seriously. Don't think that somehow you should be protected from misfortunes that befall others…*

6 *"You can't please everybody. Don't let criticism worry you…*

7 *"Don't let your neighbour set your standards. Be yourself…*

8 *"Do the things you enjoy doing, but stay out of debt…"*

9 Let us pray:

God our Father,
  you are very pleased
  when you see people living fully,
  developing their talents,
  living a balanced life,
  and being of service to others.
We ask you to inspire us
  to live as you would have us live
  and walk in your presence.
Amen.

❖❖❖❖❖❖❖❖❖❖❖❖❖❖❖❖

✐ *Robert Louis Stevenson: 13/11/1850-3/12/1894. He suffered from tuberculosis (TB) and travelled abroad to find a more suitable climate. He died of a brain haemorrhage on the island of Samoa in the South Pacific, aged 44. He also wrote 'The Black Arrow' and 'The Master of Ballantrae'.*

✐ *It is important to pause after each of these six points. See 12 November for his remaining six points.*

𝄞 Come, come, follow me; Do not worry; Father, I place; Seek ye first

11 NOVEMBER

1 On this day in 1918, at 11.00am - the 11th hour of the 11th day of the 11th month - the First World War came to an end. Much of the war had been fought in dug-out trenches across Belgium and France. It is thought that about 9 million soldiers lost their lives, and about 27 million were wounded - many of them permanently disabled.

2 At 11.00am, the fighting stopped everywhere, six hours after the Armistice was signed in a railway carriage in Compiègne, northern France.

3 Two years later the body of an unknown British soldier from one of the battlefields was laid in a coffin and brought over to England. On this day in 1920 the coffin of the unknown soldier was taken in procession to Westminster Abbey, past thousands of people lining the streets. During the service, the coffin was laid to rest with some soil from France in the floor of the central aisle of Westminster Abbey. The tomb commemorates all British casualties, especially those who have no known grave, and all who suffered during that war and since.

4 Lying there amongst the tombs of kings and queens and many famous people, this *"Tomb of the Unknown Warrior"* bears the inscription, *"Beneath this stone rests the body of a British warrior, unknown by name or rank, brought from France to be among the most illustrious of the land."*

5 During that service, the hymn *"Lead Kindly Light"* was sung, and we make that our prayer today:

6 **Lead, kindly light,**
    amid th'encircling gloom:
lead thou me on.
The night is dark,

and I am far from home,
    lead thou me on.
Keep thou my feet;
    I do not ask to see
the distant scene;
    one step enough for me.

7 **I was not ever thus, nor prayed that thou**
    shouldst lead me on.
I loved to choose and see my path;
but now
lead thou me on.
I loved the garish day,
    and, 'spite of fears,
pride ruled my will;
    remember not past years.

8 **So long thy power hath blest me,**
sure it still
will lead me on
o'er moor and fen,
    o'er crag and torrent, till
the night is gone,
and with the morn
    those angel faces smile
which I have loved long since
    and lost awhile.

9 During the First World War, the soldiers in their dug-outs could see red poppies growing in the fields of Flanders - the name for an area that covers parts of Belgium, the Netherlands and France. Each year, the Royal British Legion sells artificial red poppies to raise money for injured soldiers, sailors and airmen who have served their country up to the present day.

10 Some countries mark Remembrance Day on the 11th of November itself, and others on the nearest Sunday. At 11.00am, many people remain silent for two minutes.

✍ *By midnight of the 11th November 1920, following the service in Westminster Abbey, about 100,000 people also filed past the newly-built Cenotaph in Whitehall, where the national annual wreath-laying now takes place. Other countries, too, have a Tomb of the Unknown Warrior - France, for example, has its tomb under the Arc de Triomphe in Paris. People always walk around these tombs, and never over them.*

✍ *In addition to the 9 million soldiers killed, it is thought that 10 million civilians lost their lives indirectly because of the war.*

✍ *The same railway carriage in Compiègne in which the Germans had been humiliated in signing the Armistice for the end of the First World War, Hitler made use of for the signing of the surrender of France to Germany at the start of the Second World War. He then had the railway carriage blown up. A replica carriage stands in the woods of Compiègne nowadays.*

✍ *See 28 January for the poem of John Magee, an RAF pilot killed during the Second World War. See also 28 June.*

✍ *The Kohima Epitaph of the Burma Star Association of the Second World War is:*

> *"When you go home*
> *Tell them of us and say:*
> *'For your tomorrow*
> *We gave our today.' "*

✍ *"Lead kindly light" was written by Cardinal John Henry Newman - see 21 February.*

✍ *Poem: Rupert Brooke: "The Soldier"*

🎼 Abide with me; Blest be the Lord *(sung slowly)*; Lead kindly light

12 NOVEMBER

1 Robert Louis Stevenson was born in Edinburgh on tomorrow's date in 1850. He is known for having written *'Treasure Island'*, *'Kidnapped'* and *'The Strange Case of Dr Jekyll and Mr Hyde'*.

2 We are going to listen to 6 of the 12 points which he called his *"Pattern for Living"*. We'll **pause** for a moment after each one:

3 *"Don't borrow trouble. Imaginary things are harder to bear than the actual ones…*

4 *"Since hate poisons the soul, do not cherish enmities or grudges. Avoid people who make you unhappy…*

5 *"Have many interests. If you can't travel, read about new places…*

6 *"Don't hold post-mortems. Don't spend your life brooding over sorrows and mistakes. Don't be one who never gets over things…*

7 *"Do what you can for those less fortunate than yourself…*

8 *"Keep busy at something. A very busy person never has time to be unhappy…"*

9 *Let us pray:*

**Your glory, God our Father,
is seen in people
who are fully alive.
Inspire us to live fully
and discover your kingdom
within us.
Amen.**

✍ *It is important to pause after each of the 6 reflections. See 10 November for the remaining 6.*

✍ *"Enmity" = the state of people being enemies of one another.*

🎼 Come, come, follow me; Do not worry; Father I place; Seek ye first

1 The Vietnam War of the 1960s and 70s provokes mixed feelings amongst the people of the United States. Their government drafted young men to go to Vietnam in south-east Asia to stop the spread of Communism. America eventually withdrew in 1975 as South Vietnam surrendered to the Communist North.

2 Whatever people's feelings are about that war, 58,000 Americans were amongst those who were killed. Many veterans returning to the United States felt themselves being rejected by people and by the government, all of whom simply wanted to forget Vietnam. One of the returning veterans wrote: *"All we want is for people to recognise the sacrifices and contributions we made because the country we love told us it was right."*

3 A small group of veterans began to organise the raising of money for a memorial to those who had died, hoping that it would be a means towards peace and reconciliation.

4 It was decided that the memorial would be simple in style, and a competition was held to choose the best. As the foundations were being laid, a navy pilot in uniform brought to the site his dead brother's *"Purple Heart"* medal for bravery, and said: *"He and I flew together. I'd like to put his medal into the concrete foundations as they are being poured."* He saluted as he did so.

5 The Vietnam Veterans' Memorial in Washington is of two 250-foot walls of black polished granite, cut into the earth. The two walls are set at an angle to make a V-shape. On the walls are carved the names of all the 58,000 Americans who had died, and they are listed according to the date on which they were killed.

6 On this day in 1982 the Vietnam Veterans' Memorial was dedicated. To emphasise that each person was unique, all 58,000 names were read out in a 56-hour vigil in Washington's National Cathedral nearby. One of the volunteers who was to read names had been awarded a *'Congressional Medal of Honour'*. He lasted only five minutes before he broke down and cried. The rest of the names allocated to him he read out kneeling down. Time slots were announced in advance so that relatives a great distance away would know precisely when the name of their loved one would be read.

7 Many who visit the memorial nowadays, place paper over a relative's name and rub over it with a crayon. Some leave photographs and other reminders. Many people are overwhelmed on seeing all the 58,000 individual names. As visitors look at the long walls that bear the names, they see themselves in the reflection of the polished granite.

8 *Let us pray:*

**I leave my own past
  to your mercy, Lord.
I entrust the present
  to your love,
  and the future
  to your providence.   Amen.**

✍ *For alternative prayers, see 22,23 January.*

✍ *A "veteran" is someone who has served for a long time, and especially is used to refer to those who have fought in a war.*

✍ *Sadly, further controversy arose once the winning design was discovered to be by a young American woman of Chinese origin. It was remembered that China had helped back the opposing soldiers of North Vietnam.*

♪ Abide with me; Blest be the Lord *("the terrors of the night" - sung slowly)*; I am with you forever; In you, my God; Lord of all hopefulness

14 NOVEMBER

1. On the night of 14th November 1940, the city of Coventry in the Midlands suffered the longest air-raid of any British city during the Second World War. High explosive bombs were dropped by the German Air Force (the Luftwaffe). On other parts of the city, fire bombs fell, gutting many buildings, including the beautiful medieval cathedral.

2. The following day, some of the debris was cleared from the ruins of the cathedral. With only its stone walls left standing (and the stained glass destroyed) Coventry simply had an 'open-air' cathedral. From the ruins were taken two charred wooden beams that had held up the roof. These were bound with wire and made into a large cross, and set up in a bin of sand near the ruined high altar.

3. 16 years after the cathedral's destruction, the first stone of a new cathedral was laid. It is linked to the old ruined church whose walls still stand.

4. Every day at midday a brief service of reconciliation is held. On Fridays the service is held at the high altar of the ruined cathedral. The cross of charred beams remains there, with the words *"Father, forgive"* inscribed on the altar.

5. If we think about "forgiveness", we may remember that there is only one condition in the prayer of Jesus that we call the *"Our Father"*. The condition is that we are forgiven **as** we set out to forgive those who have hurt us.

6. On the cross, Jesus prayed, *"Father, forgive."* There may be a time in my life when I find that I can't say those words because I wouldn't mean them. Perhaps, then, I can say:
   *"Father, I **want** to forgive."*

7. Maybe the hurt is so deeply felt that, at the moment, I can only **genuinely** say:
   *"Father, I **want** to want to forgive."*

8. Then, at a later date, I will be able to progress through those three stages and finally be able to say:
   "Father, forgive."

9. Let's pray in silence for a moment, simply repeating those two words:
   "Father, forgive."

✍ The prayer of 17 January could be used.

✍ The "Medieval" Period - the "Middle Ages" - generally refers to the period in European history between the Fall of the Roman Empire in the West (about the 5th Century) and the Renaissance (in the 15th Century).

✍ So total was the aim to destroy a city, that the Nazis coined a new word - to be "coventrated". The bombing of such picturesque cities as Coventry led to the naming of the 'Baedeker Raids', after a famous set of guide books for travellers to places of culture throughout Europe.

✍ See also 8 November regarding the attitude of forgiveness of Mr Gordon Wilson in Enniskillen.

✍ A group could prepare a set of 4 or 5 short prayers about some elements of today's society. The response could be, "Father, forgive" . e.g.
For our misuse of the goodness of the earth:
   - Father, forgive.

For not being concerned about the poor and those on the margins of our society:
   - Father, forgive.

For not valuing people as individuals:
   - Father, forgive.

♩ God forgave my sin; Laudato sii ("those who spread forgiveness"); Lord, make me a means; Make me a channel; O Lord, all the world

1 In the war film, *"The Great Escape"*, the actor Steve McQueen played a prisoner-of-war who is seen trying to escape from the Nazis on a motor-bike, through fields near the barbed-wire border with Switzerland.

2 Steve McQueen is also remembered for playing in the Western, *"The Magnificent Seven"*, in *"Bullitt"*, *"Papillon"*, and as the fire-chief in the disaster-movie, *"The Towering Inferno"*.

3 In his last years, Steve McQueen had cancer, and said:
"I expect to win
my battle against cancer,
but no matter how it goes,
I'm at peace with God
- and so I can't lose."
He died in November 1980.

4 *Let us pray:*

We place ourselves into your hands,
God our Father,
knowing that whatever difficulties
we face,
we can never be losers
because nothing can ever separate us
from your love.
May we live in your peace.
Amen.

📖 *Steve McQueen: 1930-7/11/1980.*

📖 *"Papillon", the French word for "butterfly", is pronounced "pap-ee-on".*

📖 *For similar thoughts, see 2 September - Roy Castle.*

🎵 Do not be afraid; Do not worry; Father, I place *(sung slowly)*; In you, my God

1 The Polish scientist, Marie Curie, and her husband (Pierre) discovered 2 new elements which they called "polonium" and "radium". The elements were radioactive.

2 Marie Curie's work in radioactivity was of great benefit in medicine. It was discovered that cancerous cells could be killed by the use of small amounts of radioactivity (such as from radium), without seriously damaging nearby healthy tissue.

3 The Curies refused to "patent" ("to own with the intention of making profit from") their work and discoveries, saying that *"Physicists should always publish their researches completely. If our discovery has a commercial future, that is a circumstance from which we should not profit. If radium is to be used in the treatment of disease, it is impossible for us to take advantage of that."*

4 Marie Curie - born in November 1867 - became world-famous, and was awarded two Nobel Prizes. Unaware in those days of the dangers of radioactivity. She died from radiation poisoning at the age of 65.

5 *Let us pray:*

Lord,
   there is so much that I don't know,
   and I ask you to inspire me
   with a thirst for knowledge.
I pray, too, for wisdom
   that I may use my knowledge well.
I give thanks
   for many people I have never met
   whose knowledge and understanding
   have been passed on to me.
I ask that I may benefit
   from their work and experience
   and may contribute, in turn,
   to the well-being of others. Amen.

🖎 *Marie Curie: 1867-1934*

🖎 *Still today, Marie's scientific notebooks are too contaminated with radioactivity to touch.*

♪ All that I am; Lay your hands; Take my hands

1 Born in November 1821, Dostoyevsky became one of Russia's finest writers. His book called 'The Brothers Karamazov' is considered to be one of the world's greatest pieces of literature. The book is a murder mystery which sets the scene for the struggle of good and evil.

2 In that novel, a character speaks to a woman who has committed a serious crime and is about to die:
"No-one can commit a sin so great
as to exhaust the infinite love of God.
Can there be a sin
which could exceed the love of God?
Believe that God loves you
as you cannot conceive,
that he loves you with your sin
and in your sin.
All things are atoned for,
all things are saved by love.
If I, a sinner, even as you are,
am tender with you
and have pity on you,
how much more will God."

3 *Let us pray:*

Loving Lord,
   you tell us in the Bible
   that whatever wrong we have done
   you tread down our faults
   to the bottom of the sea.   *Mic 7¹⁹*
We know there is no need
   to keep thinking
   about what we have done
   in the past,   *Is 43¹⁸*
   because you pardon
   the wrongs we have done,
   and you delight
   in showing mercy.   *Mic 7¹⁸*
You bind up all our wounds   *Ps 147³*
   and you renew us by your love. *Zeph 3¹⁷*

4 Lord, you love
   all that you have made,   *Wis 11²⁴*
   and it is your very nature
to love and forgive.
Lead us to be generous
   in accepting and forgiving others
   in the same way
   as you accept and forgive us.
Amen.

📖 *An alternative prayer would be that of 8 October.*

📖 *See the first footnote of 27 December.*

📖 "God will forgive me. It's his job", *were the last words of Heinrich Heine (one of Germany's greatest poets), quoting from Voltaire's 'Candide'.*

📖 "You need not hold on to your sins forever. You can give them to God. If you are truly sorry for what you have done wrong, he will take away your sins" - *Hildegard of Bingen (Scivias - 3.5.4).*

📖 "So shall the world be created each morning anew, **forgiven** - in Thee, by Thee."
                    - Dag Hammarskjöld

📖 *Fyodor Mikhaylovich Dostoyevsky: 11/11/1821-9/2/1881. He also wrote 'Crime and Punishment' and said:*
"If you want to be respected by others, the great thing is to respect yourself."

🎼 Amazing grace; Do not be afraid; Freely, freely; I will never forget you; Lay your hands; Oh the love of my Lord

1 On this day in 1991 the English hostage, Terry Waite, was released from his 5 years of captivity in the Lebanon. He had been captured whilst trying to negotiate the freeing of other hostages. For a long time he was held in solitary confinement.

2 A month after his release, in an interview on TV, Terry Waite described how his faith had helped him during his years of captivity, which had included long periods of solitude, physical and psychological torture, and mock executions. Terry Waite said:

3 *"My faith came to my aid.*
The remarkable thing about faith
is that it isn't a sudden flash from heaven,
or a sudden insight of that kind.
It is just something that quietly sustains.
I would say to myself:
'You can do your worst,
but you can't destroy me - never.'
And they didn't."

4 He told of the three resolutions he had made when first captured:
"No regrets,
no sentimentality,
and no self-pity.
I had to stick by that, and it helped me
through the whole process
of interrogation.
Self-pity kills. It absolutely destroys."

5 *Let us pray:*

God our Father,
    in *good* times
    may I live in such a way
    that I will be strengthened
    for the difficult times
    that all of us face in our lives.
Lead me now
    to make positive choices
    to value friendship and loyalty,

and develop attitudes and values,
    treasuring all that is lasting
    and important.
Throughout *difficult* times
    may I build on
    the positive choices of my past,
    looking outward
    in the service of others
    and avoiding self-pity.
May I grow in the faith
    that, whatever my circumstances,
    I need have no regrets
    but may entrust
    my past to your mercy,
    my present to your love,
    and my future to your Providence.
May I know, too,
    that my faith in you
    is only a shadow
    of your faith in me
    and your love for me.
Amen.

📖 *See also 24 January. 29 July offers an alternative prayer.*

📖 *Terry Waite gave his interview on 22/12/91.*

📖 *Eleanor Roosevelt (1884-1962) said:*
"No-one can make you feel inferior without your consent."

🎼 God's Spirit is in my heart (*"prisoners no more"*); He who would valiant be; In you, my God; Lay your hands (*"free the broken-hearted"*); O Lord all the world belongs to you; Only a shadow (*"my faith in you"*); Walk with me

1 The President of Egypt in the 1970s was Anwar Sadat. Egypt and other Arab countries had been at war with their neighbour, Israel, for many years.

2 With great courage (and risking hostility from people on both sides), President Sadat flew on a mission of peace from his capital city of Cairo, to Jerusalem. It was the 18th of November, 1977.

3 All the countries involved in the on-going hostilities had suffered. Whilst in Israel, President Sadat spoke to the Israeli Parliament, quoting from the Jewish scriptures and from the Islamic Koran, stating that it is not possible to build happiness on the misery of others. He said:

4 *"I speak to you the bewailing mother, you the widowed wife, you the child who lost a brother or a father - you, the victims of all wars."*

5 President Sadat's initiative was courageous and generous. He wanted to consign the past **to** the past, and promote understanding and peace. The name *"Jerusalem"* means *"city of peace"*, and it is a place that is holy to followers of Judaism and Islam (as well as to Christians).

6 We'll pray using words from the psalms of the Jewish scriptures, acknowledging that President Sadat said: *"Until now, the distance between Cairo and Jerusalem seemed very great."*

7 *Let us pray:*

Happy are those, Lord
who long in their hearts
to walk the roads
that lead to Jerusalem,
the City of Peace. Ps 84[6]

Now that I stand in Jerusalem,
I pray:
"Peace be upon everyone." Ps 122[2,8]
I know that in your presence, Lord,
justice and peace Ps 85[14]
will come about. Amen.

📖 *Jerusalem is a sacred city to the Jews - the "Wailing Wall" is the remnant of the huge Temple where God's Presence was deemed to focus on the Holy of Holies where Moses' stone tablets of the Ten Commandments were kept in the Ark of the Covenant.*

Jerusalem is sacred to Christians as the site of the last days of Jesus, from Palm Sunday and the Last Supper to his betrayal, trial and crucifixion, and from where the Resurrection took place.

Muslims, the followers of Islam, hold Jerusalem to be holy, worshipping in the golden-roofed mosque, the "Dome of the Rock", that is built on the site of the Jewish Temple, over the rock on which Abraham is thought to have been about to sacrifice his son, Isaac (and from where Mohammed is said to have ascended to heaven). Abraham is considered "our father in faith" of the three mono-theistic religions (i.e. worshipping one God) - Judaism, Christianity and Islam - and therefore Jerusalem is a unique place.

📖 *The name "Jerusalem" means "city of peace", with "salem" in Arabic and "shalom" in Hebrew being words that mean "peace".*

The following words are said by practising Muslims five times a day, at the conclusion of their formal prayer:
"Lord, you are peace, and peace is from you. Blessed are you, enrobed with majesty and honour."

📖 *Anwar al-Sadat: 25/12/1918-6/10/1981 (assassinated).*

🎵 Come, let us go up to the Lord *("to Jerusalem - peace")*; Lord, make me a means of your peace; Make me a channel

1 Abraham Lincoln was elected U.S. President in this month in 1860. In one of the biographies of Lincoln we can read that he and a friend were walking in the countryside one night. Lincoln turned his eyes to the clear night sky and named some of the stars. He said to his friend:

2 *"I feel that I am looking*
in the face of God.
I can see how it might be possible
for someone to look around on earth
and not believe in God,
but I cannot conceive
how anyone could look up into the heavens
and say there is no God."

3 Throughout the winter months, we can see in the night sky the set of stars called **"Orion".** The Orion Constellation is easy to recognise as it is shaped like the letter "H".

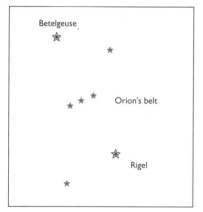

Betelgeuse

Orion's belt

Rigel

4 **Rigel** is the star at "the bottom right" as we look at the constellation. It is 900 light-years away from us. In other words, it is so far away that it takes light 900 years to reach us, and light travels at 186,000 miles per second. So, when we look at Rigel, we are actually seeing it as it was 900 years ago - we are seeing it as it was at the time of William the Conqueror!

5 **Betelgeuse** is the star at the "top left" as we look at the constellation of Orion. This reddish star is so large that our own sun could "fit" into it 64 million times! If Betelgeuse was placed where our Sun is, it would extend beyond the orbit of Earth, to that of Mars - but we know of stars that are even 50 times bigger than that!

6 *Let us pray:*

God our Father,
   open our eyes
   to the wonder
   of all your creation
   - from the beauty
   of all that is close to us,
   to the fascination
   of far-away places
   on our own planet and far beyond.
Heighten our awareness,
   deepen our understanding,
   and extend our horizons
   that we may have respect
   for all that is around us
   and discover your kingdom
   deep within us.   Amen.

✍ *Abraham Lincoln was elected on 6/11/1860.*

✍ *"Betelgeuse" is pronounced "beetle-jers". From November to March, the Constellation of Orion can be seen in the night sky, looking in the following directions at about 9pm:*
November: eastern horizon.
December: south-east.
January and February: south.
March: south-west.

♪ Colours of day; I watch the sunrise; O Lord my God, the Father of creation; O Lord my God, when I in awesome wonder *(I see the stars")*; The light of Christ; Yahweh I know you are near *("if I climb to the heavens")*

1 One of the early Christian writers was called Eusebius, and he died about the year 340A.D. He wrote these words which we will make our prayer today:

2 May I be no-one's enemy,
   and God's friend.
May I never quarrel
   with those nearest me
   but, if I do,
   may I be reconciled quickly.
May I never plot evil against others,
   and if anyone plots evil against me
   may I escape unharmed
   and without the need
   to hurt anyone else.

3 May I love and seek and achieve
   only what is good.
May I desire happiness for all,
   and may I envy no-one.
May I never find pleasure
   at the misfortune of someone
   who has done wrong to me.

4 May I gain no victory
   that harms either me
   or my opponent.
May I reconcile friends
   who become angry with one another.
May I, insofar as I can,
   give all necessary help
   to those who are in need,
   and never fail a friend in trouble.

5 May I respect myself
   and always keep in control of myself,
   being gentle in attitude
   and never letting circumstances
   make me angry with others.
May I never discuss the wicked
   or what they have done wrong,
   but know good people
   and follow in their footsteps.
Amen.

❖❖❖❖❖❖❖❖❖❖❖❖❖❖❖❖❖❖❖

✍ *Bishop Eusebius of Caesarea, c.260-c.340A.D. His name is pronounced "You-see-be-uss". He was a theologian, scholar and historian.*

✍ *This prayer is appropriate for use in a ceremony for those leaving school (or who have left and returned for their exam certificates - as also is Prayer 55 in the Appendix to Volume 2, along with Rudyard Kipling's poem "If" (perhaps omitting the 3rd verse).*

♪ Christ be beside me; Do not worry; Follow me; Lord of all hopefulness; O Lord all the world; Take my hands

1 In the early 1960s many primary schools still issued their students with blotting paper. It was used to absorb excess ink from writing with wooden pens that had metal nibs. After only a few words those pens had to be dipped into the inkwell to take up more ink.

2 In the 1930s in Hungary, Ladislao Biro produced thick quick-drying ink. He placed that ink into a thin capillary tube in a plastic casing. The pen had a rotating ball of metal at its point. No longer would people have to use inkwells or fountain pens, but his "biros" (as they became known) were very expensive at first.

3 Thousands of "biros" were used by members of the armed forces in Britain and America, and so became very popular, and they were then produced more cheaply. It was on this day in 1946 that they first went on sale in Britain.

4 *Let us pray:*

God our Father,
   until the time
   of the printing press,
   people copied the Gospel,
   writing it by hand.
Slowly the Gospel took shape
   - both on the page
   and deep within themselves.
I ask that the Gospel
   - the Good News of your love -
   may be written in me
   not with ink
   but with the Spirit of God.   *2 Cor 3³*
Only then
   will I grow as a credible witness
   of the wealth of your love.

5 Day by day,
   as the pages of my own life turn over,
   remind me

that you write my name
on the palm of your hand.   *Is 49¹⁶*
I ask this prayer
   through Jesus,
   who is your Word,
   living amongst us. Amen.

✍ *The surname of Ladislao Biro was pronounced "bee-row", rather than "by-row" as we now name the pen. His Christian name is pronounced "lad-iss-l-ow".*

✍ *Ladislao Biro left his country of Hungary in 1939 to escape from the Nazis, and moved to South America. Later he sold his pen business in England, and it is now owned by the French firm called "BIC", which produces millions of biros every day, as well as retractable pencils.*

✍ *See 8 June for the Jewish hymn about quills and ink and God's love.*

✍ *In Chapter 5 of the Book of Daniel in the Old Testament can be found details of Belshazzar's Feast and the Writing on the Wall.*

✍ *Jesus wrote on the ground - see John 7⁶,⁸*

✍ *Until the times of the printing press (invented by Johann Gutenberg in the 15th Century), people down the ages copied the gospel by hand, copy by copy.*

✍ *A bizarre example of wanting to be fully "part of" a book, was performed in August 1997 as, at his own request, the ashes of Mark Gruenwald (the late editor of Marvel Comics) were mixed into printers' ink at an Ohio printing plant. A re-print was then made of a limited edition of a 1985 comic that Gruenwald had written. The editor-in-chief commented: "He wanted to be part of his work in a very real sense!"*

✍ *President John F Kennedy was assassinated in Dallas, Texas, on this day in 1963.*

♪ Christ be beside me; Come, come, follow me; Do not worry; Follow me; Sing a simple song; Take my hands

1 On his return to Britain from the Far East at the end of the Second World War, Bishop Leonard Wilson spoke on the radio. Like many others, he had been tortured in the Japanese concentration camp that was called Changi Jail, in Singapore. The Japanese had taken it in turn to beat him, and some enjoyed their cruelty.

2 On the radio, Leonard Wilson said:
"By the grace of God
I saw those men
- not as they were then,
but as they had been.
Once they were little children
with their brothers and sisters,
happy in their parents' love,
in those far-off days
before they had been conditioned
by their false nationalist ideas.
And it is hard to hate little children.
So I saw them
- not as they were in the present -
but as they were capable of becoming,
redeemed by the power of Christ,
and I knew that I should say:
'Father, forgive.'"

3 *Let us pray:*

Lord, in my *better* times
it is easy for me
to ask in prayer
that I may never allow
the negative actions of others
to dictate
that I should act in a negative way.
In the *difficult* times
that I may face in the future,
I ask that I may be true
to my inner convictions
and still look for the best in others,
remaining generous towards them.

Remind me, too,
that, as time moves on,
people can change
and their attitude can change
for the better.
Amen.

Dom Helder Camara, Archbishop of San Recife in Brazil, has written the following prayer to Jesus (who had been a Child), asking to discover the "child" within others:
"Child, dear Child,
help me to discover
even in the most overpowering people
and in the most severe people,
the child asleep in their hearts."

"We should not pursue those who have done harm to us. To do that, would be a betrayal of God, who does not pursue us. We can only expect God's mercy, if we ourselves show mercy to others."
- Hildegard of Bingen

"Nationalist ideas" refers to the Japanese propaganda that had so convinced (conditioned) the Japanese people to believe that their nation was superior to all others.

In the 20 years before the Second World War, the British built up Singapore as its vital naval base in East Asia. It was considered an impregnable fortress but its mighty guns were only able to point out to the sea, as it was considered impossible for an army to travel through the jungle of Malaya, to the north. The consequent Japanese invasion led to the surrender of 70,000 British and Commonwealth soldiers.

Amazing grace; Be still and know I am with you; Do not be afraid *("my child")*; For to those; God forgave my sin; He who would valiant be; If God is for us; Oh the word of my Lord *("my child", & calling)*; O Lord all the world *("loving enemies")*

1 Before the Age of the Railways in Britain, clocks were set at various times in towns and villages, varying by as much as 20 minutes. By 1850, the railways throughout the nation had a regular timetable, but "Railway Time" did not always agree with "Local Time". This caused further confusion as some towns installed clocks with two faces - one for "Local Time" and the other for "Railway Time"!

2 On this day in 1858, a court case was held in Dorset, set to start at 1.00pm. One of the men involved in the court case was not in court on time, and so the judge awarded the case in favour of his opponent. At that moment, the other man arrived - only to be told that he was late. He disagreed with the judge, saying that he was on time according to his watch which he had set according to the station clock in his own town of Carlisle.

3 Because different "times" were in use in different places, the court case had to be re-tried. The matter received a lot of publicity. Then, in 1880, Parliament finally decided that the whole nation should follow 'Greenwich Mean Time', standardised at the Greenwich Observatory in London.

4 **Let's think of those who look back and wish they had an extra day or more time:**
   - those who have too little time
   for what they are expected to do;
   - those who have lost a sense of balance
   and proportion in their lives;
   - those who feel
   that they have made a mess
   of everything
   and would like to be able
   to start again.

5 **We pray, too,**
   for those who might wish for less time:
   - those who are worried
   about what might happen;
   - those who are in despair;
   - those who suffer hours
   of pain and illness;
   - those who are in prison
   or are being tortured;
   - those who wish to die.

6 **On all these people, Lord,**
   we ask your blessing.
   Amen.

📖 *See also 23 May. An alternative prayer would be that of Michel Quoist, "Lord, I have time", from his book, "Prayers of Life".*

📖 *Dietrich Bonhoeffer, the German theologian executed in Nazi Germany, said:*
   "Time lost
   is time in which we have failed
   to live a human life,
   gain experience,
   learn, create, enjoy and suffer.
   It is time that has been filled up
   - but left empty."

🎼 All that I am; Be still and know I am with you; Do not worry; Here I am, Lord; I watch the sunrise; Lord of all hopefulness *("at the break/noon/eve/end of the day")*

1 Diane Modahl was 5-times the British 800 metre champion, and also held a Commonwealth title.

2 She was one of the British athletes at the 1984 Olympic Games in Seoul, South Korea. Diane made it through the heats and became one of the eight to run in the final. Knowing that it could be a lonely experience for her, she prayed Psalm 23 quietly as she began to walk through the tunnel into the stadium itself.

3 As we listen to the words of Psalm 23 which Diane prayed, we can picture her walking in the darkness of the athletes' tunnel, approaching the light of the stadium:

4 Lord, you are like a shepherd to me,
   and so I have all that I need.
You give me rest
   in meadows of green grass,
   and you lead me to flowing water
   where I gain new life and strength.
You guide me
   along the way that is best for me.

5 Even when I walk in darkness
   and everything around
   seems like death,
   you are there, walking with me,
   and the promise
   of your love and faithfulness
   helps to conquer my fear.

6 In the sight of those who do me down,
   you invite me
   to sit at table with you.
There you offer me
   even more than I need,
   and you remind me
   that I am significant and special.

7 You call me to goodness and kindness

every day of my life,
and your house will be my home
my whole life long.

(Psalm 23)

📝 *See also 26 November.*

📝 *Seoul is pronounced "sole".*

🎵 All that I am; Do not worry *("trust and pray, go do your best today")*; I give my hands; I will be with you *("go now throughout the world")*; Like a shepherd; The Lord's my shepherd; Though the mountains may fall *("you will run, never tire")*; Yahweh, I know you are near *("where can I run from your love?")*

1 Manchester athlete Diane Modahl was 5-times the British 800 metre champion. In 1994 she was sent home in disgrace from the Commonwealth Games in Victoria, British Columbia, Canada. Like other athletes, she was routinely tested for drugs, and the Games' officials concluded that she had been taking performance-enhancing drugs.

2 Diane fought extremely hard to clear her name and restore her good reputation, yet the Games officials stated that they had been given proof by the scientists who had analysed a sample that she had given.

3 It was over a year later that other scientists showed that the initial tests on Diane's sample were unreliable and at fault.

4 Meanwhile, amidst her difficulties, Diane gave birth to a daughter whom she and her Norwegian husband decided to call *"Imani"*, which is the Norwegian word for *"hope"*.

5 Four years after being condemned, Diane Modahl spoke on TV. She said that, at times of profound difficulty, we can feel totally alone, and we can ask where God is amidst it all. At her worst time, Diane came across the following words which are called *"Footprints"*. As we listen to the words, we can think of difficult times in our own lives:

6 'One night a man had a dream. He dreamt he was walking along the beach with the Lord. Across the sky flashed scenes from his life. For each scene he noticed two sets of footprints in the sand - one belonging to him, the other to the Lord.

7 When the last scene in his life flashed before him, he looked back at the footprints in the sand. He noticed that many times along the path of his life there was only one set of footprints. He also noticed that it happened at the very lowest and saddest times of his life. This really bothered him, and he questioned the Lord about it. "Lord, you said that, once I decided to follow you, you would walk with me all the way. But I've noticed that during the most difficult times in my life there is only one set of footprints. I don't understand why, in times when I needed you most, you would leave me."

8 The Lord replied, "My precious child, I love you and would never leave you during your trials and sufferings. When you see only one set of footprints, it was then that I carried you."'

📖 *See also 25 November.*

📖 *The source of "Footprints" is unknown.*

📖 *A plaque in Nottingham Cathedral marks the new burial place (2/12/97) of Mother Mary Potter, who had founded the Sisters of the Little Company of Mary (died in 1913). The plaque bears her words:* "We have travelled on and on, and we have felt the presence of our God. There are parts of the way that we have not walked - but God has carried us."

𝄞 Christ be beside me; In you, my God; Walk with me, O my Lord

1 Two trapeze artists were interviewed. They said that there has to be the greatest of trust between the one who flies through the air and the one who catches.

2 We might think that it is the flier who grabs the one who is hanging from the trapeze but, that way, the wrists of either of them could be broken. Instead, it is for the flier to stretch out his arms and place complete trust in the catcher, who will grab him with split-second timing. The flyer has to fly, and the catcher has to catch, bringing his partner to safety.

3 *"I place myself into your hands, Father,"* were the words of Jesus as he lay dying on the cross.

4 *'Dying is trusting in the Catcher!* **Caring** *for the dying is saying: "Don't be afraid! Remember that you are a beloved son or daughter of God. He will be there when you make your long jump... Don't try to catch him, he will grab you... Just stretch out your arms and hands, and trust... trust... trust."'*

5 *Let us pray:*

**Help us to grow in trust, Father,
and place ourselves
into your hands,
both now
and at the time of our death.
Amen.**

✍ *If thought more appropriate on the particular occasion, the words* "both now and at the time of our death" *could be omitted. An alternative prayer:*

**Help me to grow in trust, Father,
so that I can more readily
place myself into your hands,
confident that all shall be well.
Amen.**

✍ *Ps (30) 31[6]:* "Into your hands, Lord, I commend my spirit." *Jesus' words on the cross are found in Luke 23[46].*

✍ "I have held many things in my hands, and I have lost them all; but whatever I have placed in God's hands, that I still possess."
- Martin Luther

✍ *The quote that is the final paragraph above is from* 'Our Greatest Gift: a Meditation on Dying and Caring' *by Henri Nouwen (Hodder & Stoughton, 1994).*

✍ *The Parable of the Prodigal Son is found in Luke 15[11-32]. Jesus invites us to live the relationship that God the Father offers. In the moving story, the father is already looking out for the son, and takes the initiative in running towards his son, clasping him in his arms with a warm embrace, kissing him tenderly. Another book by Henri Nouwen is* 'The Return of the Prodigal Son', *in which he reflects in a very touching way on this parable in the light of Rembrandt's glowing painting of the same name.*

✍ *See also the quote of Julian of Norwich on 1 December.*

♩ Do not worry *("leave it in the hands of the Lord")*; Father, in my life I see *("you hold my life in your hands")*; Father, I place into your hands; Take my hands

28 NOVEMBER

1 In the summer of 1620, a group of 120 people set sail from Plymouth on the south coast of Devon. They had experienced persecution in England because of their religious beliefs. In their ship, the *'Mayflower'*, these *"Pilgrims"* (or *"Pilgrim Fathers"*) crossed the Atlantic. They called their place of landing *"New Plymouth"*, and the area became known as *"New England"*, which is on the northeast coast of what we now call "the United States".

2 Half of the small colony's number died during their first winter. Then they received help from the Native Americans. Joining together, both groups celebrated a day of thanksgiving for the harvest in the autumn of 1621.

3 "Thanksgiving Day" in the United States is an important national holiday which is celebrated in family groups. It is held on the fourth Thursday each November.

4 **Let's pause**
to remember and give thanks
for what has been good in our lives:
- for people who have given us
love and care,
friendship and support...

5 **Let's pause**
to remember and give thanks
- for our health and talents,
and for the opportunities
that come to us...

6 **Let's pause**
to remember and give thanks
- for the beauty that we can see
and for the inspiration we receive...

7 **Let's pause**
to remember and give thanks
- for the happy memories we treasure
and for all that has been good
over the years...

✍ *See also 23 April and 31 October regarding thankfulness.*

✍ *Canada holds "Thanksgiving Day" on the second Monday in October.*

✍ *"Eucharist" is the Greek word for "thanksgiving".*

✍ *It has been said that unexpressed gratitude is like smiling at someone in the dark. The person smiling is the only one who knows about the smile.*

✍ *Only one of the ten cured of leprosy by Jesus returned to give thanks - Luke 17[11-19]*

✍ *"For all things give thanks to God" - St Paul: 1 Thess 5[18]*

♩ Thank you; Thank you for fathers

1 Tomorrow (the 30th) records the birth in 1874 of Winston Churchill, who would lead Britain as Prime Minister through the Second World War.

2 Winston Churchill spoke the following words about relating with people:

3 *"I have no secret.*
You haven't learned life's lesson very well
 if you haven't noticed
 that you can decide
 the reaction you want of people
 in advance.
It's unbelievably simple.
If you want them to smile, smile first.
If you want them to take an interest in you,
 take an interest in them first.
If you want to make them nervous,
 become nervous yourself.
If you want them to shout and raise their voices,
 raise yours and shout.
If you want them to strike you,
 strike first.
It's as simple as that.
People will treat you
 like you treat them.
It's no secret.
Look about you.
You can prove it with the next person you meet."

4 *Let us pray:*

Inspire me, Lord,
to be of good influence
on people I will meet today.
Amen.

✍ *See also 3 Feb, 15 May, 10 July, 20 and 22 Oct for "touching hearts".*

✍ "Treat people
 as if they were what they ought to be,
 and you help them to become
 what they are capable of becoming."
 - Johann Goethe (1749-1832), a German writer.

✍ *Today's words of Churchill are also suitable for use with school-leavers.* "The secret of education is respecting the pupil," *said Ralph Waldo Emerson.*

✍ *Winston Spencer Churchill: 30/11/1874-24/1/1965.*

♪ Do not worry; If I am lacking love; I give my hands; Make me a channel; O Lord all the world

30 NOVEMBER

1 We pray today for all who are Scottish, as this is the feastday of the Patron of Scotland - Saint Andrew.

2 When Pope John Paul visited Britain in 1982, he spoke to the young people of Scotland. He mentioned Saint Andrew - Scotland's patron saint - as the disciple who led to Jesus the boy who had five loaves and two fish. Meanwhile the huge crowd were far from anywhere and had nothing to eat.

This is what Pope John Paul said:

3 *"Jesus had been teaching*
a crowd of five thousand people
about the Kingdom of God...
As evening approached,
one of the disciples
- it was Saint Andrew - said:
'There is a small boy here
with five loaves and two fish;
but what is that among so many?'
Jesus took the loaves and blessed them...
Later the disciples collected twelve baskets
of the fragments that were left over...
(Jn 6$^{1-14}$)

4 *"Saint Andrew gave Jesus*
all that there was available,
and Jesus miraculously fed
those five thousand people
and still had something left over.
It is exactly the same with your lives.
Left alone to face the difficult challenges
of life today,
you feel conscious of your own inadequacy
and feel afraid
of what the future may hold for you.
But what I say to you is this:
place your lives in the hands of Jesus.
He will accept you and bless you,
and he will make such use of your lives
as will be beyond
your greatest expectations!

5 *In other words:*
surrender yourselves
- like so many loaves and fishes -
into the all-powerful,
sustaining hands of God
*and you will find yourselves **transformed***
with "newness of life",
with "fullness of life".

6 *Let us pray:*

Lord,
you were given
five loaves and two fish.
I give you
all that I have
and all that I am,
ready to be transformed.
Amen.

❖❖❖❖❖❖❖❖❖❖❖❖❖❖❖❖❖

✍ *Or could use Prayer 17 from the Appendix of this volume.*

✍ *For the Feeding of the Five Thousand, see John 6$^{1-14}$. For "newness" and "fullness" of life, see Romans 6^4 and John 10^{10}.*

✍ *The white diagonal cross (the 'saltire') against a navy blue background of the flag of Scotland reflects the death of St Andrew who, according to tradition, was crucified on an X-shaped cross.*

✍ *In 1606 that flag of St Andrew was combined with the flag of St George to form the first "Union Jack" - the first flag of Great Britain (which did not bear the red diagonal stripes, added in 1801, following the Union of Ireland with Great Britain - see also the footnotes of 5 November.)*

 All that I am; Come, come, follow me; Do not worry *("leave it in the hands of the Lord")*; Father, in my life I see; Father, I place into your hands; Lay your hands; The love I have for you

1 One of the 'Peanuts' cartoons has Lucy promising not to laugh at what Charlie Brown wants to tell her.
"You have my solemn promise
not to laugh," she states.

2 So he says to her:
"Sometimes I lie awake at night
listening for a voice that will say:
'We like you, Charlie Brown.'"
As expected, Lucy laughs at him, but people can sympathise with Charlie Brown because he needs encouragement.

3 In the Gospel we can read of a young man who approaches Jesus and says,
"Master, I have tried to do
all that I think God wants me to do."
The Gospel then states that
'Jesus looked steadily at him,
and loved him'.

4 Many people find those
to be very touching words
that reflect what the Good News is:
that God looks steadily at **me**
and loves **me**.

5 *Let us pray:*

Lord Jesus
you treasure
and hold a special place
for each and every person,
as though
only that one individual exists,
and you accept us as we are,
in the reality of our lives this day.
May I grow in the faith
that you look steadily at me
and love me.
Amen.

6 | Jesus looked steadily at him, and loved him. |

📖 *The Gospel passage that records the meeting of Jesus with the rich young man is found in Mark 10^{17-22}. The encounter is presented differently in Matthew 19 and Luke 18.*

📖 *Hildegard (1098-1179) of Bingen in Germany wrote:*
"Remember that you were made
in the image and likeness of God.
And so you should love yourself,
recognising your own beauty
as a mirror of God's beauty."
Hildegard was in charge of an abbey, and composed some remarkable hymns and poetry. She experienced visions which she recorded in writing, and was widely consulted by religious leaders and state rulers.

📖 "He is quick to clasp us to himself,
for we are his joy and his delight,
and he is our life and our salvation."
- *Julian of Norwich (1342-1420).*

🎼 Amazing grace; Do not be afraid; Father, in my life; I will be with you; Lay your hands; Oh the word of my Lord; The love I have for you; Sing a simple song *("I see that you love me")*; This, then, is my prayer; Yahweh, I know you are near *("you have searched my heart")*

2 DECEMBER

1 Each December, the Jewish community celebrates a festival of lights, called 'Hanukkah'.

2 Over 2,100 years ago, King Antiochus (the Greek ruler of Syria) had control over the land of Israel, his southern neighbour. Whilst the Jews believed in one God, the king insisted that they worship many gods, including himself.

3 A Jewish rebellion started against the far greater forces of the occupying armies. After 3 years of war, the Jewish leader - Judah Maccabee - re-took Jerusalem's Temple, built by the Jews for the worship of God. The Temple had been desecrated - abused - by worshipping pagan gods whose statues had been placed there.

4 The Jews set about re-dedicating the Temple to God. There were 8 days of festivities. In the Temple, the oil lamps of the Menorah - a branched candlestick - were lit again, but there was only enough oil for them to burn for one day. Miraculously, the oil burnt for 8 days until new oil was obtained, and so 'Hanukkah' has become an 8-day festival.

5 Nowadays, as Hanukkah is celebrated, recalling the re-dedication of the Temple in Jerusalem, Jews re-dedicate themselves to God. It is a happy time, and presents are given. Pancakes are eaten, and children play a game with a spinning top that bears 4 Hebrew letters, standing for the words: *"A great miracle happened here."*

6 At nightfall on the first day of Hanukkah, one candle is lit. Each night another branch of the candlestick is lit, until by the end of the Festival, all 8 are alight.

7 *Let us pray, basing our words on Jewish prayers used at this time:*

8 **Blessed are you, Lord God,**
   King of the universe.
We light these candles
   to remind ourselves
   of the wonders you have performed
   for your people down the ages.
Create new miracles for us
   and, as the days go by,
   may your light
   grow brighter and brighter within us.
Amen.

✍ *"Antiochus" is pronounced "Ant-eye-o-kuss".*

✍ *Hanukkah (variously spelt Hanukah, Chanukah or Chanukkah) is sometimes known as 'The Festival of Lights' or 'The Feast of Dedication' (of the Temple).*

✍ *The 'Menorah', the branched candlestick, normally has 7 candles (Exodus 25$^{31-40}$). The Hanukkah Menorah has 8 candles for the 8-day festival.*

✍ *As the Jewish Calendar is lunar-based, the festival of Hanukkah may start on any day in December. Psalms 113-118 are used during the festival. Psalm 117 is the shortest psalm in the Bible:*
   Praise the Lord, all you nations.
   Speak to him, all people of the earth
   because his love is great
   and he is always faithful.

✍ *Unlike the RC Church, Protestant Churches tend not to include the two Books of Maccabees as part of the Bible, as such. The two books recount the details of the Jewish resistance and the rededication of the Temple. 'Judas the Maccabee' is sometimes called 'Judas Maccabaeus', meaning 'Judas the Hammer'. In 164 B.C.E. (i.e. "Before the Christian Era") he established the feast as an annual reminder to remain faithful to God no matter how society or a political situation may influence them otherwise.*

♦ Be not afraid; Be still and know I am with you *("you fear the light may be fading")*; Colours of day; In you, my God; Seek ye first; The light of Christ

1 In the late 1300s a lady called Juliana, living in Norwich, became seriously ill. As she was recovering, she experienced a number of visions of Jesus. She wrote down for others what she had experienced. For example:

2 *"God showed me a little thing,*
the size of a hazelnut,
in the palm of my hand...
I looked at it with my mind's eye
and I thought:
'What can this be?'
And an answer came:
'It represents all that is made.'

3 *I marvelled that it could continue to exist*
because I thought
that it would have crumbled to nothing,
it was so small.
And the answer came into my mind:
'It exists and always will
because God loves it.'
All things have their being
through the love of God.
In this little thing I saw three truths:
the first is that God made it;
the second is that God loves it;
the third is that God looks after it."

4 Mother Julian of Norwich (as she is generally known) was making the point that God has made all things, that he loves all that he has made, and that in his love he looks after all that he has made.

5 She also wrote that, in God's love,
"all shall be well
and all manner of thing
shall be well."

6 *Let us pray:*

God our Father,
in your love
you have a special care
for all that you have made.

May we grow in the faith
that you *"enfold us in your love"*
and that everything
does work out for good
for those who love you:
that *"all shall be well*
and all manner of thing
shall be well". Amen.

✏ *"Norwich" is pronounced "nor-idge", and is the county town of Norfolk.*

✏ *Juliana's name is normally shortened to "Julian", being known as "Mother Julian (or Dame Julian) of Norwich" (1342-1420). She also wrote:*
"The fullness of joy
is to behold God in everything."
"We shall see God face to face,
simply and wholly."

✏ *If the circumstances are appropriate, and if the group is settled and at peace, each person could be given a round hazelnut to hold in the palm of the hand.*

✏ *The last six lines of the long quote should be emphasised, and the whole of that passage should be read slowly.*

✏ *"You love all that you have made..."*
- Wisdom 11$^{24-26}$.

✏ "Faith is an inner conviction of being overwhelmed by God" - *Gustaf Aulen.*
"Faith is being a friend of God", said *Pope Saint Gregory.*
The five letters of the word FAITH can be used to construct phrases about faith, e.g.

Faith is a Fantastic Adventure In Trusting Him.
Feeling Afraid, I Trust Him.
Faith Asks Impossible Things Humbly.
For All, I Thank Him.

🎼 Father, in my life I see *("you hold my life in your hands")*; For to those who love God; If God is for us; Sing a simple song; *("I see that you love me")*; The love I have for you; This, then, is my prayer

4 DECEMBER

1 The world's worst industrial accident took place in the early hours of yesterday - the 3rd of December - in 1984, as poisonous gas escaped from a pesticide factory. The cloud of highly toxic methyl isocyanate moved through the streets, engulfing people as they slept, over an area of 40 square kilometres. 800,000 people were living in the city. Of those people, 300,000 were injured, and as many as 10,000 people were killed.

2 Many of the survivors were blinded, or suffered liver and kidney failure. All had breathing difficulties. Doctors stated that most of those who survived will have long-term health problems.

3 This disaster took place in Bhopal, a city in central India.

4 *Let us pray:*

We pray today, Father,
for the injured and sick
who are still suffering
from the after-effects
of man-made or natural disasters.
We pray that those
who have responsibilities
may have a "feeling" for others
and so grow in care and respect
for those
whose lives they may influence.
For ourselves
and those that *we* care for,
lead us to make our choices wisely,
and accept responsibility
for our own lives
and for our choices and actions
and their consequences.
Amen.

✎ *Methyl iso-cyanate is CH_3NCO. 2,000 people died immediately, and about another 8,000 have died since from their injuries.*

✎ *$470 million was eventually paid out in compensation (to the Indian government) by the United States-owned parent-company of 'Union Carbide'. Accordingly the Indian government dropped its criminal charges against the company and its personnel.*

✎ *Bhopal (the first syllable rhymes with "go") is the capital of Madhya Pradesh State in central India. The city has the largest mosque in India, that of Taj-ul-Masjid.*

✎ *In the text that appears above the prayer, the location of the city was not stated until the last paragraph. Might people have reacted differently if 10,000 people had been killed and 300,000 seriously injured in a country of the "West", rather than in a "Developing" ("Third World") country? Would financial compensation and the prosecution of those responsible have been different? Would international reaction have been even greater if this had taken place in a country with a ready presence of the mass media and a good transport and telecommunications system?*

✎ *The accident took place whilst there was a temperature inversion, confining the gas below cooler air that was above the city.*

✎ *The world's worst **nuclear** accident was Chernobyl - see 26 April.*

✎ *On this day in 1154, Nicholas Breakspeare was elected Pope Adrian IV. He has been the only person from Britain to have been elected Pope.*

♩ Abide with me *("Help of the helpless");*
In you, my God; Lay your hands

Good Shepherd

Lord,
may the care we experience
remind us of your presence,
because you are the Good Shepherd,
caring for us.

(Jn 10[14])
(see page 183)

1 Britain's first stretch of motorway was opened on this day in 1958. This 8-mile length of the M6 motorway by-passed Preston in Lancashire, and was opened by the then Prime Minister, Harold Macmillan.

2 When another motorway (the M62) was being built across the Pennine hills between Lancashire and Yorkshire, it was often the case that the tops of hills would be pushed into valleys, filling them in. This helped to create level ground and a smooth path for vehicles to travel along.

3 Between Junctions 22 and 23 of the M62, one farmer stubbornly resisted the "compulsory purchase order" which would have led to good financial compensation for the forced purchase of his land, through which the motorway was to be built. As was his right, he appealed against that compulsory purchase order, causing delays for the completion of the road. He refused to move out of his house.

4 It was then decided simply to by-pass his farmhouse. And so the motorway splits at that point, with the two carriageways isolating the farmhouse in the middle of the motorway, but giving access by tunnels to fields on either side.

5 The building techniques of the M62 across the Pennines are similar to images used by the prophet Isaiah. During the Church's Season of Advent, his words are often read, because they point the way forward to God coming amongst us.

6 This is what Isaiah says:
'A voice cries out:
"In the wilderness
prepare a way for the Lord.
Level the mountains
and fill in the valleys.
Make the uneven ground level
and so make a straight road in the desert
for our God to approach
and come amongst us.
From the top of a high mountain
we proclaim
that God is approaching:
he is coming amongst us.
This is his promise,
and he is faithful to what he says.'''
Is 40³⁻⁵,⁹,42¹⁶

7 *Let us pray:*

Loving Father,
we ask you
to show us how to level
any *'mountains'* we might have
of feeling 'superior'
or 'better' than others,
or of making judgements
about people.
Raise us from any *'valleys'*
of despair
or a poor self-image
or a sense of worthlessness.
Lift us up
from whatever kind of poverty
may affect our lives.
Lift us up, we pray,
from anything that makes us
less than fully human.
Raise us from sinfulness,
and lead us to prepare a straight path
for the coming anew into our lives
of Jesus, your Son.
Amen.

✏ *The first stretch of the M1 was opened in November 1959 - 11 months after the opening of the M6 Preston By-Pass.*

✏ *In Britain, the main 'A' ("Arterial" or "Trunk") roads are named as follows, radiating (clockwise) like the spokes of a wheel from the capital cities of England and Scotland:*
A1 - London to Edinburgh
A2 - London to Dover
A3 - London to Portsmouth
A4 - London to Bristol
A5 - London to Holyhead (Anglesey)
A6 - London to Carlisle
A7 - Edinburgh to Carlisle
A8 - Edinburgh to Glasgow
A9 - Edinburgh to John O'Groats.

All roads within the sector bounded by two of the above-named roads (e.g. between the A4 and the A5) are named according to the first number. This explains, for example, why most of the roads in Wales start with "A4__" e.g. A479, A483, A44, A4103. The 'B'-roads follow the same pattern as, in a general way, do the Motorways.

✏ *Chapters 40-66 of the Book of Isaiah (often called "Second Isaiah") were written about the time of the Fall of Babylon in 593 B.C., as Cyrus of Persia was about to allow the Jews to return to their own land from their Exile in Babylon.*

✏ *The passage from Isaiah is one of the texts set to music by Handel (see 22 Aug) in his oratorio 'The Messiah', often performed before Christmas and before Easter.*

✏ *"Prepare ye the way of the Lord" is a song from the musical 'Godspel', being the words of John the Baptist (as he quotes Isaiah), preparing the way for Jesus.*

🎼 Come let us go up *("walk in his paths.... the mountain")*; In your coming and going *("you look at the mountains")*; Though the mountains may fall; Walk with me *("the road.... the steepest mountain-side")*

✏ *Even on a national road atlas map, the deviation of the M62 around the farm can be seen - between J22 and J23, 4 miles to the west of Huddersfield.*

6 DECEMBER

1 Today is the feastday of the patron saint of children, Saint Nicholas, whose name is altered to give us "Santa Claus". Today we might picture various situations of children and young people across the world.

2 During the football season and approaching Christmas, we can remind ourselves that there are children of 9 and 10 who spend the whole day sitting in a crowded room, stitching pieces of leather together to make footballs for a few pennies an hour.

3 There are reports in the newspapers of orphans from Romania being taken in groups to Berlin, and sent out every day by their minders to rob and steal. If they do not bring back the goods in the evening, they get beaten.

4 We know of towns in India where the street kids survive by getting up early in the morning to spend most of the day picking through the city's rubbish. If they can find something worthwhile, it is sold to get something to eat.

5 Bangkok, the capital of Thailand, is so big, and the rubbish dumps are so enormous, that whole families go and live on the tip to make sure they get a good spot to start picking. Children are born and brought up on the rubbish dump, with no chance of going to school unless someone is able to offer them some help.

6 It is thought that there are about 8 million street-children in Brazil. They were sleeping on the city streets at night, but many now have to sleep in hidden places like the sewers, because death-squads move around at night, shooting the children.

7 In contrast, we are going to listen to some words about how children and young people learn best. We can think about the way **we** treat others, whatever our age and theirs:

8 *"A child living with criticism learns to condemn.*

9 *A child living with hostility learns to fight.*

10 *A child living with ridicule learns to be shy.*

11 *A child living with shame learns to feel guilty.*

12 *But
A child living with encouragement learns confidence.*

13 *A child living with praise learns to appreciate.*

14 *A child living with fairness learns justice.*

15 *A child living with security learns to have faith.*

16 *A child living with approval learns love of self.*

17 *A child
living with acceptance and friendship learns to find love in the world."*

(Dorothy Law Holte
- adapted to inclusive language.)

"Your faith leads you to see the young people entrusted to you as the living images of Jesus Christ. By the quality of your care, let it be seen that you have a real love for them."

✍ *See 6 October for the UN 'Declaration of the Rights of the Child'.*

✍ *In the 1600s, Dutch immigrants to Nieuw Amsterdam (now New York) in the United States, took with them their Christmas tradition of Sinter Klaas (derived from the name of St Nicholas, the patron saint of children). The name soon became transformed into "**Santa Claus**", whose image combined with "Father Christmas", who had been introduced into Britain from Germany in the mid-1800s (based on a mediaeval figure, the "Spirit of Christmas").*

For 20 years in the late 1800s, an American cartoonist called Thomas Nast published drawings in a magazine each Christmas. They showed Santa Claus with sledge, reindeer, snow, sacks of presents, and elves working at Santa's workshop at the North Pole. 25 years earlier, a poem by Clement Moore gave such details as the names of the reindeer. These images caught the public's imagination.

Whether we call him "Santa Claus" or "Father Christmas", the warm image delights in children, and is derived from stories about St Nicholas who showed care, love and generosity. One such traditional story has Nicholas (the 4th century Bishop of Myra in what is now Turkey), protecting a poor family by secretly throwing a bag of gold through their window on three separate occasions, thereby giving dowries that enabled the three vulnerable girls to marry. This evolved into the custom of giving presents on the saint's feastday. German Protestants were responsible for the re-focussing of the giving of gifts, transferring the occasion to Christmas itself, the birth of God's Gift to mankind.

✍ *Poem: 'Christmas' by John Betjeman.*

♪ If I am lacking love; Lord, make me a means; Make me a channel; Oh the word of my Lord *("I know that you are very young")*; Thank you for fathers

✍ *Paragraphs 2-5 are from an article by Terence Collins FSC, May 1998.*

✍ *The words of Dorothy Law Holte should be read slowly, with feeling, and in a reflective way, with a pause between each. Regarding those words, see the quote of Winston Churchill on 29 November about taking the initiative in influencing people to behave in certain ways.*

✍ *The patron saint of teachers - John Baptist De La Salle wrote a meditation for this feastday of the patron of children:*

1 Our nearest star, of course, is the Sun. Stars that are relatively close to each other are said to form a "galaxy".

2 There are about 1,000 million stars in our own galaxy which is often called "The Milky Way".

3 There are about 100,000 million galaxies throughout the whole of the Universe.

4 We can't begin to grasp these numbers, but the Earth is a small planet travelling around one sun amongst about 100 million million million stars!

5 *Let us pray:*

God our Father,
  we thank you
  that in the vastness of your creation
  there is something special
  about the beauty of this earth.
Into our world
  which you love so much   *Jn 3*[16]
  you sent Jesus, your Son
  - your Word
  who became a human being *Jn 1*[14]
  and made his home among us.
Breathe your Holy Spirit into us
  once again
  that we may grow in a sense of wonder
  and proclaim to be good
  all that you have made.   *Gen 1*[31]
May we live more fully
  as brothers and sisters of one another
  and of Jesus, your Son.
Amen.

See the footnote of 9 October regarding our own galaxy.

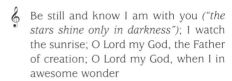

Be still and know I am with you *("the stars shine only in darkness")*; I watch the sunrise; O Lord my God, the Father of creation; O Lord my God, when I in awesome wonder

1 Philip Lawrence was headteacher of St George's Comprehensive School in Maida Vale, in west London. He always made a point of saying goodbye to his students at the school gates each evening. He had been headteacher for two years when, on this day in 1995, standing outside the school gates, he saw a student being attacked by a group of teenagers on the street. Going to protect that student, Philip Lawrence was stabbed to death.

2 300 years earlier, the patron saint of teachers - John Baptist De La Salle - had written:
"As someone chosen by God
to proclaim the gospel to others,
your commitment and enthusiasm
must go so far
that you are ready to give your very life,
so dear to you
are the young people entrusted to you."

3 The tragedy for Philip Lawrence's family and the school and his friends, provoked discussion nationally about violence and the availability of knives.

4 Mrs Lawrence remarked that when young people felt unloved and undervalued, they tended to search in the darkness for something to fill the emptiness. A minority develop aggressive behaviour, violence and complete disregard for human life.

5 It was said of Philip Lawrence that he understood education as offering options to young people that they might appreciate all beauty, so that there is no room inside them for ugliness.

6 *Let us pray:*

Teach us, good Lord,
to give and not to count the cost,
to fight and not to heed the wounds,
to toil and not to seek for rest,
to labour and to ask for no reward,
save that of knowing
that we do your will.
Amen.

✍ *On the first anniversary of Philip Lawrence's death, his 9-year old son, Lucien, unveiled a plaque outside his father's school. Present at the Catholic school with the Lawrence family were the Duchess of Kent, and Cardinal Hume, and the then Home Secretary.*

✍ *Posthumously Philip Lawrence was awarded the Binney Police Bravery Award, as well as the Queen's Gallantry Medal in the Queen's Birthday Honours in 1997.*

✍ *The prayer is by St Ignatius of Loyola. Or could use the prayer of 14 August.*

✍ *"No-one can have greater love than to lay down their life for their friends" - John 15[13].*

✍ *Today is the Feast of the Immaculate Conception of Mary. It* **doesn't** *refer to Mary conceiving Jesus. In the words of Pope Pius IX:* "From the first moment of her conception, the Blessed Virgin Mary was, by a singular grace and privilege of Almighty God, and in view of the merits of Jesus Christ, Saviour of mankind, kept free from all stain of original sin."

♪ Christ be beside me; Father, in my life; He who would valiant be; If I am lacking love; In you, my God; This is what Yahweh asks

1 We'll reflect and pray today using a few sentences from some Christmas carols.

2 *'O Little Town of Bethlehem'* includes these words:

> *"The hopes and fears of all the years are met in thee" (Bethlehem) "tonight."*

3 *Let us pray:*

As we are about to focus
on your birth, Lord,
we bring our *fears* to you,
remembering that you assured us
that *"There is no need
to be afraid".*   Mt 10[31]
We also bring our *hopes* to you,
knowing that you said to us:
"Place your trust in me."   Jn 14[1]

4 Let's pause for a moment to name some *"hopes and fears"* and place them into God's hands...

                    (Pause...)

5 *'Once in Royal David's City'* has these words:

> *"He was little, weak and helpless...
> "With the poor... and lowly
> laid on earth our Saviour holy...
> "He feeleth for our sadness
> and he shareth in our gladness."*

6 *Let us pray:*

You placed yourself, Lord,
with the poor and helpless,
and identified fully with them,
seeking no advantage for yourself.
Inspire us
to "feel" for how other people are,
that we may try to understand them
and be willing
to place ourselves
alongside those in need.
Amen.

7 The Advent carol,
'O Come, O Come, Emmanuel', says:

> *"From depths of hell thy people save...
> And close the path to misery."*

8 *Let us pray:*

We remember, Lord,
those who are experiencing
the hell of poverty, drugs,
alcoholism, abuse,
homelessness, persecution,
and the other forms of hell
that are to be found
in our world today.
We bring before you, Lord,
those who feel unloved
and all who have little joy
and little hope
in their lives. Amen.

9 Most carols focus on the birth of Jesus.
' While Shepherds Watched'
reminds us
of the message of the angel:

> *"And on the earth be peace:
> goodwill henceforth from heaven to men
> begin and never cease",*

yet there is much tension in the Holy Land in our own times,
between Jews and Palestinians.

10 We also sing:

> *"And with true love and brotherhood
> Each other now embrace"*

from the carol
'God Rest Ye Merry Gentlemen'.

11 *Let us pray:*

We think of ordinary people, Lord,
   caught up in war
   in man-made divisions
   between people
   of different race or belief,
   or background or culture.
We pray for justice and peace
   for all who feel threatened.
We pray, too,
   for greater love and acceptance
   for those experiencing difficulties
   in family life.
In praying for these things,
   we are praying, too,
   that you inspire and enable us
   to be instruments
   of your justice and peace today.
Amen.

✍ *If today's words are to be read in public, they need to be read slowly and clearly and not rushed. There should be a short pause between each of the four sections.*

✍ *For another carol, see* 'Silent Night' *- 24 December.*

✍ *Members of a group could gather appropriate pictures from newspapers and magazines to match lines of the carols. If photocopied onto acetates, the pictures can be projected to good effect in black and white via an overhead projector. Slides could be used with some of the passages.*

♪ Appropriate verses from each carol could be sung.

1 As Alfred Nobel read the newspaper one morning, he saw his own obituary printed - his own death notice! Whilst a journalist had obviously made an error, Nobel was quite shaken by what he read - not simply because others would think he had died, but because what was written about him seemed to give a false picture of who he was. The newspaper sensationalised that he was *"The Dynamite King"*.

2 His younger brother and four others had been killed in a factory explosion whilst handling nitro-glycerine. Alfred Nobel had set about making the explosive much more safe to handle by having it in solid form, which he called 'dynamite'. His hope was that his discovery would put an end to war. He wrote - hopefully - that:

   "On the day two army groups
   realise that (with dynamite)
   they can annihilate each other
   in one second,
   all civilised nations
   will recoil from war in horror."

3 Having read his obituary and realising that his good intentions for peace and understanding were not even mentioned, Nobel decided he would invest for a good purpose the fortune that he had made from his invention of dynamite. When he died on this day in 1896, his Will stated that most of his fortune was to be placed in trust. The interest on that money would fund annual prizes *"to those who, in the preceding year, shall have conferred the greatest benefit upon mankind."*

4 On this day each year (the anniversary of his death) the Prizes are presented by the King of Sweden in Stockholm, the city where Alfred Nobel was born. The Nobel Prizes are among the most highly-regarded honours anyone can receive. Winners are given a gold medal and a diploma, as well as a large cash award. People are named for contributions in six categories: Chemistry, Economics, Literature, Peace, Physics, and Medicine.

5 *Let us pray:*

Lord,
   you have enriched our lives
   in many ways,
   and we are grateful
   for all who have influenced our lives
   for the better.
Show us how best
   to use the time and talents
   you have given each one of us,
   and inspire us to live fully
   and bring benefit
   to our own part of the world.
Amen.

📝 Since 1969, "Economics" has been added to Nobel's original list of five categories, but that Prize is paid for by the Swedish National Bank.

📝 Some of the more famous recipients of the Nobel Prizes are as follows:

Chemistry:
1908 - Ernest Rutherford (UK)
1911 - Marie Curie (Fr) (see 16 Nov)

Economics:
1976 - Milton Friedman (US)

Literature:
1907 - Rudyard Kipling (UK)
1923 - W.B.Yeats (Ire)
1925 - George Bernard Shaw (UK)
1948 - T.S.Eliot (UK)
1953 - Winston Churchill (UK) (see Index)
1954 - Ernest Hemingway (US)
1957 - Albert Camus (Fr) (see 7 Nov)
1958 - Boris Pasternak (USSR)
1970 - Alexander Solzhenitsyn (USSR)
                                 (see 28 Dec)
1983 - William Golding (UK)
1995 - Seamus Heeney (Ire)

Peace:
1901 - Jean-Henri Dunant (Switz) (see 9 May)
1952 - Albert Schweitzer (Fr) (see 14 Jan)
1961 - Dag Hammarskjöld (Sw) (see Index)
1964 - Martin Luther King (US) (see Index)
1977 - Amnesty International (see Index)
1978 - Anwar al-Sadat (Egy) (see 19 Nov)
1979 - Mother Teresa (Ind) (see Index)
1993 - Nelson Mandela (S.Afr) (see Index)

Physics:
1901 - William Röntgen - 1901 (Ger) (see 10 Feb)
1903 - Marie Curie (Fr) (see 16 Nov)
1909 - Guglielmo Marconi (It) (see 27 March)
1921 - Albert Einstein (US) (see Index)

Physiology and Medicine:
1902 - Sir Ronald Ross (UK)
1904 - Ivan Pavlov (Russ)
1905 - Robert Koch (Ger)
1945 - Sir Alexander Fleming (UK) (see Index)
1973 - Konrad Lorenz (Aust)

❖❖❖❖❖❖❖❖❖❖❖❖❖❖❖❖❖❖❖

📝 Alfred Nobel - his surname is pronounced "know-bell": 21/10/1833 - 10/12/1896.

📝 An obituary is an account of the life and achievements of someone who has just died.

📝 Nitroglycerine is $C_3H_5(NO_3)_3$. In solid form it is called 'dynamite'. When detonated, the explosion is due to the sudden production of about 10,000 times its own volume of gas. Nobel also invented gelignite. Some of his large fortune was derived from investments in the Baku oilfields in Azerbaijan, near the Caspian Sea.

📝 Today's materials could be linked to a school's annual Prize Giving/Certificate Evening - see prayer 55 in the Appendix to Volume 2. See also "Certificate Evening" in the Index.

🎼 All that I am; In the love of God and neighbour ("talents, gifts and skills")

Paralysed man
let down through the roof

We read in the Gospel, Lord,
that some people were such good friends
of a man who was weak and paralysed
that they made their way
through the crowds,
carried him on to the roof,
and gently lowered him down,
so that he could be right in front of you.
There are times when each of us
becomes weak or strong,
reminding us
that we all need the support of others
at one time or another.
As we gather together in your presence,
we come as friends
who are concerned for each other.
In our strengths and weaknesses
we bring one another to meet you,
face-to-face.

(Lk 5[17-26]; Mk 2[1-12])

(see page 179)

1 Yesterday, the 10th of December, marked the anniversary in 1948 of the United Nations adopting the *"Universal Declaration of Human Rights"*. As we listen to excerpts about some of those rights, we can bear in mind people in different parts of the world who do not share our own experience of human rights being respected.

2 *"All human beings*
are born free and equal
in dignity and rights.　　　　(1)

3 *"No-one shall be held in slavery."*　(4)

4 *"No-one shall be subjected to torture."*　(5)

5 *"Everyone has the right*
to recognition everywhere
as a person
before the law."　　　　(6)

6 *"Everyone charged with a penal offence*
has the right to be presumed innocent
until proved guilty."　　　(11)

7 *"Everyone has the right*
to freedom of thought,
conscience, and religion."　　(18)

8 *Let us pray:*

Lord, it's good
　to be actively concerned
　about the abuses of human rights
　in other countries,
　but I must not lose sight
　of the mis-treatment of others
　closer to me.
Most particularly, Lord,
　point out to me
　my own failings
　in lacking respect
　for those who come into my daily life.

9 I readily condemn slavery,
　but help me to liberate those I know
　who are overburdened.

I condemn torture,
　but lead me to discourage the use
　of cruel words and actions
　to those I will meet today.
Remind me
　that those who degrade others
　are themselves diminished.

10 Enlighten me
　so that I do not
　jump to conclusions about people,
　or be judgmental.
Lead me
　always to respect individuals
　for who they are,
　realising that their experiences
　may be different from my own,
　as each follows paths in life
　that are particular to them.
May I grow in appreciation
　that those
　who think differently from me
　can hold equally valid views.

11 In these and other ways, Lord,
　may I grow in respect for all people.
This day, may others respect me
　as much as I respect them.
Amen.

📖 *See also 12 May.*

📖 *It has been said that the character of a person can be assessed according to how they treat someone who can do nothing for them in return.*

🎼 Christ is our king; God's Spirit is in my heart; If I am lacking love; Make me a channel; There is a world

12 DECEMBER

1 On this day in 1653, Oliver Cromwell was declared "Lord Protector" of England. The country had become a republic, and King Charles I had been executed five years previously. Cromwell would have almost absolute power for the following five years.

2 A painting of the Lord Protector was commissioned. The artist felt that he should paint the feared Cromwell as favourably as possible. The problem lay in the fact that Cromwell was far from looking attractive, and had pimples and warts on his face. He said to the artist:

3 *"Use your skill*
to paint my picture truly like me,
and do not flatter me at all.
Show me as I am - warts and all.
Otherwise I will never pay a farthing
for it."

4 That phrase - *"warts and all"* - has passed into the English language, as a reminder to accept people fully as they are: accepting not just a person's positive points, but valuing the whole person, *"warts and all"*.

5 *Let us pray:*

God our Father,
as you welcome me
and accept me fully
and love me as the person I am,
so inspire me
to be generous to others
in the welcome and acceptance,
and the love and the care
that I offer.
Amen.

📖 *The artist was a Mr Lely. Horace Walpole, in his "Anecdotes of Painting in England" (Vol 3), gives fuller details.*

📖 *Oliver Cromwell: 1599-1658. He had been MP for Huntingdon and later for Cambridge. He was made "Lord Protector" almost 5 years after the execution of King Charles I. Parliament offered the crown to Cromwell, but he declined. He is sometimes referred to as* "the uncrowned king of England". *It was on 16 December 1653 that Oliver Cromwell was formally installed as Lord Protector of the Commonwealth (meaning 'Republic' at that time). The period of the Republic (later called 'The Interregnum') would last for 11 years until the 'Restoration' of Charles II.*

📖 *Cromwell struggled against the tyranny of Charles I, who ruled for 11 years without a parliament. Yet in the eyes of many, including those who suffered under him (especially the people of Ireland), Cromwell himself became a tyrant, although he did contribute to the development of a constitutional form of government, in which an elected parliament would become the ultimate authority. Accordingly, a statue of Oliver Cromwell on a horse is in a prominent position outside the Houses of Parliament.*

🎵 All that I am; Come, come, follow me; Do not worry; He who would valiant be; I give my hands; I will never forget you; Take my hands; The love I have for you

1 The comedy series 'Blackadder' stars Rowan Atkinson. One series was set in the times of Queen Elizabeth I, and another in the trenches of the First World War. Edmund Blackadder also appears as the butler to George, the Prince Regent. One of the characters in that series is Doctor Johnson, who is seen to be compiling a dictionary.

2 The **real** Doctor Samuel Johnson - who died on this day in 1784 - spent 8 years preparing his dictionary of about 40,000 definitions. He was also a poet, and is remembered for short phrases (sometimes comical) that sum up a situation.

3 He wrote this simple statement:
"True greatness
consists in being great
in little things."

4 *Let us pray:*
Lord, I need to keep an eye
    on the small things in life
    as well as the bigger issues,
    because my thoughts
    become my attitude,
    my attitude becomes my words,
    my words become my actions,
    and my actions form my character.
Be there, Lord,
    in that instant before every thought,
    that I may choose wisely
    my thoughts and my attitude,
    my words and my actions,
    so that I may grow in friendship
    with those
    who become part of my life.
Show me, too,
    how best to encourage others
    to reach their potential.
Amen.

5 | *"True greatness*
consists in being great
in little things."

📖 *Dr Samuel Johnson: 18/9/1709-13/12/1784. See also 17 September.*

📖 *If the 'dictionary' theme is to be followed, the prayer of 22 November concerns 'words'.*

📖 *For some similar ideas, see 13 September, the quote of Charles Dickens on 9 June, and "little" in the index. An alternative prayer would be that of Blaise Pascal - 24 June - "Teach us, Lord, to do the little things as though they were great..."*

📖 *Helen Keller (see 1,3 June; 1 September) wrote:*
"I long to accomplish
a great and noble task,
but it is my chief duty
to accomplish small tasks
as if they were great and noble."

📖 *The Prince Regent became King George IV - see 26 June.*

🎵 Do not worry; Father, I place; I give my hands; Oh the word of my Lord

1 Many Christmas customs were lost in Britain when the feast of Christmas itself was abolished by Oliver Cromwell and the Puritans in the 17th Century. They said that Christmas was only to be a solemn time.

2 Many of the customs we have today were introduced to Britain in the 19th Century. For example, Prince Albert (the husband of Queen Victoria) brought from his own country of Germany the tradition of having a decorated Christmas Tree.

3 An edition of *"The Illustrated London News"* for 1848, stated that:

"The Christmas Tree is prepared annually
by her Majesty's command
for the Royal children…
The tree employed for this festive purpose
is a young fir
about eight feet high.
On each branch
are arranged a dozen wax tapers…
Fancy cakes and gingerbread
are suspended by coloured ribbons
from the branches.
On the top of the tree
stands the small figure of an angel
with outstretched wings."

4 The custom of the Christmas Tree - brought to Britain by Prince Albert - soon spread throughout the country. Prince Albert died on this day in 1861, aged only 42.

5 One of the best-known Christmas Trees stands in Trafalgar Square in London. Each year a huge fir tree is shipped over from Norway - a present from the Norwegian people, in gratitude for Britain's help during the Second World War.

6 It is thought that 500 years ago, Martin Luther (the German church reformer) was the first to put candles on a Christmas tree. He said that the lights would remind people of the stars that shone above Bethlehem on the night of the birth of Jesus.

7 *Let us pray:*

God our Father,
 at this time of year
 we think of loved ones,
 and remember with gratitude
 what others have done for us.
As the stars shone over Bethlehem,
 so may we shine in the world
 like bright stars *Phil 2¹⁵*
 as we share the Word of Life
 - Jesus, your Son,
 your Word amongst us. *Jn 1¹⁴*
Amen.

vived once Charles II became King in England, but Scotland tended to keep to the Puritan ways. Christmas in Scotland is still marked differently from in England, Wales and Ireland. Tending to keep distinct the sacred and the secular, Scotland's secular festivities are held on Hogmanay - see 31 December.

✍ Queen Victoria was devastated at the unexpected death of her young husband, Prince Albert (often called the "Prince Consort"). The Queen wore black as an expression of mourning (and would continue to do so until her own death, 50 years later in 1901). The nation joined the Queen in her mourning, and shops sold out of black cloth. People with iron railings in front of their houses even painted those black. Before Albert's death, iron railings had been painted in the colour of the house. So long was the sense of mourning that it has since become "traditional" to paint railings black! An archbishop-to-be sent a letter to the Queen on the death of her husband. Hoping to comfort her, he wrote: "From now on, your husband will be Christ." Across his letter the Queen wrote: "Twaddle"!

✍ Martin Luther: 10/11/1483 - 18/2/1546.

✍ Another image of the Christmas Tree was given after the Apollo 15 moon-landing in July 1971. A Christmas Tree ornament could be held suspended as the following words of astronaut James Irwin are read:
"You can see the Earth like a beautiful Christmas Tree ornament against the blackness of space. It's as if you can reach out and hold it in your hand... As we flew into space we had a new sense of ourselves, of the Earth, and of the nearness of God. I was touched by a desire to convince mankind that we have a unique place to live, that we are unique creatures, and that we must learn to live with our neighbours."

✿✿✿✿✿✿✿✿✿✿✿✿✿✿✿✿✿✿✿

✍ St Boniface was born about 680 in Crediton, Devon. He felt called to be a missionary in the then pagan lands of Germany, and would later be known as "the Apostle of the Germans". The pagan people considered a certain oak tree to be sacred. The oak tree of Donar was at the summit of Mount Gudenberg (at Geismar, 100 miles east of what is now the city of Dusseldorf). Boniface hit the tree with an axe. Far from being struck down by pagan gods, his few blows demolished the mighty tree. It was seen as a 'sign' that the pagan 'gods' did not exist. Amidst the roots of the oak tree on that December day was seen to be growing a little fir tree. Boniface is said to have remarked to the people that "the fir tree is a sign of eternal life, as its leaves are ever-green. From now on it shall be called the tree of the Christ-Child." It is from Boniface that the custom of the Christmas Tree is thought to have originated.

✍ For Oliver Cromwell, see 12 December. Regarding Christmas, Cromwell's aim was to focus on the simplicity of the event, having seen gluttony and other apparent abuses of festivity. Some of the traditions of Christmas were re-

𝄢 Be still and know I am with you ("the stars shine"); O little town of Bethlehem (vv 1 & 3; "the silent stars"); Sing a simple song; The light of Christ; The love I have for you ("your light in me will shine")

15 DECEMBER

1 The American poet and author, Carl Sandburg, wrote:
> "Shakespeare, Leonardo da Vinci,
> Benjamin Franklin, and Abraham Lincoln...
> were not afraid of being lonely,
> because they knew
> that was when
> the creative mood in them
> would work."

2 Another person who is renowned for being very creative, was the musical composer, Ludwig van Beethoven, who was born on tomorrow's date in 1770.

3 Beethoven wrote these words:
> "You will ask where I find my ideas;
> I hardly know.
> They come uninvited, directly or indirectly.
> I can almost grasp them with my hands
> in the open air,
> in the woods while walking,
> in the stillness of the night,
> early in the morning,
> called up by the moods
> which the poet translates into words
> and I translate into musical tones.
> They ring and roar and swirl about me
> until I write them down in notes."

4 *Let us pray:*

God our Father,
   amidst the busy-ness and noise
   of daily life,
   I ask you to bring it home to me
   how much I need
   time and quiet for myself,
   in which I can become
   more attuned with myself
   and more at one
   with you, my God.
As I am then able to grow more
   in your image and likeness
   and be re-created,
   inspire me to be creative
and develop to the full
the talents you have given me
for the benefit of those people
you place into my life.
Amen.

✦✦✦✦✦✦✦✦✦✦✦✦✦✦✦✦✦✦✦

✎ *Carl Sandburg: 6/1/1878-22/7/1967.*
William Shakespeare: 1564-1616 (see Index)
Leonardo da Vinci: 1452-1519
   (see 2 Sept and Maundy Thursday)
Benjamin Franklin: 1706-1790 (see 17 April)
Ludwig van Beethoven: 1770-1827
   (see 3 March, 28 April, 7 May)
Abraham Lincoln: 1809-1865
   (see 4 March, 9 April, 20 Nov)

✎ *Beethoven's birthday is an occasion marked in Peanuts' cartoons.*

✎ "Let me make my life simple,
   and as straight as a recorder,
   for you to fill with music"
                    - *Rabindranath Tagore.*

✎ "The person who fears to be alone will never be anything but lonely" - *Thomas Merton.*
See also 26 September re 'loneliness', and 27 July about time and quiet for self.

♪ All that I am; I give my hands; Take my hands

Praying in lonely places

We read in the Gospel, Lord,
that you would go away to lonely places,
and there you would pray.
Not alone now, but here with others,
we thank you for being with us
and joining us in prayer to our Father.

(Lk 5:16)

(see page 179)

16 DECEMBER

1 At dawn on this day in 1944, the Germans started their last major counter-attack of the Second World War. They took advantage of heavy mists that lay over the Ardennes region on Germany's border with Belgium and Luxembourg.

2 The Germans were thought no longer capable of launching a major offensive, yet they managed to reach 50 miles within the Allied lines before they had to retreat.

3 One of the leaders of the American forces of this "Battle of the Ardennes" (also called "The Battle of the Bulge") was General Omar Bradley.

4 Some years after the end of the Second World War, and as some nations were spending vast amounts of money on stock-piling nuclear and other weapons, General Omar Bradley spoke the following words:

5 "We have too many men of science,
   too few men of God.
We have grasped the mystery of the atom,
   and rejected the Sermon on the Mount.
The world has achieved
   brilliance without wisdom,
   power without conscience.
Ours is a world
   of nuclear giants
   and ethical infants.
We know more about war
   than we do about peace;
   more about killing
   than we do about living."

6 General Omar Bradley mentioned the "Sermon on the Mount". Those words of Jesus include the "Beatitudes", which are a set of 8 statements of choices which lead to a person being happy or blessed. We can reflect and pray today, using the words of those Beatitudes:

7 "Happy are the poor in spirit
   - for the Kingdom of Heaven is theirs.

8 Happy are those who mourn
   - for they will be given
   courage and comfort.

9 Happy are the gentle and humble
   - for they shall have the earth
   as their heritage.

10 Happy are those who hunger and thirst
   for what is good and right
   - for they will be fully satisfied.

11 Happy are those
   who are merciful to others
   - for they will have mercy
   shown to them.

12 Happy are the utterly sincere
   - for they will see God.

13 Happy are those who promote peace
   - for they will be called God's children.

14 Happy are those who suffer persecution
   for the cause of goodness
   - for the Kingdom of Heaven is theirs."

✍ *General Omar Bradley: 1893-1981. He worked with the famous General George Patton. The two are depicted in the film, "Patton - Lust for Glory", which includes footage of today's battle.*

✍ *"Beatitude" is pronounced "be-attitude". It has been said that "the 'Beatitudes' are 'good attitudes' to have in life." Some translations of the gospel use "Happy" for each of the Beatitudes, whilst others use the word "Blessed". Printed above, they need to be read slowly and meaningfully, preferably pausing between each.*

✍ *The Sermon on the Mount is found in Matthew's Gospel, Chapters 5, 6 and 7. Matthew, writing for Jewish Christians, is keen to draw parallels between Jesus and Moses, who had led the people from slavery in Egypt (about 1250 BC) and who then received "the Law" of the 10 Commandments on Mount Sinai (also called Mount Horeb). Accordingly, Matthew portrays Jesus as speaking the heart of the Good News (this 'Sermon') on a mountain. Luke, on the other hand, writing for Gentiles (i.e. non-Jews) locates Jesus' words of "the Sermon" on a plain (Lk 6$^{17-49}$) - conveying a sense of openness and availability of God's Word to everyone, and not only to Jews.*

✍ *"Ethical" in paragraph 5 means a sense of what is right and wrong.*

✍ *Each of us could think about specific incidents in our own lives (or in the lives of friends, well-known figures, or saints) that reflect particular Beatitudes. Newspaper articles or photographs could be chosen to illustrate each Beatitude, possibly as photocopiable acetates on an overhead projector.*

🎶 Blest are you, O poor in spirit *(the Beatitudes)*; Christ is our king; Come, let us go up to the Lord; Make me a channel; O Lord all the world *("turning the world upside-down")*; Take my hands; Whatsoever you do

1 Often shown as a film at Christmas is Charles Dickens' story, *'A Christmas Carol'.* The rich and miserly Scrooge is known to be selfish and uncaring towards everyone. When asked to donate some money for the poor, he says:

"I don't make merry myself at Christmas, and I can't afford to make idle people merry."

2 His partner in business had been Jacob Marley, but he had died and now sends three messengers to Ebenezer Scrooge. The first is called the *'Ghost of Christmas Past'* . He shows Scrooge the happiness that he **could** have had, if he had made different choices in his life.

3 The second messenger is the *"Ghost of Christmas Present"*. He shows Scrooge how happy his married nephew is, despite not having his uncle's great wealth. He is also shown the family of one of his employees, Bob Cratchit, who is very poor yet has a very happy life at home. One of his children is called 'Tiny Tim', who is disabled. Tiny Tim says that he hopes that those who have seen him in church (with his disability)

"might recall on Christmas Day
who it was
who made lame beggars walk
and the blind see."

4 Scrooge's third visitor is the *'Ghost of Christmas Yet to Come'.* He shows Scrooge that, in the future, he will sack Bob Cratchit. With no income for the family, Tiny Tim will die. The Ghost then takes Scrooge to a tomb - it is his own - and no-one will mourn his passing. Yet Scrooge learns that, if he changes, life will be different, and the negative things he has seen will not then take place.

5 The next day is Christmas Day. As he awakes, Ebenezer Scrooge is a changed person. He gives a pay-rise to Bob Cratchit and visits his family, meeting Tiny Tim, who says,

"God bless us everyone."

6 Scrooge now chooses to live in a positive and cheerful way, and so discovers happiness himself.

7 *'A Christmas Carol'* is one of many books by Charles Dickens, and it was published on this day in 1843.

8 Our prayer today is simply those words of Tiny Tim. So let us pray for all whom we love and all who share our lives:

9 **"God bless us everyone."**

📖 *The word "Scrooge" has entered the English language to mean someone who is miserly and, in Mrs Cratchit's words, "odious, stingy, hard and unfeeling."*

📖 *Charles Dickens: 7/2/1812 - 9/6/1870. See also 9 and 10 June. Also in "A Christmas Carol" (ch.2) we can read: "In came Mrs Fezziwig, one vast substantial smile!"*

📖 *A custom at Christmas is the pulling of **crackers**. They were invented in the late 1800s by Tom Smith, who was an English baker. By the turn of the century, the company he had set up was producing millions of crackers.*

🎼 Christ is our king *("the crippled and lame")*; If I am lacking love; I give my hands; Lord have mercy *("Give me the heart of stone within you")*; O Lord, all the world belongs to you

1 On TV in the United States, programmes and films are often interrupted by adverts. Which was the first film to be shown on American TV without any breaks for adverts? It will have been a serious film which created an atmosphere which adverts would have destroyed.

2 The film was *"Schindler's List"*, about the protection of some Jewish people during the Second World War. Before reaching TV, it was first shown at the cinema, being released as a film in mid-December 1993.

3 Spielberg's film shows how a German-Czech businessman deals with Nazi leaders. Oskar Schindler bribes them, managing to protect a group of over a thousand Jews who would otherwise have been killed in a concentration camp.

4 As the war ends, a gold ring is presented to Oskar Schindler. The ring is made from the gold fillings from the mouths of some of the survivors. It is engraved with these words:
  "Whoever saves one life saves the world entire."

5 The picture was filmed in Kracow, using the actual factory that Schindler operated. At one point during the filming, Steven Spielberg found himself walking amongst the many "extras" - the people needed for crowd scenes. In haste, and not being able to speak their language, Spielberg realised that he was gesturing people to the right or to the left.
  "I felt like a Nazi,"
he said, remembering those who ran the concentration camps who would divide people to the right or to the left as Jews arrived in cattle trucks at the concentration camps - dividing them to one side for **life**, or in the other direction for immediate **death** in the gas chambers.

6 Spielberg said that his worst days in filming were when he had to have the actors take their clothes off as they approached the gas chambers. It was humiliating and stripped the people of their human dignity.

7 *Let us pray:*

Lord God of all people,
  lead me not to judge others
  or discriminate
  and divide into different groups.
Inspire me to live in such a way
  that I am not destructive
  or negative.
Empower me with your Spirit
  that I may choose wisely
  and live positively
  and so promote all that is life-giving.
Amen.

✍ *Oskar Schindler: 1908 - 1974.*

✍ *The film lasted 3 hours and 15 minutes, and received 7 Oscars in 1993.*

✍ *"Whoever saves one life..." are words from the Talmud, a collection of Jewish teachings. A ring with the same inscription is still worn by Nicholas Winton, who saved more than 600 Jewish children from the Nazis, taking them from Czechoslovakia to Wales.*

✍ *Sadly and tragically, Jews (and others) have been persecuted down the ages. Until more recent times, the greatest prejudice and discrimination towards the Jews was brought about by those who professed to be Christians (see 4 May). Jews have been segregated into "ghettoes", taking their name from the ghetto in Venice (formed in 1516). The Venetian Jews were confined to an area beside a foundry - and the word for 'foundry' in Italian is 'getto'.*

✍ *See also the prayer of 4 May.*

19 DECEMBER

1 Many would say that Turner was one of Britain's greatest artists. He died on this day in 1851. It has been said that before Turner, nobody painted sunsets. He taught people to *"really see"* sunsets, even though they were so obvious. In Turner's water scenes, both the water and the sky are filled with brilliant, golden and hazy light, and it is difficult to see where the water finishes and the sky begins.

2 Living at the same time as Turner was another English painter, John Constable, who saw and painted the beauty in ordinary country scenes. He said:

"There is nothing ugly;
I never saw an ugly thing in my life.
Let the form of an object
be what it may
- light, shade and perspective
will always make it beautiful."

3 Both artists - Turner and Constable - remind us that the physical world and the spiritual are not separate, but overlap and are intermingled - the *"veil"* between them is thin. God's coming to us as a human being ("the Incarnation") reminds us that it is not helpful to try to draw lines between what is "sacred" and what is "secular".

4 *Let us pray:*

God our Father,
you created light
and all that we can see.
Show us how to grow
in a sense of wonder
that we may *"really see"*
and appreciate
all the beauty that is around us.
Lead us to discover
how inter-connected
are so many things in life
and how inter-woven
with your presence.
May the coming into our world
of Jesus, your Son,
- who lived fully as a human being -
remind us that we are all called
to be at-one with you.
Show us how to transform
all that might be ordinary
in our daily lives
and, through your Spirit,
become more fully alive,
to your greater glory. Amen.

📖 "I am constantly aware
that there is another reality
which inter-penetrates our own"
                              - Philip Toynbee.

📖 *As with mention of Turner's portrayal of an indistinct 'partition' between land (or sea) and sky, George Macleod (who founded the Iona Community in 1938) talked of*
"a place where the veil
between heaven and earth
is particularly thin."
He was referring to the island of Iona, and this concept of everything being interwoven with God's presence is integral to 'Celtic Spirituality'.

📖 *Joseph (J.M.W.) Turner: 23/4/1775-19/12/1851. Often portrayed are his several views of Venice, 'Shipwreck', 'Steamboat in a Snowstorm', 'Rain, Steam and Speed - the Great Western Railway', 'Burning of the Houses of Parliament', and 'Calais Pier'.*

📖 *John Constable (11/6/1776-31/3/1837) felt it a great compliment when he overheard someone say to some visitors: "This is Constable country" referring to the area of Dedham and East Bergholt around the River Stour in Suffolk which he painted the most. Some of his most renowned paintings are 'Flatford Mill', 'The Hay Wain', 'The Cornfield', 'The White Horse', and several views of Salisbury Cathedral.*

🎼 Christ is our king *("sunlight", "vision")*; I watch the sunrise; Oh the word of my Lord; The light of Christ

1 An American writer told a short story about self-sacrifice at Christmas. Two young people who were very much in love wanted to give a present to each other, but both were poor. Without telling each other, they decided what they would do.

2 The girl was proud of her long hair that flowed down her back. She approached a wig-maker who gave her money as long as strands of her hair were cut off. Now she was able to buy her friend a present.

3 Meanwhile, her boyfriend sold his most precious possession - an old-fashioned watch of sentimental value, as it had been given to him by his grandfather. He, too, then bought a present.

4 That day, Christmas Eve, the two had arranged to meet, as usual - she with her remaining hair covered by a scarf, and he a little late because he no longer had a watch. What were their presents? She had bought him a special watch-chain so that he could hang his watch from his coat pocket! He had bought her a set of expensive combs for her long, flowing hair!

5 They shed tears as they appreciated the sacrifice in love that each had made - and they laughed!

6 *Let us pray:*

Lord Jesus,
   as we prepare to celebrate
   the gift of yourself
   to our world,
   we think too of our loved ones,
   remembering that you said
   that there is *"more joy in giving*
   than in receiving."   Acts 20[35]
We ask you to bless us
   and those we love.
Amen.

🖎 *The story is by O.Henry, a pseudonym for William Porter, 1862-1910.*

🖎 *Could use the prayer 'Christmas love' in 'Pause for Thought with Frank Topping', pg 149 (ISBN: 0-7188-2524-1).*

🖎 *As well as giving presents, it has become a custom to send* **Christmas cards**. *It is thought that the first Christmas card as such was designed in London for Christmas 1843. It cost a shilling (5 pence) - then about 10 times the price of a loaf of bread. The idea of Christmas cards was slow to catch on until the 1870s with cheaper ways of printing and an inexpensive postal service.*

The 1836 winter of very heavy snowstorms was still remembered when people designed Christmas cards. At that time, mail coaches were delayed or caught in snow drifts, probably inspiring the secular pictures of stagecoaches amidst the snow.

🖎 *Nowadays the Royal Mail produces special* **Christmas stamps**. *In odd-numbered years the stamps are religious in design (e.g. showing the shepherds visiting the stable in Bethlehem). In even-numbered years the designs are secular (e.g. a robin and Father Christmas).*

 If I am lacking love

21 DECEMBER

1 On the 21st of December 1968, the Apollo 8 spacecraft blasted off on its 6-day mission. It was the first manned flight to leave Earth's orbit. The mission was successful because of the hard work and co-operation of many people with skills in maths, science and technology.

2 Apollo 8 travelled to the Moon, making 10 orbits, taking many photos of the surface of the Moon. Frank Borman, one of the astronauts, said:

"The more we learn
about the wonders of our universe,
the more clearly we are going to perceive
the hand of God."

3 As the spacecraft began to orbit the Moon, it lost radio contact with Earth each time it travelled around the far side of the Moon. Coming back into radio contact, the craft was facing the Earth, and the astronauts referred to *"the good Earth"*. They said that they wished to send a Christmas greeting to all who were listening. Then the astronauts took it in turn to read the opening verses of the Bible from the Book of Genesis. They are a poem about God's goodness and blessing in creating the world.

4 Frank Borman then read a prayer - now called *"the Astronauts' Prayer"*. As we pray those same words, we ask for vision and inspiration:

5 *Let us pray:*

"Give us, O God, the vision
which can see your love in the world
in spite of human failure.
Give us the faith, the trust,
and the goodness
in spite of our ignorance
and weakness.
Give us the knowledge
that we may continue to pray

with understanding hearts,
and show us
what each one of us can do
to set forth
the coming of the day
of universal peace.
Amen."

❖❖❖❖❖❖❖❖❖❖❖❖❖❖❖❖❖❖❖❖

📖 *Apollo 8 was crewed by Frank Borman, Bill Anders, and Commander Jim Lovell (who would later lead the ill-fated Apollo 13 - see 25 May).*

📖 *As we look at the Moon from the Earth, and as the astronauts looked at both from space, the Moon and the Earth reflect the light of the Sun. St Paul writes to the Christians in Corinth:*
"We are like mirrors,
reflecting the brightness of the Lord,
and we grow brighter and brighter
as we are turned into
the very image that we reflect."
(2 Cor 3[18])

📖 *See 12 January re Genesis 1-2.*

📖 *On 20/2/62, 10 months after Yuri Gagarin (see 12 April) of the Soviet Union became the first person to orbit the Earth, John Glenn became the first American to do so. He said:*
"The God I worship
is too big for space to contain."

📖 *See also the last footnote of 14 December, which quotes the Apollo 15 words about the Earth looking like a fragile Christmas ornament.*

🎼 I watch the sunrise *("moonlight")*

1. 400 years ago, **Christmas mince pies** were made of chopped meat, rather than fruit. The crust on top was formed from a piece of pastry in the shape of a baby. The mince pie was rectangular in shape, representing the Christ-Child in the Manger.

2. Nowadays mince pies are made with mixed fruit of currants, sultanas, and the peel of lemons and oranges. At Christmastime, nuts and dates are often bought, along with some less-common fruits such as mandarins, clementines, nectarines and satsumas - all varieties of orange.

3. 720,000 tons of oranges were destroyed in Europe in 1993. They were fit for human consumption, as were the apples - nearly a million tons of them - also destroyed that year by the European Union. Nearly three million tons of perfectly good fruit and vegetables were destroyed that year - mostly by being buried in the ground and allowed to rot.

4. This was done according to the agricultural policy of the European Union, paying farmers to destroy some of their crops rather than have *"too much food"* on the market, causing prices to drop. This policy cost British taxpayers £57 million in 1993.

5. *Let us pray:*

God our loving Father,
our governments
spend money in our name
to subsidise farmers to "set aside"
good agricultural land
so that less food is produced.
Some potatoes and other good crops
are sprayed with dyes
to make them unfit
for human consumption,
and it is policy
to destroy good harvests
of fruit and vegetables.

Yet our brothers and sisters
go hungry and die
across the world.
Lead us to grow
in valuing the dignity
of all people,
as well as in respect
for the fruit of the earth
and the work of human hands.
Inspire us to be of influence
in our own part of the world
so that injustices -wherever they exist-
may be challenged,
and all people learn to grow together
as caring and responsible
brothers and sisters.
Amen.

✍ *Currants and sultanas are dried grapes.*

✍ *As with mince pies, "**Christmas Pudding**" used to be savoury, made with meat. Beef and veal were often boiled in wine and sherry, along with sugar, spices, currants, raisins and prunes (which, being dried plums, gave us the alternative name of "Plum Pudding"). The pudding was thickened with the addition of brown bread.*

✍ *The stated figures were given in reply to parliamentary questions tabled by Labour MP Stephen Byers and published in newspapers on 7/8/95.*

✍ *There are instances of groups of farmers donating some of their grain crops to charities for overseas aid.*

✍ *CAFOD, Romero Close, Stockwell Road, London SW9 9BR is the 'Catholic Fund for Overseas Development'.*
Christian Aid, P.O.Box 100, London SE1 7RT.

♭ Come, let us go up to the Lord; God's Spirit is in my heart; If I am lacking love; O Lord, all the world *("turning the world upside down")*; This is what Yahweh asks of you *("act justly")*

23 DECEMBER

1 We're going to listen to an account of how St Francis of Assisi created the first **Christmas Crib**.

2 For many people,
one of the most beautiful
and peaceful
towns in the world
is that of Assisi,
set on a hillside in northern Italy.

3 There it was in the year 1223
that St Francis
thought how best he might portray
the simplicity
of the Birth of the Son of God
into our world.

4 In the darkness of Christmas Eve
and in the days before electricity,
people brought candles
and burning torches
which lit up the hillside
as they travelled from around:
all converging on a cave on the hillside.

5 As the people arrived,
hay was spread out,
and local farmers and shepherds
led into the cave
an ox and a donkey and a few sheep.
The animals were at peace;
the people were hopeful.

6 Then Francis himself
placed on a stone altar
cloths that were wrapped
to resemble a baby.
All the people prayed and sang.
The Christmas Midnight Mass began.
Francis himself read the Gospel,
telling how Mary and Joseph had travelled
and found no room available in Bethlehem,
whose name means *"the House of Bread"*.

7 There they sheltered with animals,
and Mary gave birth to Jesus
in poverty and simplicity,

placing into a manger
(from which the animals ate hay)
the Child
who would later declare himself to be
"the Bread of life".

8 As the Mass ended,
the people left the cave.
They had repeated the words of the angel
and had, indeed,
given *"Glory to God in the highest!"*
They returned to their homes,
joyful, and living in peace with one another:
"Peace to all people of good will!"

9 We have heard how Francis of Assisi created the first Christmas Crib, and placed an image of Jesus there, amidst the ordinary surroundings of the lives of the local people.

10 *Let us pray:*

**God our Father,
may the simplicity of the birth
of Jesus, your Son,
remind us
that we can readily discover him
in the ordinariness of our daily lives.
Amen.**

📖 *Francis of Assisi (see the Index) was not a priest. He lived from about 1182 until 1226. Francis made his crib in Greccio.*

📖 *A "manger" - normally made of wooden slats - is a container holding hay or other feed for animals ("manger" in French is the verb meaning "to eat").*

📖 *Could make use of the 'Prayer of the Donkey' by Carmen Bernos de Gasztold in 'Prayers from the Ark' (ISBN 0-330-32438-1).*

📖 *Martin Luther (1483-1546) wrote:*
"God is the God of the humble, the miserable, the oppressed, and the desperate, and of those who are brought even to nothing, and his nature is to give sight to the blind, to comfort the broken-hearted, to justify sinners."

📖 *It is a custom in Mexican villages*
on the nine nights before Christmas
to enact the journey to Bethlehem
of Mary and Joseph.
Each night the villagers gather
and process with candles and music,
carrying figures
that represent Mary and Joseph.
They make their way
to another house in the village.
There they knock at the door
and ask if there is room
for Mary and Joseph to stay.
In this way
the welcome that was not evident in Bethlehem
is given by the Mexican villagers
who sense that Jesus is brought to birth
in their own homes.

🎼 Angels we have heard on high; Away in a manger; Come and join the celebration; Go tell it on the mountain; Hark the herald angels; In the bleak mid-winter; O come, all ye faithful; Once in royal David's city; On Christmas night all Christians sing; Sing a simple song; Unto us is born a Son; While shepherds watched

1 It was Christmas Eve, 1818, in the picturesque village of Oberdorf, near Salzburg, in German-speaking Austria. The 26-year-old priest, Joseph Mohr, discovered that the church's organ was damaged - a mouse had eaten through one of the leather bellows of the organ. No music could be played.

2 Later that day, Joseph would be celebrating the Christmas Eve Midnight Mass - it would not be the same without any music. What could be done? Joseph could play the guitar, but he realised that the Christmas hymns they all knew, would not sound their best on a guitar. He decided to write some words as a new Christmas carol.

3 As he sat down, he remembered a family he had visited recently. There, with the cold winter's snow around them, he had blessed the mother and her newly-born child, and it had touched him to see how the mother protected her child from the winter's cold. This was the picture in his mind as he began to think of the Birth of Jesus, and he started to write the carol that we now know as *"Silent Night"*.

4 With the words he had written, Joseph walked as quickly as he could through the snow to the nearby village of Arnsdorf. There he met his friend, Franz Gruber, who was the village teacher and a musician.

5 Joseph left the simple poem with him, and Franz set about creating a tune that would somehow match the words and the simplicity of the Gospel story. He composed a lullaby, and took it back to Father Joseph. They had little time left to practice it but, at the Midnight Christmas Mass in the Church of St Nicholas, Joseph Mohr played the guitar and sang tenor, and Franz Gruber sang bass. The church choir joined in a 4-part harmony in the simple refrain. The song touched many people and reminded them of the simplicity of Christmas.

6 In the months and years ahead, the organ at the church of St Nicholas continued to have problems! Repairs did not last and so, in 1824 or 1825, a repairman was called in to reconstruct the organ. As he worked, he tried out the organ by playing from sheets of music that were stored nearby. One of these was "Silent Night", and he asked for a copy from Franz Gruber (the organist and musician).

7 As the organ-repairer travelled from one church to another, he introduced many others to the delightful carol. Very soon, groups of Austrian singers added "Silent Night" to the collection of music that they sang throughout Europe - even travelling to the United States, where the song was translated into English. It took a few years before the carol was traced back to Joseph Mohr and Franz Gruber.

8 A hundred years later, the First World War started. France and Britain and Belgium opposed the invaders from the empires of Germany and Austro-Hungary. As the first Christmas of the War approached in 1914, each side had lost nearly a million men. The two sides lay in trenches that stretched about 500 miles from Switzerland to the French coastline on the North Sea. Soldiers in opposing trenches were only the width of a football pitch apart, with "No-Man's Land" in-between.

9 On Christmas Eve, in the section where the British opposed the Germans, the British gathered holly, and the Germans set up small Christmas trees which they lit up. It was an unofficial "truce". German soldiers started to sing *"Stille Nacht"*, and the British joined in the carol in English: *"Silent Night"*.

10 An English soldier later wrote:

> "It was a beautiful, moonlit night, frost on the ground, white almost everywhere, About 7 or 8 in the evening, there was a lot of commotion in the German trenches, and there were lights. And then they sang 'Stille Nacht - Silent Night'. I shall never forget it as long as I live. It was one of the highlights of my life."

11 Let us pray:

In silence, Lord,
I place myself amongst all those
in many parts of the world
and in various circumstances
who are praying for peace
on this day,
as I, too, pray for peace.

12 The soldiers shook hands with their enemies, exchanged small gifts, and even played football!

❖❖❖❖❖❖❖❖❖❖❖❖❖❖❖❖❖

✍ *"Stille Nacht" is pronounced "steel-a nakt". "Bass" in the last-but-one sentence in paragraph 5 is pronounced "base".*

✍ *The lengthy reading about 'Silent Night' could be shortened by omitting paragraphs 6 & 7 (the organ repair and the spread of the carol). Alternatives would be to stop at the end of paragraph 5 (before mention of the organ-repair) or at the end of paragraph 7 (before mention of the First World War).*

✍ *30 years after writing the words, Fr Joseph Mohr died in poverty during the winter of 1848 in the nearby village of Wagrain. He had contracted pneumonia after a lengthy walk to visit a sick parishioner. Nowadays on Christmas Eve every year a choir sings "Stille Nacht" at his graveside.*

✍ *The term "All quiet on the Western Front" originates from the time of this unofficial truce. Some of the British officers who had taken part, were later court-martialled. Sir Arthur Conan Doyle (the writer of 'Sherlock Holmes'), in his history of 1914, wrote that the unofficial truce in the First World War was "one human episode amid all the atrocities which have stained the memory of war."*

✍ *The English soldier quoted was Albert Moren, a Private in the 2nd Queen's Regiment, then stationed at the front line, close to the village of Armentières, near Lille.*

✍ *A month after the Armistice that ended the First World War (see 11 Nov), Christmas Eve in 1918 saw a new Service being held in the Chapel of King's College, Cambridge. It was the "Festival of Nine Lessons and Carols" which has since become very popular, and is always broadcast on the radio on the afternoon of Christmas Eve.*

✍ *Could use the prayer 'Christmas Eve' from 'Pause for Thought with Frank Topping', pg 223 (ISBN: 0-7188-2524-1).*

✍ *"**Wassailing**" used to take place in parts of England on Christmas Eve and on 6th January. After singing, a group would be offered food and drink, and would toast the health of all present. The word "wassail" comes from Old English meaning "be in health; be whole". The term "good health" is still used in toasting others with a drink. The words "whole" and "holy" come from the same stem.*

🎵 Silent night

25 DECEMBER

1 We'll reflect today on St Luke's gospel, as he writes of the birth of Jesus. We'll pause after each section.

2 For the taking of the census,

> 'everyone went to his own town
> to be registered.
> And so Joseph and Mary
> went to Bethlehem
> because Joseph was a descendant
> of King David who was born there.'

(Lk 2$^{1-4}$)

3 At this time I think of some of the places and some of the people who form part of **my** 'roots'…

(Pause…)

4 'Mary gave birth to her son…
She laid him in a manger
because there was no room for them
in the inn.'

(Lk 2^7)

5 I can think of occasions when I have felt excluded, not part of what is going on, and I think of when I have not fully "included" other people…

(Pause…)

6 'The shepherds watched their flocks during the night.'

(Lk 2^8)

7 I think of particular people who have expressed care for me, and those for whom I have cared…

(Pause…)

8 'The angel
said to the shepherds in the fields:
"Do not be afraid!"'

(Lk 2^{10})

9 Those words - *"Do not be afraid!"* - occur 366 times throughout the Bible, as though they are a reminder for every day of the year. I name in God's presence anything in my life of which I am afraid, nervous, unsure, apprehensive. As I think of anything I say to myself,
"Do not be afraid…",
and I place those fears in God's hands…

(Pause…)

10 'The angel said to the shepherds:
"I bring you news of great joy."'

(Lk 2^{10})

11 I can think back to times when I have experienced great joy…

(Pause…)

12 The angel told the shepherds that
"Today in the town of David
the Saviour is born."

(Lk2^{11})

13 I repeat to myself those words of the angel, but replace the words *"the town of David"* with my own name: *"Today in (me) the Saviour is born…"*

(Pause…)

14 'The shepherds hurried from the fields
and found Mary and Joseph,
and the baby lying in the manger,
as they had been told.'

(Lk 2^{16})

15 I can think of special moments throughout my life when I have been more aware than at other times of God's presence…

(Pause…)

16 *'Mary treasured all these things*
   and thought deeply about them
   in her heart.'

   (Lk 2¹⁹)

17 I pray to remain thoughtful, reflective,
   and prayerful.

   (Pause...)

18 *'The shepherds went back,*
   praising God
   for all that they had seen and heard.'

   (Lk 2²⁰)

19 For what can I give praise and thanks to
   God at this time?...

   (Pause...)

20 *Let us pray, using some words of Robert*
   Louis Stevenson:

   "O God, our loving Father,
   help us rightly to remember
   the birth of Jesus,
   that we may share in
   the song of the angels,
   the gladness of the shepherds,
   and the worship of the wise men...
   May Christmas morning
   make us happy to be your children,
   and Christmas evening
   bring us to our beds
   with grateful thoughts,
   forgiving and forgiven,
   for Jesus' sake. Amen."

✍ "Utterly at home,
   God lives in us forever"
                    - Julian of Norwich (see 3 Dec).

✍ "If Jesus Christ is not true God,
   how could he help us?
   If he is not true man,
   how could he help us?"
                    - Dietrich Bonhoeffer .

♪ Angels we have heard on high; Away in
   a manger; Come and join the celebration; Go tell it on the mountain; Hark
   the herald angels; O come, all ye faithful; Once in royal David's city; On Christmas night all Christians sing; Sing a simple song; Unto us is born a Son; While
   shepherds watched

1 For Christians who are Catholic or Protestant, Christmas Day itself is the focus for prayer and celebration at Christmas-time.

2 Christians of the Orthodox Church (such as in Russia and Greece) have a quiet celebration on Christmas Day, but have the Epiphany (the 6th of January) as their main day of prayer and celebration at Christmas-time. Why do Orthodox Christians focus in a public way more on the Epiphany (when the wise men visited) than on Christmas Day itself?

3 They recall that the birth of Jesus was greeted by ordinary shepherds who recognised that he was the Son of God. The birth was quiet and almost secret. It wasn't yet time to make public the news of the birth of the Son of God. And so Orthodox Christians tend to see Christmas Day mainly for personal commitment, in the manner of the shepherds.

4 They celebrate more publicly on the 6th of January, the Epiphany - the feast that recalls the wise men travelling to worship Jesus. The birth of the Son of God is no longer a secret, and the wise men represent the people of all nations, searching for God.

5 Whilst the shepherds were invited to a personal commitment, the wise men from afar represent a broadcasting of the Good News - the Son of God has been born a human being. The 'secret' is out! Epiphany marks the 'going public' of the Good News that Jesus is present. And so Orthodox Christians celebrate Epiphany together and in a special way. The Epiphany represents a challenge and an invitation to all people to recognise who Jesus is.

6 *Let us pray:*

Jesus, God-with-us,
what gift shall we bring to you?

The angels bring their song,
the heavens bring their star,
the shepherds bring their wonder,
the animals give their manger,
the wise men bring their gifts,
and we human beings
bring the Virgin-Mother.
We bring our whole selves to you
who have so fully and generously
given yourself to us.
Amen.

❖-❖-❖-❖-❖-❖-❖-❖-❖-❖-❖-❖-❖-❖-❖-❖

✍ *The prayer is based on words of a Greek Orthodox prayer.*

✍ *See 5,6,7 January re the Epiphany.*

✍ *As Saint Stephen was the first person to die for telling others about Jesus (Acts of the Apostles 6[8]-8[2]) he was given the honour of having his feastday today, next to the day that commemorates Jesus' birth. The proximity of the feasts also serves as a harsh reminder that commitment can be costly.*

✍ *26 December is often called "Boxing Day". How did we get the name? Over 100 years ago it used to be much more common to have money boxes in churches for donations for the very poor. On this day those boxes would be opened, and the money would be distributed to the needy. This custom was later adapted in houses that employed servants, and either money or small presents would be put in boxes and handed to each servant. Nowadays a "Christmas Box" is sometimes the name used for a family's donation at Christmas to those who have delivered newspapers, the post, the milk, or have collected rubbish.*

♪ Angels we have heard on high; Away in a manger; Come and join the celebration; Go tell it on the mountain; On Christmas night all Christians sing; Sing a simple song; The first Nowell; Unto us is born a Son; While shepherds watched

Becoming a human being
and living amongst us

God our Father,
your Son became a human being
and lived among us.
We pause to remind ourselves
that he is with us now.

(Jn 1¹⁴
(see page 178)

1   When the Nazis occupied Holland during the Second World War, they soon began to round up the Jews - as they did elsewhere - to be taken away and killed. A Dutch family of watch-makers were determined to do what they could to protect Jewish people. They had a secret room built in their 3-storey house in Haarlem, above their corner-shop where they sold and mended watches and clocks. Secretly a workman created a hiding-place by building a false wall about 75 centimetres from a bedroom's end wall. The entrance was through a panel at the bottom of a built-in cupboard. If the Gestapo or soldiers arrived, the 4 or 5 Jews who were hiding upstairs at the time, could quickly climb through to the secret hiding-place, remaining there in silence.

2   Eventually the Ten Boom family was betrayed, and they were sent to a concentration camp, although the Jews they were hiding were not discovered. In the hell-on-earth that was Ravensbruck Concentration Camp, the tall chimneys belched out smoke from the incinerated bodies of those who had been done to death. Even there in Ravensbruck, Corrie Ten Boom remarked that
    "there is no pit, no hole, so deep
    that God's love is not deeper still."

3   Amidst the terror and the evil of that place, Corrie showed people how still to give thanks to God in **all** the circumstances in which they found themselves.

4   One day, as all the camp was gathered for early morning roll-call, the number by which Corrie was known was called out. She walked forward, thinking that, like other times at roll-call, this would mean being called to death. Instead, an administrative error had been made.

Corrie Ten Boom found herself being released - by mistake! Her release-papers were stamped by the Nazi guards with tomorrow's date: *"28th December, 1944."*

5   When the War was over, Corrie helped to look after people who had been severely traumatised by what had been done to them. She was invited by people of many countries to talk of her experiences, and especially how she lived in faith and encouraged others to forgive those who had hurt them.

6   *Let us pray:*

    God, Father of us all,
    you who call me by name: *Is 43¹*
    you are my hiding-place,
    my shelter,   *Ps 32⁷*
    amidst life's difficulties.
    Remind me
    that there is no pit, no hole, so deep
    that your love
    is not deeper still.
    Lead me to give thanks
    in all my circumstances,   *1 Thess 5¹⁸*
    and show me
    how to transform
    whatever suffering or difficulties
    I may experience,
    into something that will benefit others
    and will set me free.
    I make this prayer,
    knowing that you
    lavish your love on us   *1 Jn 3¹*
    and you set
    the down-trodden free.   *Is 61¹; Lk 4¹⁸*
    Amen.

📝 *Similar to the quoted words of Corrie Ten Boom are those of Pope John Paul II, spoken in Liverpool's RC Cathedral on Pentecost Sunday, 30/5/1982 (and which are now carved in wood in the Reconciliation Chapel there):*
  "No evil is more powerful
  than the infinite love of God."

📝 "The Secret Room - the story of Corrie Ten Boom" *is a 30-page booklet by David Wallington in the* 'Faith in Action' *series (RMEP): ISBN 0-08-026415-8.* "The Hiding Place" *is the name of a film about Corrie Ten Boom's war-time experiences in Haarlem and then in Ravensbruck Concentration Camp. See 22 March for a prayer found by the body of a dead child in Ravensbruck.*

📝 *See 12 March for the sheltering of Anne Frank in another secret room.*

📝 *27th December is the feastday of Saint John, the apostle and gospel-writer. The New Testament letters of 1,2, and 3 John (as quoted in the prayer above) are also attributed to him.*

🎼 Amazing grace; For to those who love God *("who can separate us from the love of Christ?")*; God's Spirit is in my heart; If God is for us *("set us free")*; In you, my God *("my refuge")*; O living water *("set us free")*

28 DECEMBER

1 Today is the Feast of the Holy Innocents - those babies murdered by King Herod. Doing that, he thought, would remove what he saw as a threat - the birth of Jesus, who was promised to be a new king in Israel. Amidst the evil that we witness in more recent times, we pray for all whose innocence and gentleness have been brutally stolen from them. We are going to listen to some words about how evil takes root.

2 In the 18th Century, the philosopher and politician, Edmund Burke, criticised the discrimination in Britain's governing of Ireland. His criticism cost him his seat as a member of Parliament. He said:
"All that is needed for evil to triumph is for good people to do nothing."

3 Albert Einstein, the great scientist, had to flee Nazi Germany in 1933 because he was a Jew. He wrote:
"The world is a dangerous place - not because of those who do evil, but because of those who watch and let it happen."

4 Martin Luther King struggled to achieve civil rights for **all** people in the United States. He was assassinated in 1968. He had said:
"The one who passively accepts evil is as much involved in it as the one who helps to perpetuate it."

5 Alexander Solzhenitsyn was imprisoned for criticising the Soviet Communist leader, Joseph Stalin, and was then exiled from his country in 1974. He said:
"In order for people to do great evil, it is first necessary for them to think they are doing a great good."

6 *Let us pray:*

Father,
 we remember before you
 those who have been abused
 in the womb, in childhood,
 and in later life.
We bring before you
 our brothers and sisters
 throughout the world
 who are victims
 of injustice, prejudice
 and persecution.
Lead us, Father,
 and lead all people of good will
 to do whatever we can
 to help turn the hearts
 of those who think themselves
 better than others,
 and who perpetrate evil.
Deliver us, Lord,
 from all that is evil. Amen.

❖❖❖❖❖❖❖❖❖❖❖❖❖❖❖❖❖

📖 *Edmund Burke, 1729-97, was highly critical of the French Revolution and of Britain's poor relationship with the then North American Colonies.*
Albert Einstein: 1879-1955 (see index).
Alexander Solzhenitsyn was born in 1918.
Martin Luther King: 1929-1968 (see index).
The quotes have been adapted to inclusive language.

📖 "This did Herod sore affray...
So he gave the word to slay
and slew the little childer"
 (from the carol, 'Unto us is Born a Son').
See Mt 2$^{13-18}$ for the Gospel account of the 'Slaughter of the Innocents'.

🎼  God's Spirit is in my heart; O Lord, all the world belongs to you; Unto us is born a son

Looking for you and finding you

Many people, Lord,
realised that they had a negative attitude
and had done things that were not good.
They looked for you and found you,
as did many sick people
whom you spoke to and cured.
As we look for you now,
may we discover you
and experience your healing in our lives.
We call to mind
that we are here in your presence.

(Lk 5^{8,15})
(see page 179)

1 In 1155 Thomas à Becket was chosen by King Henry II to be Chancellor of England. He served the king faithfully, helping to run the country, especially as Henry spent much of his time on the Continent, governing the rest of his kingdom.

2 Seven years after Thomas became Chancellor, the king - wanting to have full control of the church - thought that he should appoint his good friend as Archbishop of Canterbury. Thomas resisted, saying that his priorities and loyalties would change, and he would have to be independent of the king. Yet Henry went ahead. Thomas - who was not then a priest - first had to be ordained to the priesthood before being made Archbishop of Canterbury.

3 As he said he would, Thomas became a different person on becoming Archbishop. He wrote that he had changed from being
"a patron of play-actors
and a follower of hounds,
to being a shepherd of souls."

4 For eight years, Thomas and the king (well-renowned for his fierce temper) had many disagreements. Whilst in Normandy, the king became very angry and said:
"Will no-one rid me
of this troublesome priest?"
Although Henry probably did not intend that anything should happen, four knights left the king's presence and sailed across the English Channel.

5 On this day in 1170, the four knights drew their swords as they approached the Archbishop in his own cathedral.
"Willingly I die
for Christ and his Church,"
he said, as they stabbed and killed him. The horrific murder was condemned throughout Europe, and Thomas was seen as a martyr and saint. Only three years after Thomas' death, the Pope declared him to be a saint. King Henry II had to undergo public penance, even though it was probably not his intention that harm be done to the Archbishop.

6 For the next 400 years, the shrine of St Thomas in Canterbury Cathedral was one of Europe's main centres of pilgrimage (until destroyed by King Henry VIII).

7 "Martyr" is the Greek word for "witness", and we can think of bishops and many other good people in our own times who have been martyred.

8 *Let us pray:*

Lord, inspire us
to be credible witnesses of your love,
and good shepherds
towards those
you have entrusted to our care.
Amen.

to the sad years of division that followed. Beneath this roof Saint Thomas Becket suffered martyrdom... The great events of salvation history are retold in the ancient stained-glass windows above us... (We are) encouraged by the witness of so many who have professed their faith in Jesus Christ through the centuries - often at the cost of their own lives - a sacrifice which even today is asked of not a few." *(29 May 1982)*

📖 *Many others have met martyrs' deaths, including Catholic Archbishop Oscar Romero, murdered in **his** cathedral (see the Index), and Anglican Archbishop Janani Luwum of Uganda (see 9 July).*

📖 *'The Canterbury Tales' by Chaucer is a collection of stories about a varied group of pilgrims on their way to Thomas' shrine in Canterbury. The pilgrims (ranging from a knight to a humble ploughman) reflect 14th Century society. Chaucer's 'Canterbury Tales' influenced greatly the development of English literature. Geoffrey Chaucer is called "the Father of English Poetry".*

On 9/7/98 a 15th-century first edition of Chaucer's 'Canterbury Tales' was sold for £4,621,500 at Christie's auctioneers - making it the world's most expensive printed book. It is one of nine surviving copies from the 200 printed in England in 1477 by William Caxton.

📖 *T S Eliot's play, 'Murder in the Cathedral', tells of Thomas' martyrdom.*

📖 *King Henry II was the great-grandson of William the Conqueror, from whom he had inherited some of his lands in France. Henry was the father of King Richard the Lionheart and King John. Henry is remembered for being one of England's greatest kings, because he laid down the foundations of the country's Common Law, and founded the beginnings of the jury system.*

📖 *Thomas à Becket was born in London in 1118 and was murdered in his cathedral in 1170.*

📖 *When Pope John Paul II was invited to meet and pray in Canterbury Cathedral in 1982, he said:* "My dear brothers and sisters of the Anglican Communion 'whom I love and long for', how happy I am to be able to speak directly to you today in this great cathedral! The building itself is an eloquent witness both to our long years of common inheritance, and

🎼 Father, in my life I see; Father, I place into your hands; He who would valiant be; Lord, make me a means; Make me a channel; O Lord, all the world; Take my hands

30 DECEMBER

1 In December 1997, newspapers reported that a 5-year-old boy was re-united with his parents on Boxing Day after they had accidentally left him behind at a petrol station.

2 His parents had driven off in separate cars from the garage in Dunmow, Essex, without realising that their son, Kyle Collins, had gone into the shop to buy some sweets. The boy had slipped out of his mother's car while she paid for petrol and, when she returned, she presumed that he had got into her husband's car. The parents left the petrol station separately and were driving for an hour before they heard a police appeal on the radio.

3 We are reminded of the family of Jesus, Mary and Joseph travelling to Jerusalem for the feast of Passover, when Jesus was 12 years old. As with the Collins' family, there was a mix-up, and Jesus stayed behind in Jerusalem without his parents realising.

4 The Sunday after Christmas is normally the Feast of the Holy Family of Jesus, Mary and Joseph.

5 *Let us pray:*

God our Father,
  we pray for all families,
  that members may feel encouraged
  to live fully,
  and may discover
  the sanctity of human love
  and the value of family life.
If times are troubled
  through separation
  or difficulties in relationships,
  may people learn to be generous.
May we all learn
  how to break the cycle
  of whatever may be negative,
  growing in understanding
  and appreciation
  and in love and respect. Amen.

✐ *The Feast of* "The Holy Family of Jesus, Mary and Joseph" *is celebrated on the Sunday after Christmas Day (or on the 30th of December if there is no Sunday between 25th December and 1st January).*

✐ *The account of the boy Jesus being lost in Jerusalem (and being found in the Temple there) appears in Luke 2$^{41-52}$, which is the Gospel for the Feast in Year C of the Church's 3-year cycle for Sunday readings. The Christian writer, teacher and theologian, Origen (about 185-254 A.D.) says:*
  "Learn where those who seek him
  will find him,
  so that you, seeking with Mary and Joseph,
  may find him."

♪ Christ be beside me; Father, in my life I see; Father, I place *("my friends and family")*; Lord Jesus Christ, you have come to us *("Mary's son"; omitting v.2 =* Eucharist*)*; Lord of all hopefulness *("child-like"; "skilled at the plane and the lathe")*; Oh the word of my Lord; Thank you for fathers

1 It has been said that
   "Life can only be understood backwards,
   but it must be lived forwards."

2 The end of the old year offers an opportunity to look back and be grateful. We may even see some negative things in a better light, as we look back with the advantage of time.

3 Let's pause to give thanks for what has been good, naming some of the people and events and circumstances of the past year...

(Pause...)

4 Dag Hammarskjöld, once the Secretary-General of the United Nations, said:
   "For all that has been -Thanks!
   For all that will be - Yes!"

5 *Let us pray:*

God our Father,
   we give thanks
   for all that has been
   and, trustfully,
   we place the past into your hands.
We ask you to inspire us
   in the year ahead
   to seek and fulfil your will.
May we truly look on each new day
   as the start of the rest of our lives.
Enable us,
   with the power of your Spirit,
   to remain positive and confident,
   and live fully and joyfully
   with those people
   you have placed into our lives.
Lead us
   to bring out the best in one another
   that we may all grow
   as the people you call us to be.
Amen.

6 At the end of one year and the beginning of another, we appreciate that we have "moved on". Yet, in another sense, we have returned to where we started. The poet, T.S.Eliot, writes:
   "We shall not cease from exploration
   And the end of all our exploring
   Will be to arrive where we started
   And know the place for the first time."

7 *Let us pray:*

Lord, you call us
   not to get too set in our ways,
   but to be trustful and faithful,
   seeing the need
   for the on-going process
   of being renewed and re-vitalised.
Repeatedly you call each one of us
   to be 'born again',
   to start anew,
   to 'repent',
   to review priorities
   and re-orientate
   the direction of our lives.
Give us the fullness of your Spirit
   that we may live
   as you would have us live.
Amen.

✍ *Dag Hammarskjöld: 1905-1961* (see Index)

✍ *Could adapt prayer 50 on page 180 of Volume 2 of this book, or could use the prayer "New Year" from* "Pause for Thought with Frank Topping", *pg 71 (ISBN 0-7188-2524-1).*

✍ *The following is a prayer by Reinhold Niebuhr (21/6/1892-1/6/1971):*

8   "O Lord,
    you have made us very small,
    and we bring our years to an end
    like a tale that is told.
    Help us to remember
    that beyond our brief day
    is the eternity of your love. Amen."

✍ *See also 1 January.*

✍ *In Scotland, Christmas tends to be a private homely celebration whereas today - Hogmanay - is more public, marking the end of the old year and the start of the new.*

The name "Hogmanay" *may come from the Norman French word,* "hoguinané", *which means* "gift at New Year". *"First-footing" takes place in parts of Scotland and England's North-East, where people go from door-to-door to their neighbours with small gifts - generally of food or drink. In earlier times when wood was used to create the warmth of a fire, a small piece of wood would be carried, representing the warmth of friendship that the* "first-footer" *was bringing. A small piece of coal is now used instead.*

The spread of Scots around the world has given rise to the custom throughout the English-speaking world, of singing "Auld Lang Syne" *at midnight as the new year starts.*

❖❖❖❖❖❖❖❖❖❖❖❖❖❖❖❖❖❖❖❖❖❖

✍ *The opening quote is by Sören Kierkegaard (1813-1855).*

✍ *T.S.Eliot (1888-4/1/1965). The quote is from his 'Four Quartets: Little Gidding', pt 5, written in 1942. For similar thoughts, see 19 August, paragraph 6 (re 'The Wizard of Oz').*

♪ Alone with none but thee, my God; Do not worry; Father, I place; I watch the sunrise; I will be with you; Lord of all hopefulness; Moses, I know you're the man *("don't get too set in your ways")*; Seek ye first; The light of Christ *("born again")*; This day God gives me

Moveable
Feasts

FAMILY FAST DAY

1 Pope John Paul II has said:

"The distinctive mark of the Christian,
today, more than ever,
must be love for the poor,
the weak, the suffering.
Living out this demanding commitment
requires a total reversal
of the alleged values
which make people
seek only their own good:
- power,
- pleasure,
- the unscrupulous accumulation of wealth.
Yes, it is precisely
to this radical conversion
that Christ's disciples are called."

2 *Let us pray:*

We ask you, Lord,
to challenge us
- especially when we become
too set in our ways.
Inspire us
to review our priorities and values,
so that our attitude may always be
to give generously
without counting the cost.
Open our eyes and hearts to all people,
and particularly to those
who are vulnerable
or marginalised
or who can do nothing for us
in return.
Lead us to act justly, *(Mic 6⁸)*
love tenderly,
and walk humbly with you, our God.
Amen.

3 *Living out this demanding commitment*
requires a total reversal
of the alleged values
which make people
seek only their own good:
- power,
- pleasure,
- the unscrupulous accumulation of wealth.

❖❖❖❖❖❖❖❖❖❖❖❖❖❖❖❖❖❖

📖 *The quotation of Pope John Paul II is from his message for the World Day of Peace, 1 January 1998. The following words are from an address of his in New York in October 1979 (referring to the Parable of 'Dives and Lazarus' in Lk 16[19-31]):*

"The poor of the world
  are your brothers and sisters in Christ.
You must never be content
  to leave them
  just the crumbs from the feast.
You must give of your substance
  - and not just of abundance -
  in order to help them.
And you must treat them as guests
  at your family table."

📖 *Archbishop Helder Camara of Rio de Janeiro, Brazil, once said:*
"When I ask for bread for the poor,
they call me a saint.
When I ask why the poor have no bread,
they call me a communist."

📖 *Generosity in the use of what we have? - "It is easier for a camel to pass through the eye of a needle than for a rich person to enter the kingdom of heaven" (Mt 19[16-26]).*

📖 *See 'Family Fast Day' in the Index for further ideas.*

🎵 O Lord, all the world *("turning the world upside down")*; Seek ye first

CHRIST THE KING

1   The last Sunday of the Church's Year - the Sunday before Advent begins - is the Feast of Christ the King.

2   During the ceremony of the coronation of British Kings and Queens, a golden orb (a globe of the world with a cross on top) is handed to the monarch. These words are spoken:

3   *"When you see the orb*
set under the cross,
remember that the whole world
is subject
to the power and empire
of Christ our Redeemer."

4   The British monarch no longer has political power, but the ceremony - watched by millions on TV - calls to mind our nation's history. The presentation of the orb (the globe with its cross) to the world-famous king or queen, is a reminder to remain humble and seek first God's kingdom.

5   *Let us pray:*

Jesus, our King,
  you tell us
  that our Father has blessed us,
  and you invite us
  to take for our heritage
  the Kingdom
  that has been prepared for us
  - a Kingdom that is close at hand,
  and which is like
  the exciting and joyful discovery
  of hidden treasure.
Inspire us, Lord,
  to sort out our priorities,
  and set our hearts first
  on your Kingdom. Amen.

(Mt 25[34], Mk 1[5], Mt 13[44], Mt 6[33])

✐ *"Orb" is Latin for 'circle', as in 'orbit'.*

✐ *One of the Gospel readings for this feast (in Year A of the 3-year cycle) is Matthew 25[31-46]:* "When did we see you hungry... Take for your heritage the Kingdom prepared for you" - *see October 20 & 22.*

✐ "Whoever works for the kingdom of God,
  does much;
Whoever prays for the kingdom of God,
  does more;
Whoever suffers for the kingdom of God,
  does all."
- Pope John Paul II, quoted in
Osservatore Romano, 8/3/85

✐ *One of the early Christian saints - Cyril of Jerusalem - writes about receiving Communion:* "As you approach,
hollow the palms of your hands,
placing one hand under the other,
making a throne
to receive the Body of Christ,
your King."

✐ *The foundation-stone of Liverpool's RC Cathedral was laid in 1933, 8 years after Pope Pius XI established the feast of Christ the King, and he suggested that the new cathedral be dedicated in that name. Instead of retaining the original Lutyens' design, the modern circular Cathedral of Christ the King has 2 large crowns. The canopy above the altar represents the Crown of Thorns; outside, the top of the tower is designed as the Crown of Victory of the Resurrection.*

𝄞 Be thou my vision *("High King of Heaven")*; Christ is our king; Hail Redeemer, King Divine; Seek ye first the kingdom of God; Take my hands *("use them for your kingdom")*; This day God gives me *("king of my heart")*

THE ADVENT WREATH

The following words may be used with a group as an explanation of the Advent Wreath.

1 The death of an old year, the birth of a new,
and ADVENT, the season of WAITING,
waiting for God to fulfil his ancient promise
to come and save us,
and to complete the salvation
already given us
through Christ our Lord.

2 We wait impatiently
through the winter months
for the renewal of the earth,
and for the birth of the Saviour in our hearts.

3 As a symbol of our waiting in hope
we have made this wreath
from the leaves of evergreen trees
- leaves that remain green in winter
and which the frost cannot kill.
They are a sign of our new life in Christ
and a reminder of his promise
to be **e v e r** with us.

4 Our wreath is in the shape of a circle
which, like the love of God,
does not come to an end.

5 The wreath includes
some leaves and berries and seeds
of the old year
which we have just completed,
and which we now offer to God.

6 As we light the candles
- one in each week in Advent -
we remember
the saints of the Old Testament
who waited and waited in the darkness
and did not give up their hope.
And we remember
those who suffer in darkness today
- in the darkness of poverty or fear,
of imprisonment or despair.

7 We shall see this wreath
as a symbol of God's faithfulness
in his promise
to be ever with us,
remembering that we are called
to be the light of the world,
a tree ever-green,
living branches joined to Christ,
who is our light and our salvation:
our King,
crowned with a wreath of victory.

8 *Let us pray:*

**God our Father,
we thank you
for the promise made to your people
to send us a Saviour.
Inspire us to prepare our hearts
and wait in joyful hope
for his coming anew into our lives.
Bless us as we gather in his name
and as we consider
the symbolism of this wreath
- a sign of your promises
that come to fulfilment
in Jesus, your Son,
the Light of our world.
Amen.**

✍ *The Advent Wreath is circular and is made from evergreen leaves. Some versions include old, decaying leaves as well as coloured berries - a walk in the woods or in a park may also reveal some acorns and winged sycamore seeds. Inclusion of the old and the seeds of the new, represents an offering of the past and the potential for the future (otherwise you will need to omit or alter Paragraph 5).*

The wreath includes 4 candles, one for each week of Advent. Sometimes 3 of the candles are purple (the reflective, penitential colour of Advent), with a rose/pink candle for the 3rd Sunday of Advent, which used to be called "Gaudete (Rejoice) Sunday", named for the first word in Latin of the Entrance Antiphon for the Mass of that day. It may be preferable to use 4 white candles, in that they do not introduce further symbolism which may not be meaningful to particular groups.

✍ *In the Scandinavian countries of Norway, Sweden, Denmark and Iceland, what we know as "holly" is called "Christ-thorn". The word "holly" is likely to have come from the word "holy", as the prickly leaves are seen as a reminder of Jesus' Crown of Thorns, and the red berries as drops of his blood. Amidst the joy of welcoming the arrival of God-made-Man, holly is a reminder of the commitment of Jesus, leading to his rejection and death.*

In North America it is customary to place a round wreath of holly at the front door of houses at Christmas. Some homes in Britain have adopted the custom, which probably started in Germany.

Remembering God's Presence
- 60 prayers based on Gospel passages

Your presence enables me

On the cross, Lord,
your dying words
were to forgive
those who had done you harm.
My own efforts alone, Lord,
are often not enough
for me to live as positively
as I know I can live.
Your presence, Lord, here and now,
and the power of your Spirit,
transform me
and enable me
to choose to live in a positive way.
And so I pause for a moment, Lord,
to remind myself
that I am in your presence.

(Lk 23¹⁴)
(see page 185)

Introduction

We may not appreciate that radio waves are travelling around us at this moment, but 'tuning in' with a radio enables us to value and become more aware of what is already present, though invisible. The prayers that follow may be of some help - like the use of a radio - in 'tuning in' to the Presence of God, already with us, yet invisible. Although the sixty prayers are worded for use with a group of people, they may readily be adapted for personal prayer. They are written around Gospel passages, but reflections could be made in similar ways on other parts of the Bible. For many, "focussing" on God's Presence is an ideal starting-point in prayer.

John Baptist De La Salle, the patron saint of teachers, strongly encouraged teachers to pause regularly throughout the busy day to call to mind - with the students - that they were in God's Presence. Why? In God's Presence we are surely enabled to be who we are called to be, and empowered to live out God's call to us in ministry, in mission. It is not simply by our own efforts that we can change ourselves. No attempts to convince Zacchaeus, the tax-collector, could cause him to change his ways. It was only in the Presence of Jesus that he was enabled to achieve the impossible, and the little person could then walk tall! Nor is it by force of argument that people (and most especially adults!) are changed, but with this practice we can bring ourselves (and others) into God's loving and healing Presence, as the few loaves and fish were transformed and became more than enough for over five thousand people! Recalling God's Presence can enable us to remain positive, because *"in his Presence, we can only love"*, as Evelyn Underhill records.

The calling-to-mind of the Presence of God is life-promoting in itself, and encompasses a growing awareness and a "surrender" to God - and hence the possibility of transformation of all that we are. Regularly pausing to remember God's Presence is instrumental in transforming many people at various stages of their lives - not least of all some who are sick and housebound. The author knows a lady who is severely ill and in much pain, yet often sets a small, clockwork timer as a reminder every hour to recall that she is in the Presence of God. She then spends moments in prayer (whether of words, or of the offering of her suffering) to name particular people in God's Presence. For this lady, a sense of God's Presence can pervade her day, despite her considerable suffering. Of what 'value' and 'benefit' to others is her prayer of intercession! That approach is reflected in*"the Little Way"* of St Teresa of Lisieux, explored on 1st October.

Other resources for helping to recall God's Presence may be found throughout the book, but especially in the material of February 10,13,24,25; March 8,17,26,27,31; April 1,7,12,22,25; May 9,24,28; June 19,20,30; August 4,24,28; November 26; December 19; Vol 2 Appendix of Prayers 1-3,27; Ash Wednesday; Palm Sunday; Good Friday, Pentecost, Trinity Sunday.

♩ Christ be beside me; Father, I place into your hands *("and in your presence rest")*; In you, my God *("here in your presence my troubles/sorrow/yearning will cease)*; Walk with me, O my Lord.

1

BECOMING A HUMAN BEING AND LIVING AMONGST US

God our Father,
  your Son became a human being
  and lived among us.
We pause to remind ourselves
  that he is with us now.

(Jn 1¹⁴)

2

THE MARRIAGE AT CANA

Lord Jesus,
  you were present as a guest
  at a wedding at Cana in Galilee.
There, when the wine for the celebration
  ran out,
  you changed water into wine,
  helping the people
  to continue to celebrate with joy.
We can celebrate, too,
  as we remind ourselves now
  that you choose to be with us
  as we gather to pray.

(Jn 2¹⁻¹²)

3

YOU CARE FOR US

Lord, your care is for each one of us
  and you know what is deep in our hearts.
We come to you as we are,
  placing ourselves now in your presence.

(Jn 2²⁵)

4

INCREASE IN US,
THAT WE MAY DECREASE

Here in your presence, Lord,
  we can live more fully
  as we let you
  become more fully part of our lives.

As we 'decrease',
  you 'increase'.
We spend a few moments in silence,
  becoming more aware of your presence.

(Jn 4⁴²)

5

LAY YOUR HANDS ON US

Lord Jesus,
  we read in the Gospel
  that all those with friends who were sick
  brought them to you,
  and you healed them.
As we are friends gathered together
  in your presence,
  we ask you to lay your hands
  on each one of us
  and bring us healing,
  so that we may live more fully
  in your presence.

(Lk 4⁴⁰)

6

GATHERED ON THE LAKESIDE

Lord, by the side of the Sea of Galilee,
  there were so many
  gathered around you,
  that you got into the boat
  of Simon Peter the fisherman.
You asked him to push out into the water
  so that the people
  could see and hear you better.
Years later, we are another group of people
  keen to encounter you.
Show us how to see and hear you better
  as we pause now
  to remind ourselves
  that we are in your presence.

(Lk 5¹⁻³)

7

PRAYING IN LONELY PLACES

We read in the Gospel, Lord,
  that you would go away to lonely places,
  and there you would pray.
Not alone now, but here with others,
  we thank you for being with us
  and joining us in prayer to our Father.

(Lk 5^{16})

8

GO AWAY FROM ME, LORD;
I AM SINFUL

Lord Jesus, Simon Peter the fisherman
  soon realised
  that there was something special
  about you.
He had seen what you could do,
  and he called you *"Lord"*.
Peter said:
  "You know what I'm like, Lord;
  you'd be better off away from me."
As with Peter, Lord,
  you choose to stay with us,
  accepting and loving us as we are.
We thank you
  for choosing to be with us now.

(Lk 5$^{1-8}$)

9

IN THE BOAT, IN THE STORM

Lord, there was a storm on the Lake,
  and you were with your friends in the boat.
Whilst they were afraid,
  you were asleep
  - even with your head on a cushion!
They woke you, frightened,
  and you calmed the storm.
You are with each of us,
  in the boat that is our lives.
We pause for a moment, Lord,
  to remember
  that you are with us now.

(Mk 4$^{35-41}$) (see also 21 August in Volume 2)

10

JESUS WALKS ON THE WATER

Lord, with a strong wind blowing,
  upsetting your friends in the boat,
  you approach them,
  walking on the water.
Remind us now, Lord,
  of your saving presence with us,
  ready to calm the storms that threaten us.

(Jn 6$^{16-21}$; Mt 14$^{22-33}$; Mk 6$^{45-52}$)

11

LOOKING FOR YOU AND FINDING YOU

Many people, Lord,
  realised that they had a negative attitude
  and had done things that were not good.
They looked for you and found you,
  as did many sick people
  whom you spoke to and cured.
As we look for you now,
  may we discover you
  and experience your healing in our lives.
We call to mind
  that we are here in your presence.

(Lk 5$^{8.15}$)

12

PARALYSED MAN
LET DOWN THROUGH THE ROOF

We read in the Gospel, Lord,
  that some people were such good friends
  of a man who was weak and paralysed
  that they made their way
  through the crowds,
  carried him on to the roof,
  and gently lowered him down,
  so that he could be right in front of you.
There are times when each of us
  becomes weak or strong,
  reminding us
  that we all need the support of others
  at one time or another.
As we gather together in your presence,

we come as friends
who are concerned for each other.
In our strengths and weaknesses
we bring one another to meet you,
face-to-face.

(Lk 5¹⁷⁻²⁶; Mk 2¹⁻¹²)

13
JESUS PRAYS
BEFORE CHOOSING THE TWELVE

God our Father,
Jesus went up a hill to pray
and spent the whole night there in prayer
before choosing twelve of his followers
to be his apostles.
We now pause for a moment
to place ourselves with Jesus in prayer
before we go about
the ordinary and special events
of this day.

(Lk 6¹²⁻¹³)

14
IN QUIETNESS AND STILLNESS

I am setting out, Lord,
to spend a moment of quietness
amidst the noise and busy-ness of the day.
I will spend a moment in silence,
making myself more aware
of the noises around me
- both within this room and beyond…
The silence within me
and the gentle noises around me
remind me that as I close myself
to all that makes me
busy and pre-occupied,
I can open myself
to the quietness and gentleness
of your loving presence with me.

15
THE ROMAN OFFICER
AND HIS SERVANT

Lord, the Roman officer
whose servant was ill
sent you a message:
*"I am not worthy to receive you,
but only say the word
and my servant will get better."*
We, too, can say
that we are not worthy
to have you with us,
but isn't your message all along
that you wish and choose
to be with us?
We spend a moment reminding ourselves
that you choose to be here
with us now.

(Lk 7¹⁻¹⁰; Mt 8⁵⁻¹³)

16
THE WIDOW'S SON RAISED TO LIFE

Lord,
we read in the Gospel
that you felt deeply
for a widow whose only son had just died.
You touched him and raised him to life.
Now that you are with us,
we ask you
to touch us and give us new life.
We join with the people of that occasion,
saying:
"God has come to us to save his people!"
We pause, Lord,
to remember that you are present with us.

(Lk 7¹¹⁻¹⁷)

17
FEEDING THE FIVE THOUSAND

Over five thousand people, Lord,
gathered to hear you speak.
They thought it was more important
to be with you

than to bring some food with them.
Yet, in your concern and care
for everything about each person,
you transformed five loaves and two fish
to be more than enough
for everyone to eat.
Gathered together today,
we are fewer than those five thousand,
and, in your presence,
each of us can feel significant.
We pause, Lord, to remember
that you are present with us,
ready to do the impossible.

(Lk 9$^{10-17}$) (see 30 November)

18

TRANSFIGURATION

Lord, three of your friends
- Peter, James and John -
accompanied you up a mountain.
There they saw you in a different light
and they heard your Father say:
"This is my own dear Son."
They said to you:
*"Lord, it is good
that we are here,"*
and now, as you call us *"friends"*, Lord,
we too are glad
to be in your presence.

(Mk 9$^{2-8}$, 1^{11}; Mt 17$^{1-8}$; Lk 9$^{28-36}$)

19

LOOKING WITH LOVE
ON THE RICH YOUNG MAN

Lord, we find in the Gospel
that a rich young man
spoke to you,
asking what he should do
to live in God's kingdom.
You looked steadily at him
with love.
As we are gathered now,
remembering that we are in your presence,
lead us to realise

that you look steadily at each of us
with great love.

(Mk 10$^{17-22}$)

(See also 1st December)

20

WORTH MORE
THAN HUNDREDS OF SPARROWS

Lord Jesus,
you tell us
that even though sparrows
are very common,
not one sparrow is forgotten
by God our Father.
You say to each of us
that we are worth more
than hundreds of sparrows
- how precious we are!
Confident of our Father's
love and acceptance,
we pause to remember
that you are present with us.

(Lk 12$^{6-7}$; Mt 10$^{29-31}$)

21

DO NOT BE ANXIOUS OR AFRAID

Lord, you tell us
not to be anxious or afraid,
but to trust
in the care and love
of our Father.
We pause to remember
that you are with us, Lord,
as we are about to pray trustfully
to God our Father.

(Lk 12$^{22-31}$; Mt 6$^{25-34}$)

22

THE PRODIGAL SON

One of your most famous stories, Lord,
is that of the Prodigal Son.
You gave us a picture
of a generous father

who wants his lost and spendthrift son
to return.
He takes the initiative
and looks out for him
and, when he sees him from a distance,
he runs to his son,
clasps him in his arms
and kisses him tenderly.
You were letting us know
of the warm, welcoming embrace
that God our Father
has for each of us.
We pause for a moment, Lord,
to place ourselves in the presence
of God our Father,
who welcomes us warmly.

(Lk 15$^{11-32}$)

23
NOT IN MEANINGLESS WORDS

Lord, we come to you to pray
- not in many meaningless words
but simply by being in your presence.
And so we spend a moment of quietness,
growing in faith that you are with us now.

(Mt 6^7)

24
YOUR PRESENCE - ONE OF OUR PRIORITIES

Lord, you said
that our heart will always be
wherever our riches are.
We want to be able to choose wisely
and get out priorities right in life,
and so we now place ourselves
in the quietness of your presence.

(Mt 6$^{21.33}$ / Lk 12^{31})

25
BEARING FRUIT IN YOUR PRESENCE

If we live each day
aware of your presence, Lord,
we will be like healthy trees
that bear much good fruit.
We pause for a moment now,
reminding ourselves that you are with us.

(Lk 6^{43}; Mt 7^{17})

26
LOVING OURSELVES

Lord, you tell each of us
to love our neighbour
as we love ourselves.
Sometimes we focus simply
on doing good to our neighbour,
but we might forget
how important it is
to love ourselves.
Now, in your presence,
as you look warmly at each one of us,
lead us to be genuinely loving
in the way we treat ourselves.
We pause to remember
that you are with us.

(Mk 12^{31}; Mt 22^{39})

27
GROWING IN YOUR LIFE

Lord, we come to you
so that we may have life.
Remind us now
of your life-giving presence
so that we may live fully in your love.

(Jn 10^{10})

28
HAVING LIFE TO THE FULL

Lord, you said
that you came amongst us
so that we might have life,
and have it to the full.
May happy times in our lives
remind us of your presence with us.

(Jn 10^{10})

29
GOOD SHEPHERD

Lord,
>may the care we experience
>remind us of your presence,
>because you are the Good Shepherd,
>caring for us.

>>>*(Jn 10¹⁴)*

30
THE WAY, THE TRUTH AND THE LIFE

Lord,
>may the journeys we take
>remind us that you are present with us,
>because you are the Way,
>the Truth and the Life.

>>>*(Jn 14⁶)*

31
LIGHT OF THE WORLD

Lord,
>may the light that we see around us
>remind us
>of your presence with us now
>- you who are the Light of the world.

>>>*(Jn 8¹², 9⁵)*

32
SITTING BESIDE THE BLIND MAN

Lord,
>a blind man was sitting by the road,
>and he asked you to take pity on him.
>We now sit with him
>>in your presence,
>>and we hear you
>>address your words to us
>>as well as to him,
>>as you say:
>*"What do you want me to do for you?"*

>>>*(Lk 18³⁵⁻⁴³; Mk 10⁴⁶⁻⁵²)*

33
HERE IN YOUR PRESENCE, TRANSFORM US

Lord,
>it was in your presence
>that those who were blind
>began to see.
>The deaf began to hear,
>>the paralysed began to walk,
>>and those who were ill
>>were made whole.
>Your presence and your words and your touch
>>transformed their lives.
>We pause for a moment
>>to call to mind that you are with us,
>>loving and healing.

34
ZACCHAEUS - A CHANGED PERSON

The little man, Zacchaeus,
>was the tax-collector
>who cheated people
>and was isolated by others.
No force of argument could change him,
>nor any name-calling
>by those he had mis-treated.
It was only in your presence, Lord Jesus,
>that he changed
>and became a better person.
It was only in your presence
>that this little man
>learned to walk tall.
Influence us, Lord,
>as we now pause to remind ourselves
>that you are with us.

>>>*(Lk 19¹⁻⁹)*
>>*(See also 23 February and 29 April)*

35
CHANGED FOR THE BETTER

We spend a moment, Lord,
>reminding ourselves
>that you are present with us,

knowing that when you are present
people are changed for the better.

(e.g. Lk 19¹⁻⁹)

36
BECOMING LIKE LITTLE CHILDREN

God our Father,
    your Son told his friends
    that they needed to change
    and become like little children.
As we gather together now,
    we ask you, Father,
    to lead us to grow
    in our relationship with you,
    that we may become
    like little children,
    dependent on our Father,
    and always happy
    in our Father's presence.

(Mt 18¹⁻⁵)

37
SALT

A little salt, Lord,
    helps to bring out
    the real taste of what we eat.
Be like salt for us, Lord,
    bringing out the best in us,
    and then we, too,
    will be enabled to be "salt" for others,
    helping to bring out the best in them.
We spend a few moments, Lord,
    reminding ourselves
    that you are with us,
    ready to be of influence in our lives.

(Mt 5¹³)

38
AT HOME WITH JESUS

Just as when we have a guest
    in our homes, Lord,
    we welcome you warmly
    amongst us,

remembering that you said:
"Make your home in me."

(Jn 15⁴)

39
IN YOUR PRESENCE AND FRIENDSHIP

We pause for a moment, Lord,
    to remind ourselves
    that you call us to friendship with you,
    and you promise to be with us always.

(Jn 15¹⁴⁻¹⁵)

40
INVITED TO FRIENDSHIP

Lord, when Lazarus was ill,
    you were sent this message:
    "Lord, your dear friend is ill."
May the love and friendship we experience
    remind us that you are here with us,
    calling us by name
    and inviting us
    to friendship with you.

(Jn 11³)

41
LAZARUS IS CALLED TO LIFE

Lord,
    when your good friend Lazarus died,
    we are told that you wept
    and were deeply moved.
Others said of you:
    "See how much he loved him,"
    and you went on
    to raise him to life.
Help us to appreciate
    that you are present with us now,
    loving us
    and calling us out of "death" into "life".

(Jn 11³²⁻⁴⁴)

42
BELIEVING AS WE PRAY

Lord, you said
    that if we really believe,
    then whatever we ask for in prayer
    we will receive.
We ask first of all, Lord,
    that we may grow more aware
    of your presence with us.

(Mt 7⁷⁻¹¹, 21²²)

43
WHEN TWO OR THREE GATHER

Lord, you said
    that when two or three
    get together in your name,
    then you would be present with us.
Remind us now of your presence
    as we gather in your name.

(Mt 18²⁰)

44
IN A CHURCH OR CHAPEL

Father, at the Last Supper
    your Son took bread,
    blessed it, gave you thanks,
    and broke the bread,
    giving it to his friends, saying:
    "Take and eat; this is my body."
Here, in this church,
    is kept
    the bread which has become his body.
Jesus - the 'Blessed Sacrament' - is here,
    both to be taken to the sick
    and to pray before.
And so we thank you, Father,
    that Jesus, your Son,
    is now with us in this special way.

(Mt 26²⁶; Mk 14²²; Lk 22¹⁹)

45
STRENGTHENING AND SUPPORTING

Lord, you prayed
    that Simon Peter's faith
    would not fail,
    yet he went on to deny you.
You prayed
    that when he would later turn back to you
    he would bring strength to others.
Remind us now
    that you are with us,
    and then lead us
    to bring strength and support
    to those who share our lives.

(Lk 22³¹⁻³⁴)

46
YOUR PRESENCE ENABLES ME

On the cross, Lord,
    your dying words
    were to forgive
    those who had done you harm.
My own efforts alone, Lord,
    are often not enough
    for me to live as positively
    as I know I *can* live.
Your presence, Lord, here and now,
    and the power of your Spirit,
    transform me
    and enable me
    to choose to live in a positive way.
And so I pause for a moment, Lord,
    to remind myself
    that I am in your presence.

(Lk 23³⁴)

47
THE GOOD THIEF - REMEMBER ME

The Good Thief on the cross
   somehow realised, Lord,
   just who it was
   who was dying beside him.
As you are beside us now, Lord,
   we can join in the words
   that the Good Thief spoke to you:
   "Jesus, remember me,
   when you come into your kingdom."
We pause to remind ourselves
   that you are beside us.   *(Lk 23³⁸⁻⁴³)*

48
THE FATHER'S PRESENCE
AS JESUS DIES

God our Father,
   in the Jewish Temple in Jerusalem
   there was a large curtain
   that separated everyone
   from the 'holy place'
   that was the focus of your presence
   on Earth.
We read in the Gospel, Father,
   that at the moment
   of your Son's death on the cross,
   that curtain was torn in two.
It was a sign
   that your presence is available to everyone.
In silence for a moment, Father,
   we remind ourselves
   that you are present with us.
                              (Lk 23⁴⁵; Mk 15³⁸)

49
BROUGHT TOGETHER AS ONE BODY

Lord,
   you died to bring together
   into one body
   all God's people
   scattered far and wide.

As we are gathered together now
   in your name,
   remind us of your presence with us.
                              (Jn 11⁵²)

50
"LET LOOSE ON THE WORLD"

Two days
   after you were laid in the tomb, Lord,
   the women returned
   and found the tomb was empty.
You had risen from the dead,
   and you are present here with us now.
We pause for a moment
   to remind ourselves
   that you are with us
   as you promised.
                        (Lk 24¹⁻⁷; Mt 28¹⁻⁸)
                  ("Let loose on the world" is a quote from
                  John Masefield's 'The Trial of Jesus'.)

51
RISEN, BRINGING PEACE

Lord, you are not to be found
   in the emptiness of a tomb.
Instead, you are risen from the dead
   and present with us now
   as you promised to be.
We pause to remind ourselves
   that you are with us,
   and you offer us your peace.
         (Lk 24¹⁻⁸; Mt 28¹⁻¹⁰; Mk 16¹⁻⁸; Jn 20¹⁻¹⁰)

52
MARY MAGDALENE
- CALLED BY NAME

After your death, Lord Jesus,
   you appeared to Mary Magdalene,
   but she only recognised you
   when you called her by her name.
Remind us now
   that you are with us,
   and you call us by name.
                              (Jn 20¹¹⁻¹⁸)

53
PEACE AND THE SPIRIT

Lord Jesus,
    after your death
    the doors were locked
    in the room where your followers
    were gathered.
You appeared amongst them,
    saying: *"Peace be with you;*
    receive the Holy Spirit."
As we now gather together,
    empower us with your Holy Spirit.
Bring us your peace
    and remind us of your presence.

(Jn 20$^{19-23}$)

54
WALKING TO EMMAUS

Two days
    after you had been killed, Lord,
    two of your followers
    were walking to a village
    called Emmaus.
They were saddened
    at what had happened.
As they were talking,
    you joined them on their journey
    but, at first, they did not recognise you.
Risen Lord, we ask you
    to lead us to recognise you
    more clearly
    as you walk with us now
    on our journey through life.

(Lk 24$^{13-32}$)

55
STANDING AMONG THEM

After you had been killed, Lord,
    you appeared to two of your friends.
They rushed off
    to tell the other apostles
    that you had risen from the dead.

Then you appeared
    and stood among them all
    as they were gathered together.
    You said: *"Peace be with you."*
Remind us now, Lord,
    as we are gathered together,
    that you stand amongst us
    and offer us your peace.

(Lk 24$^{36-53}$)

56
RECOGNISING JESUS
AT THE START OF THE DAY

Lord Jesus,
    after you had died,
    you stood at the water's edge
    as the sun was rising
    over the Sea of Galilee.
You asked your disciples about their fishing,
    but they were slow to recognise you.
Here, at the start of our day,
    as we become busy,
    lead us to recognise that you are present,
    standing beside us.

(Jn 21)

57
YOUR PRESENCE INFLUENCES US
FOR GOOD

People are changed as they place themselves
    in the warmth of the sun.
So we are influenced for good
    as we realise more and more
    that you are with us, Lord.
We pause for a moment
    to remind ourselves
    of your loving presence with us.

(Jn 21^4)

58
WITH YOU ALWAYS

St Matthew in his Gospel
    records your last words, Lord,
    as these:
    "I will be with you always."
And so, Lord,
    we remind ourselves
    that you are with us at this moment,
    as you promised to be.

(Mt 28²⁰)

59
BECOMING MORE AWARE

We may not have noticed
    so far today, Lord,
    the little things in nature
    or the unspoken messages
    of people we have met.
Lead us to become more aware, Lord,
    of all that is around us.
May we grow more conscious, too,
    of your life-giving presence with us.

60
LET US REMEMBER

Let us remember
    that we are in the presence of God,
And let us adore him.

Index

INDEX

Aberfan - 21 Oct
"Abide With me" - 17 May
Abortion - 28 April
Achievements - 1,29 May
Ackroyd, Dan - 24 Oct
Advent Wreath - Appendix of Vol 3
Advertising - 30 Aug
Aesop - Intro.
Afraid - see 'Fear'
Agca, Mehmet Ali - 13 May
Aged - see 'Elderly'
Alban, St - 27 May; 20 June
Albert, Prince - 14 Dec
Alcoholics Anon. - 11 May
Aldrin, Buzz - 21,22,25 July
Algeria - 28 Aug
Ali, Mohammed - 23 July
Alone - see 'loneliness'
'All Saints' - 1 Nov
'All Souls' - 2 Nov
Altar - 14 Jan
"Amazing grace" - 24 July
Ambrose, St - Family Fast Day, Vol 1
'American Graffiti' - 2 May
Amnesty International - 24 Jan, 5 March
Andes - 13 March
Andrew, St - 30 Nov
Anglican Cathedral, Liverpool - 8,9 Feb
Annunciation - 25 March
Apartheid - 21 March
Apollo space programme - 11 April; 25 May;
     20 July; 7 Aug; 21 Dec
Appreciating - 8,10,14,22 Jan;
     8,9,14,19,20 Feb; 1,23,31 March; 11
     April; 2 June; 3 July; 5 Sept - see also
     'Thanksgiving'
Arc de Triomphe - 11 Nov
Archaeology - 16 Feb; 1 Aug
Archery - 12 June
Architecture - 16 Oct
Ardennes - 16 Dec
Argentina - 13 March
Armistice - 11 Nov
Armstrong, Neil - 20-22,25 July
Arrafat, Yasser - 8 Nov

Art - 18,23 Feb; 16 May; 3 Aug; 2 Sept; 14,16
     Oct; 15,19 Dec; Maundy Thurs, Vol 1
Arthritis - 6 March
Ascension - Vol 2
Ashes, The - 15 March
Ash Wednesday - Vol 1
Aspirin - 6 March
Asquith, Herbert - 11 Oct
Assumption of BVM - 15 Aug
Astronomy - 11 Aug; see
'Apollo','creation', 'space', 'stars', 'sun',
Athens - 1 Feb
Athletics - 6 May; 19 July; 25,26 Nov
Atkinson, Rowan - 13 Dec
Attitude - 7,23 Jan; 1 Feb; 19 May; 23,27
     Aug; 5 Sept; 24 Oct; Vol 2 - Appendix
     of Prayers
Attlee, Clement - 24 Oct
Augustine of Canterbury, St - 27 May
Augustine of Hippo, St - Intro.; 24 June;
     28 Aug; 12 Oct
Auschwitz - 14 Aug; 7 Oct
Australia - 12 Jan; 4 Nov
Austria - Sacred Heart, Vol 2
Autumn - 2,31 Oct
Awe - see 'wonder'

Bacteria - 14 May; 15 July
Baedeker Raids - 14 Nov
Bakr, Abu - 24 Feb
Balance in life - 3,12,14 July; 29,30,31 Oct;
     15 Dec; Vol 3 Appendix of Prayers 41
     (see 'time' and 'wonder')
Balmoral Castle - 21 Jan
Bananas - 10 April
Bandages - 14 Sept
Bank - 29 Oct
Bannister, Roger - 6 May
Baptism - 23 May; 16 Aug; 5,25 Oct;
     Pentecost, Vol 2
Barcelona - 19 July
Basil, St - Family Fast Day, Vol 1
Battle of Britain - 15 Sept
Battle of Hastings - 14 Oct
Baum, Frank - 19 Aug

Bayeux Tapestry - 14 Oct
Be/do/have - 14 July
Beatitudes - 30 May; 15 June; 16 Dec
'Beauty and the Beast' - Intro.
Becket, Sr Wendy - Intro.
Becket, Thomas - 29 Dec
Beddgelert - 10 Sept
Bede, St - 27 May
Beethoven - 3 March, 28 April, 7 May; 15 Dec
Beginnings - 1,16 Jan
Beirut - 24 Jan
Belgium - 11 Oct
Bell, Alexander G - 10 March; 2 Aug
Belshazzar - 22 Nov
Ben Hur - 8 Nov
Bernadette, St - 11 Feb
Berlin - Easter Sunday, Vol 1; 13 Aug; 9 Nov
Berwick-upon-Tweed - 13 Jan
Best - 21 Jan; 9,18 Feb; 3,15 March; 7,23 April;
    27,29; May; 9,12 June; 13 July; 15 Oct;
    Vol 2 Appendix of Prayers - 23,24,47
Betelgeuse - 20 Nov
Bethlehem - 25 July
Betrayal - 13 Feb; 10 Sept
Bhopal - 4 Dec
Bible passages/sayings - 28 Sept
BIC - 22 Nov
Biro - 22 Nov
Big Ben - 24 April
Bitterness - 4 Feb; 11 Oct
Blackadder - 13 Dec
Black Death - 12 June
Black Rod - 28 Oct
Blair, Tony - 6,23 Sept
Blessing - 16,25 Jan; 30 March; 22 Aug;
    1 Sept; Vol 2 - Appendix of Prayers
Blindness - 2 Jan, 3 March; Vol 3 Appendix
    of Prayers 32 (see also 'seeing','vision', &
    Helen Keller)
Blondin, Charles - 30 June
Bloom, Anthony - 25 April; Lent Volume 1
Blunkett, David - 2 Jan
Boat/ship- 12,22 Jan; 14 April; 3,21 Aug; 8 Sept;
    2 Nov; Prayers 6,8,9,10 in Appendix to Vol 3
Body - 21 May; 17 June

Body & Blood of Christ, Feast of - Vol 2
Bonhoeffer, Dietrich - 4 Feb; 9 July; 24 Nov;
    25 Dec
Boniface, St - 14 Dec
Books: burning - 4 May
Borman, Frank - 21 Dec
'Born again' - 31 Dec
Bosco, St John - 31 Jan
Bosnia - 28 June; 11 July
Boston - 31 May
Bournville - 19 Sept
Boxing - 23 July
Boxing Day - 26 Sept
Bradley, General Omar - 16 Dec
Braille, Louis - 2 Jan; 1 Sept
Braveheart - 7 June
Bravery - see 'Courage'
Bread - 19 Feb; 16,30 March; 21 July
Breakfast - 19 Feb
Breakspeare, Nicholas - 4 Dec
Brixham - 17 May
Brontë, Charlotte - 31 March
Brooke, Lord - 22 Sept
'Brothers Karamazov, The' - 17 Nov
Browning, E.B. - 16 Sept
Bruce, Robert the - 7 June
Bubonic plague - 12 June; 7 Sept
Buddhism - 25 Aug
Building - 26 Feb
Bulb, electric - 18 Oct
Bulge, Battle of - 16 Dec
Bullimore, Tony - 12 Jan
Bunyan, John - 24 Jan
Burdens - 14 Sept (see also 'Cross')
Burke, Edmund - 28 Dec
Burma Star - 11 Nov
Busby, Matt - 6 Feb

Cadbury, George - 19 Sept
Caesar - 17 July
CAFOD - 10 April; Family Fast Day, Vol 1
Calculator - 19 June
Calculus - 4 Jan
Calendar - 9 Sept
Calment, Jeanne - 3 Aug

Calming of the Storm - 3,21 Aug

Camara, Helder - 3 Sept; 23 Nov; Family Fast Day, Vol 3

Camp David Accord - 19 Nov

Camus, Albert - 7 Nov

Cana - Shrove Tuesday, Vol 1; Prayer 2 of Appendix to Vol 3

Cancer - 2 Sept; 15,16 Nov

'Candle in the Wind' - 6 Sept

Candlemas - 2 Feb

'Canticle of Creation' - 10 Oct

Canterbury - 29 Dec

Cardinal - 26 March

Carnarvon, Lord - 16 Feb

Carnegie, Andrew - 10 Aug

Carnival - Shrove Tuesday, Vol 1

Carols - 9,24 Dec

Carretto, Carlo - Intro.

Carter, Howard - 16 Feb

Carter, Jimmy - 19 Nov

Carton, Sydney - 10 June

Castle, Roy - 2 Sept

Cathedrals - 8,9 Feb; 19,29 May; 14 Nov

Cat's eyes - 3 April

Cavell, Edith - 11 Oct

'Certificate Evening' - see 'leaving school'

CFCs - 16 Sept

Challenge - e.g. 15 Feb; 25 Sept

Challenger - 28 Jan

Change - 11 May; 14 Oct

Changi Jail - 23 Nov

Channel, English - 5 May; 6 June; 15 Sept

Channel Tunnel - 5 May

Channel Islands - 2 July;

Chaplin, Charlie - 20 Sept

Charity work - e.g. 29 Oct

Charles I - 28 Oct; 12 Dec

Charles II - 5 March

Chaucer, Geoffrey - 29 Dec

Chernobyl - 26 April

Chesterton, G.K. - Ascension, Vol 2; 8 Nov

Children - e.g. 27 Sept; 6,7 Oct; 23 Nov; 6 Dec; Vol 3 Appendix of Prayers 36

Chile - 13 March

China - 16 Jan; 24 May

Chinese New Year - 16 Jan

Chocolate - 20 Aug; 19 Sept

Choices - 31 May; 6 June; 2,9,12,27 July; 8 Aug; 24 Oct

"Choose life, not death" - 2 July; 18 Aug; 24 Oct

Chopsticks - 16 April

Christian Unity - see 'Church Unity'

Christie, Agatha - Intro.

Christmas cards - 20,24 Dec

Christmas carols - 9,24 Dec

Christmas crackers - 17 Dec

Christmas crib - 23 Dec

Christmas pudding - 22 Dec

Christmas stamps - 20 Dec

Christmas tree - 14 Dec

Churchill, WS - 23 Jan, 11 March; 4 June; 13 July; 15 Sept; 29 Nov

Church Unity - 18,25 Jan; 8,21 Feb; 25 Oct

Circulation - 1 March

Civic dignitary - Vol 2 Appendix of Prayers - 70

Civil Rights - see 'human rights'

Civil War, American - 4 March; 9 April

Civil War, Yugoslavia - 11 July

Clarke, Arthur C - 22 July

Clemens, Samuel - see 'Mark Twain'

Clinton, President - 8 Nov

Clitherow, Margaret - 25 Oct

Coal - 21 Oct

Coca-Cola - 30 Aug

Coffee - 10 April

Coin - 27 Sept

Cold War - Easter Sunday, Vol 1; 1 May; 13 Aug; 9 Nov

Collins, Michael (astronaut) - 22,25 July

Colombia - 30 July

Columba, St - 25,27 May

Comets - 8 Jan; 13 April

Commandments - 15 Jan; 14 May; 8 June; 18 Aug

'Common Good' The - Intro.; 18 March; 26 May

Commons, House of - see 'Parliament'

Commonwealth - 7 March

Communion - Christ the King, Vol 3 (& see 'Eucharist')

Denmark - 29 July
Derby - 2 June
'Derry Air' - 6 Sept
Devon - 16 Aug
Diamond (dog) - 20 March
Diana, Princess - 31 Aug; 6 Sept; Vol 2 - Appendix of Prayers - 32
Dickens, Charles - Intro.; 9,10 June; 26 July; 17 Dec
Differences - 8 Feb
Dillinger, John - 6 July
Disability - 19 Jan; 3 March; 19 July; 1,3 June; 25 Sept *(see also 'illness')*
Disaster - 3,28 Jan; 11,14,15,26 April; 25 May; 16 Aug; 7 Sept; 21 Oct
Discernment - Vol 2 Appendix of Prayers - 28
Discrimination - *see 'prejudice'*
Dix, Dom Gregory - 'Body & Blood of Christ', Vol 2
Dog - 20 March; 10 Sept
Door - 1 Jan, 26 Feb
Dostoyevsky, F - 17 Nov
Dowding, Air Chief Marshall Sir Hugh - 15 Sept
Downing Street - 23 Sept
Dream - 4 April
Dunant, JH - 9 May
Dunblane - 3 March *(error: took place on 13 March)*
Dunkerley, William - 2 Oct
Dunkirk - 4 June
Duties - see *'responsibilities'*
Dying - 5 April; 3,22,25,31 Aug; 2,5,6 Sept; 20,21,22 Oct; 2,15,27 Nov; Prayers 65-67 of Appendix to Vol 2 *(& see 'Death')*

'Each day and in every way' - 29 Sept
Easter - Vol 1
Eclipse - 11 Aug
Edison, Thomas - 18,19 Oct
Education - e.g. 19 Jan; 18 May (prayer), 31 May; 1 June; 6 Oct *(see also 'children' & 'touching hearts')*
Education Reform Act - Intro.
Edward the Confessor - 14 Oct

Effort - 13 July
Egypt - 16 Feb
Eichmann, Adolf - 31 May
Einstein, Albert - 14 March; 18 April; 18 May; 10 Oct; 28 Dec
Eisenhower, Dwight - 6 Nov
Elderly - 3 Aug
Election - 20 Jan; 12 May; Vol 2 Appendix of Prayers 69 *(and see 'voting')*
Electricity - 3 Feb
Elijah - Shrove Tuesday, Vol 1
Eliot, TS - 7 Jan; Shrove Tuesday, Vol 1; 29,31 Dec
Elizabeth I, Queen - 23 March; 28,31 July; 22 Sept; 25 Oct; 5 Nov
Elizabeth II, Queen - 20 April; Maundy Thursday, Vol 1; 5,29 May; 12 July; 3,8 Nov
El Nino - 11 Sept
Emergency services - 11,12 Jan *(see also 'disaster')*
Emerson, RW - 5 Feb; 6 Oct; 29 Nov
Emmaus - Intro.; 17 May; Vol 3 Appendix of Prayers 54,55
Empathy - e.g. 3,24 Jan; 19 March; 16 April; 22,30 May; 26 Sept; 18,19,20,22,23 Oct; 4 Nov; 4,9 Dec *(see 'Family Fast Days', 'judging', 'prejudice')*
Encouragement - 26,27 Jan; 23 Feb; Vol 2 Appendix of Prayers 30
Enemies - e.g. 15 Jan *(see also 'forgiveness')*
England - e.g. 23 April
Enniskillen - 8 Nov
Enola Gay - 6 Aug
Environment - e.g. 12 Feb; 6,16 March; 6,16 Aug; 11,16 Sept; 3,14 Nov; 4,22 Dec *(see also 'Creation')*
Epiphany - 5,6,7 Jan; 25 July; 26 Dec
Escobar, Andrés - 30 July
E.T. - 11 June
"Ethnic cleansing" - 11 July
Eucharist - Holy Thursday, Vol 1; 21 July; 'Body & Blood of Christ', Vol 2; Vol 3 Appendix of Prayers 44; Christ the King, Vol 3
European Union - 7 May; 8 June; 27 Sept; 22 Dec

Eusebius - 21 Nov
Eutychus - 31 July
Everest - 29 May; 24 Aug
Evil - e.g. 29 Jan; 30 April; 31 May; 7 Oct; 28 Dec (see also 'cycle of evil/hatred', 'prejudice','war')
Evolution - 12 Feb
Exams - 23 May; Vol 2 Appendix of Prayers 53
Exiles - see 'refugees'
Exmoor - 16 Aug
Extraordinary - 7 Jan; 20 Aug; 13 Sept (see also 'Ordinariness')
Eyam - 7 Sept

Failure (see 'success') - 4 March
Fairtrade - 10 April
Faith - e.g. 30 June; 25 July; 1,17 Aug; 18 Nov; 3 Dec
Faithfulness - 13 Feb; 7,20 March; 10,17 Sept (see also 'Friends' & 'Love')
Faiths (other than Christian) - see 'Judaism', 'Islam', 'Buddhism', 'Chinese')
Family Fast Day - Appendix to Volumes 1 & 3. Also suitable: 16 March; 10 April; 13 June; 28 July; 6 Nov (also see 'Food', 'Human rights' & 'Justice')
Father Christmas - 6 Dec
Fawkes, Guy - 5 Nov
Fear -e.g. 28 Feb; 18 July; 9 Dec; Prayer 21 of Appendix to Vol 3
Feeding of 5,000 - see 'Five thousand'
Fibonacci - 16 Oct
Fifty pence piece - 27 Sept
Film projector - 19 Oct
Fingerprints - 6 July
Fire - 26 Feb; 20 March; 21 Aug; Pentecost, Vol 2; Trinity, Vol 2; 11 Sept
First-footing - 31 Dec
First Fridays - 'Body & Blood of Christ', Vol 2
First World War - 28 June; 1 July; 11 Nov; 24 Dec
'Fish' cryptogram - 5 Oct
Fisher, St John - 22 June
Fisherman - 14 July
Five thousand, feeding of - 16 July; Vol 3

Appendix of Prayers 17
Fleming, Dr Alexander - 9 Jan; 11 March
Flight - 17 Oct
Flower girl - 26 July
Flowers - 15 April
Food - 19 Feb; 16 March; 10,16 April; 28 July; 22 Dec (see 'family fast','hunger')
Foolscap paper - 16 Oct
Football - 13 Jan; 6 Feb; 29 March; 29 April; 17 May; 2,12,27 June; 30 July; 6 Dec
'Footprints' - 26 Nov
Forgiveness - 17 Jan; 26 Feb; 22,23 March; 4,11,13,22 May; 7,17 July; 8 Oct; 8,14,17,23 Nov
Forrest Gump - 20 Aug
Four-minute mile - 6 May
Francis of Assisi - 5 March; 4,10,24 Oct; 23 Dec
Frank, Anne - 12 March
Frankincense - 7 Jan
Franklin, Benjamin - 17 April; 15 Dec
Freedom - e.g 12 Oct; Trinity, Vol 2 (see 'slavery')
Freeman, Laurence - Intro.
French Revolution - 10 June
Friendship - 13 Feb; 23 April; 20 June; 4 July; 12,18,29 Aug; 17,22 Sept; 7,21 Nov; Vol 3 Appendix of Prayers 39
Fry, Elizabeth - 12 Oct
Funeral - see 'Death'

Gachet, Dr - 16 May
Gagarin, Yuri - 12 April
Gajounicezek, Franz - 14 Aug
Galaxy - 9 Oct; 7 Dec (see 'stars')
Galileo - 8 Jan
Gallipoli - 3 May
Gandhi - 29,30 Jan; 5,17 Feb; 12,17 May; 28 July; 29 Aug; 1 Oct
Garaudy, Roger - 22 May
Garland, Judy - 19 Aug
Geese - 17 Oct
Gelert - 10 Sept
General Election - 20 Jan; 7 Feb (see 'voting')

Generosity - e.g. 3 Sept
Genesis - 12 Feb; 21 Dec
George, St - 23 April
George I, King - 23 Sept
George II, King - 22 Aug
George IV, King - 26 June
George V, King - 22 Jan; 14,28 Oct
George VI, King - 1,22 Jan; 14 Oct
Germs - 15 July
Ghetto - 18 Dec
Gibson, Mel - 7 June
Gifts - e.g. 5,6,7,20 Jan; 20 Dec *(see
    'talents')*; Pentecost, Vol 2
Gladstone, W.E. - 19 May; 13 Sept
Glasgow - 30 May
Glencoe - 13 Feb
Glenn, John - 21 Dec
Globe Theatre - 21 Aug
Godspel - 5 Dec
Goering, Hermann - 15 Sept
Goethe, Johann - 29 Nov
Gold - 5,7 Jan
Golden Mean/Ratio/Rectangle - 16 Oct
Goldman Sachs - 29 Oct
Good Friday - Vol 1; 8 Nov
Good Shepherd - Vol 3 Appendix of
    Prayers 29
Gospel - e.g. 17 Feb; 21 Aug; 12 Sept
Grace - 24 July
Grace before meals - 4 Sept
Grahame, Kenneth - 8 March
Grail Prayer - 28 March
Grangemouth - 3 Nov
Gravitation - 4 Jan
'Great Britain' - 5 Nov
Great Fire of London - 26 Feb; 21 Aug
Greatness - e.g. 15 May; 9,24 June; 13
    Dec *(see 'little')*
Great Plague - 7 Sept
Greenwich - 24 Nov
Gregorian Calendar - 9 Sept
Gregory the Great, Pope St - 27 May; 30 June
Gregory XIII, Pope - 4 Jan
Grellet, Stephen - 11 March
Griffiths, Bede - Intro.

Grimm Brothers - Intro.
Gruber, Franz - 24 Dec
Gruenwald, Mark - 22 Nov
Guernsey - 22 May
Guinness Book of Records - 14 June; 3 Aug;
    2 Sept
Gunpowder Plot - 5 Nov
Guitenberg, Johann - 22 Nov
Guy Fawkes - 5 Nov

Hague, The - 10 Aug
Hale-Bopp Comet - 13 April
'Hallelujah Chorus, The' - 22 Aug
Halley's Comet - 13 April
Halloween - 31 Oct
Halo - 16 May
Hammarskjöld, Dag - 18,26 Sept; 15 Oct;
    31 Dec
Handel, GF - 22 Aug; 5 Dec
Handicap - *see 'disability'*
Hanks, Tom - 25 May; 20 Aug
Hanukkah - 2 Dec
Harold, King - 14 Oct
Harriot, John - Intro.
Harvey, Dr William - 1 April
Haskins, Minnie - 1 Jan
Hastings, Battle of - 14 Oct
Hatred - e.g. 4 Feb; 10 May; 11 Oct *(see
    'cycle of', 'prejudice' and 'war')*
Hawaii - 19 March
Healing - 11 Feb; 3,28 May; 14 Sept *(see
    also 'illness')*
Hearing - *see 'deafness'*
Heart - 1 April; 15 May
Heaven - 16 April
Hell - 16 April
Henry II, King - 29 Dec
Henry VIII, King - 7 Feb; 22 June; 24 Sept;
    29 Dec
Henry, O - 20 Dec
Herbert, Anne - 10 July
Hildegard of Bingen - 22,24 Oct; 17,23
    Nov; 1 Dec
Hill, Rowland - 10 Jan
Hillary, Edmund - 29 May

Hillsborough - 15 April
Himalayas - 29 May
Hiroshima - 6 Aug
Hitler, Adolf - 4 May; 5,18 Aug; 15 Sept; 7 Oct (& see 'concentration camps'; 'Second World War')
Hoffman, Felix - 6 March
Hogmanay - 31 Dec
Holiness - e.g. 1 Nov
Holland - 23 Oct
Holly - 'Advent Wreath' in Appendix of Vol 3
Holmes, Sherlock - 9 Oct
Holte, Dorothy Law - 6 Dec
'Holy Family' - 30 Dec
'Holy of Holies' - 8 Oct; 19 Nov; Vol 3 Appendix: Prayer 48
Holy Saturday - Vol 1
Holy Thursday - Vol 1
Hope - e.g. 8 Feb; 26 Nov; 9 Dec
Hopkins, GM - 26 May
Horace - 9 Sept
Hostages - 24 Jan; 18 Nov
Hubble Telescope - 9 Oct
Hugo, Victor - 22 May
Human being (composition) - 21 May
Human rights - 15,20,24,29 Jan; 16,18,24 March; 4,5,9,10,28 April; 14 June; 11 Sept; 3 Nov; 11 Dec (see also 'prejudice' and 'justice')
Hume, Cardinal - 13 May; 31 Aug
Hunger - 16 March; 13 June; 28 July (see 'Family Fast', 'food','Matthew 25')
Hussein, Saddam - 13 Feb

Ichthus - 5 Oct
Ideals - 12 March
Ignatius Loyola - 5 Feb; 31 March; 4 June; 31 July; 8 Dec; Pentecost, Vol 2
Illness - 11 Feb; 6 March; 3,28 May; 18 June (prayer); 5,23 July; 25 Sept; 1 Oct; 4 Dec Vol 2 Appendix of Prayers 39,62 64; Vol 3 Appendix of Prayers 5,11,12,15,32,33,40,41 (see also 'Disability' & 'Matthew 25')
Image - 23 June

'Imani' - 26 Nov
Immaculate Conception - 8 Dec
Immigrants - see 'refugees'
Imprisonment - see 'prisoners'
Incarnation - e.g. 19,25 Dec
Incense - 7 Jan
India - 4 Nov (& see 'Gandhi')
Individuality - 10,22 31 Jan; 10,12,24 Feb; 3,9,12,29 March; 7,29 April; 1,2,15,18,28,29,30 May; 3,11,25 June; 6,9,12,14,26,27 July; 19,23,27 Aug; 12,21 Sept; 1 Dec; Trinity Sunday - Vol 2; Vol 2 Appendix of Prayers
Indonesia - 26 Aug; 11 Sept
Industrial Revolution - 3 Nov
Initiative - 20 Jan
Ink - 22 Nov
Inspiration - e.g. 19 Oct
INRI - Good Friday, Vol 1
Inventions - 2,4 Jan; 10 March; 17 April; 22 July; 2,30 Aug; 18, 19 Oct (see also 'Science' & 'Space')
Iona - 27 May
Ireland - 17 March; 8 Nov
Irenaeus of Lyons - 1 Nov
Irwin, James - 7 Aug
Isaiah 2 - 27 Feb
Isaiah 40 - 5 Dec
Isaiah 49 - 12 Sept
Islam - 24 Feb; 30 March; 19 April ; 9 May; 7 July; 8 Aug; 2 Sept; 29 Oct; 19 Nov
Israel - 31 May (see 'Judaism')

Jail - 5 Feb
James I/VI, King - 5 Nov
James II, King - 13,26 Feb
Janus - 1 Jan
Jarret, Bede - 2 Nov
Jenner, Edward - 14 May
Jerusalem - 19 Nov
JN1:14 - 22 July
John, Brother - 8 April
John, Elton - 6 Sept
John, King - 15 June
John Paul I - 26 Aug

Life-giving - e.g. Shrove Tuesday, Vol 1;
Vol 2 Appendix of Prayers 25; 24 Oct;
10,12 Nov *(see also 'positive')*
Light - 1,4 Jan; 2,21 Feb; 9 March; 3 April;
Easter Sunday; 10 June; 18, 31 July;
11 Aug; 12 Sept; 4,18 Oct; 20,25 Nov;
2,19,21,23 Dec; Vol 3 Appendix of
Prayers 31 *(see 'Sun')*
Lincoln, Abraham - 4 March; 9 April; 20 Nov;
15 Dec
Lister, Joseph - 15 July
Little/small - 14 May; 24 June; 15 July;
20 Aug; 13 Dec *(see also 'greatness',
'Zacchaeus')*
Liverpool - 8,9 Feb; 15 April; 3 May;
Pentecost, Vol 2; 27 Dec; Christ the
King, Vol 3
Llewellyn - 10 Sept
'Loaves and fish' - 30 Nov
Lom, Herbert - 29 Sept
London - 11 Jan; 26 Feb
Loneliness - 26 Sept; 15 Dec
Lord's Prayer, The - 1 Aug; 2 Sept
Lourdes - 11 Feb; 3 May
Love - e.g. 4,14 Feb; 30 May; 13 July;
17 Sept; 6, 10 Oct; 1 Nov
Lovell, Jim - 25 May; 21 Dec
Lowell, Percival - 4 July
Lowry, LS - 23 Feb
Loyalty - *see 'Faithfulness'*
Loyola, St Ignatius - *see 'Ignatius'*
Lucas, George - 2 May
'Lumen Gentium' - 1 Nov
Lutyens, Sir Edwin - Christ the King, Vol 3
Luther, Martin - 27 Nov; 14,23 Dec
Luwum, Janani - 9 July
Lynmouth - 16 Aug
Lyte, Henry - 17 May

Maastricht Treaty - 1 Nov
Macleaod, George - 19 Dec
Magee, John - 28 Jan
Magna Carta - 15 June
Malta - 25 Jan
Manchester - 1 Aug

Manchester United - 6 Feb
Mandela, Nelson - Intro.; 27 April; 10
May; 12,18 July
Marconi - 27 March
Mardi Gras - Shrove Tuesday, Vol 1
Mark, St - 25 April
Marriage - 17 Aug
Mars - 4 July; 30 Oct
Martyrs - see *Alban, Becket, Bonhoeffer,
Cavell, Clitherow, Damian, Eyam, Fisher,
Gandhi, King, Kolbe, Latimer, Lawrence,
Luwum, More, Ridley, Romero, Tolpuddle*
Marx, Karl - 15 Oct
Mary (Our Lady) - 2,11,28 Feb; 25 March;
20 May; 15 Aug; 24 Sept ; 8,25 Dec
Mary Magdalene - Vol 3 Appendix of
Prayers 52
Mary, Queen - 22 Jan
Masefield, John - 12 Jan
Mass - *see 'Eucharist'*
Mathematics - 16 Oct
Matthew 25 - 5 April; 20,22 Oct
Maundy Thursday - Vol 1
Mayor - Vol 2 Appendix of Prayers, 70
McQueen, Steve - 15 Nov
M.E. - 16 June
Meal - 19 Feb; 4 Sept
Media - 23 May; 30 Aug
Meister, Joseph - 15 July
Memories - 5 Jan; 3 Aug; 28 Nov
"Messiah, The" - 22 Aug
Mexico - 23 Dec
Mezuzah - 8 Aug
Micah - 27 Feb; 22 April; 8 Oct
Michelangelo - 18 Feb
Milky Way - 9 Oct; 7 Dec
Mince pies - 22 Dec
Miracles - 3 May
Misérables, Les - 22,26 May
Mistakes - 4 July *(see also 'forgiveness')*
Mitterand, President - 5 May
Miyashima, Toki - 6 May
Moccasins - 4 Nov
Modahl, Diane - 25,26 Nov
Mohr, Joseph - 24 Dec

Molokai - 19 March
Mompesson, W - 7 Sept
Money - *see 'riches'*
Monica, St - 28 Aug
Monotheism - 8 Aug
Monroe, Marilyn - 6 Sept
Monument - 26 Feb
Moon - 11,12 April; 20-22, 25 July; 21 Dec
    (see 'Apollo)
Moonlight Sonata - 3 March
Morgan, Charles - Sacred Heart, Vol 2
More, St Thomas - 7 Feb; 5,22 June
Morse Code - 14 April
Moses - 16 Sept; Shrove Tuesday, Vol 1;
    16 Dec
Motorways - 5 Dec
Mount St Helens - 26 Aug
Mourning - 8,15 April; 17 May; 25 Aug; 2
    Nov; Prayers 65-67 of Appendix of Vol
    2; Vol 3 Appendix of Prayers 41 *(see
    also 'dying')*
Multi-cultural - 15,16,29,30 Jan; 1,2,16,
    24,25 Feb; 6,7,21,29,30 March; 19 April;
    9 May; 8,13 June; 7 July; 5,8,25 Aug;
    2,21,26 Sept; 8,13,23,27 Oct; 4,19 Nov;
    2 Dec *(see also 'prejudice', 'United Na-
    tions' & names of countries)*
Munich - 6 Feb; 9 Aug
Murphy, Eddie - 24 Oct
Muscles - 17 June
Music - 3 March; 20,28 April; 7,17,22,26
    May; 24,26 July; 19,22 Aug; 2,6 Sept;
    16 Oct; Trinity, Vol 2; 1,5,9,15,24 Dec
Muslim - *see 'Islam'*
'My Fair Lady' - 26 July
Myrrh - 6,7 Jan

Nagasaki - 6 Aug
Naked - *see 'Matthew 25'*
Name - 22 Jan; 23 Feb; 7,29 April *(see
    also 'individuality')*
Napoleon - 17 Jan; 8 June
National Anthem - 20 April
National Health Service - 5 July
Nature - 16 Oct *(& see 'creation')*

Nazis - 22 March; 4 May *(& see 'concentra-
    tion camps', 'Hitler', 'Second World War')*
"Need is greater" - 22 Sept
Netherlands - 23 Oct
New Orleans - Shrove Tuesday, Vol 1
Newman, JH - 21 Feb; Good Friday, Vol 1
Newton, Sir Isaac - 4 Jan; 20 March
Newton, John - 24 July
New Year - 1,16 Jan; 21 Sept; 8 Oct
New Zealand - 4 Nov
Niagara Falls - 30 June
Nicholas, St - 6 Dec
Nicholas II, Tsar - 17 July
Niebuhr, Reinhold - 11 May; 31 Dec
Nightingale, Florence - 16 June
Nineveh - 2 March
Noah - Shrove Tuesday, Vol 1
Nobel Prize - 14 Jan; 10 May; 14 Nov; 10 Dec
Nolan, Chris - 19 Jan
Norkay, Tenzing - 29 May
North Sea - 3 Nov
Nouwen, Henri - 27 Nov
Numbers - 16 Oct

Offering - e.g. 14 Jan; 28,30 March; 1,10
    Oct; 27,30 Nov; Vol 2 Appendix of
    Prayers 4-8
Offertory prayers - 30 March; 21 Sept
Oil - 3 Nov
Olympic Games - 6 April; 19,23 July;
    5 Aug; 25,26 Nov
'Only Fools and Horses' - 3 Feb
Open University - 30 Sept
Opportunities - 9 Jan
Oppression - *see 'human rights'*
Orb - Christ the King, Vol 3
Ordinariness - 7 Jan; 1 April; 19 May; 9
    July; 20 Aug; 13 Sept; 1,7 Oct
Orion - 20 Nov
Orthodox Churches - 25 April; Lent
    Volume 1; 17 July; 26 Dec
Oscar Ceremony - 25 Sept
'Our Father' - 1 Aug; 15 Oct
Our Lady - *see 'Mary'*
Owen, Jesse - 5 Aug

Presentation - 2 Feb
President - 20 Jan
Priesthood - 4,12,14 Aug; 25 Oct
Prime Minister - 23 Sept
'Prime Suspect' - 21 Aug
Priorities - Family Fast Days, Vols 1 & 3; 12,27,28 July; 8,10 Aug; Christ the King, Vol 3 *(see 'values')*
Prisoners - 24 Jan; 24 March; 22 May; 20 June; 12 July; 22 Aug; 12 Oct *(& see 'Matthew 25' and individual names)*
'Prize-giving' - see 'Leaving school'
Prodigal Son - Intro.; Shrove Tuesday, Vol 1; 19 July; 27 Nov; Vol 3 Appendix of Prayers 22
Prophet - 2 March, 22 April *(& see 'Isaiah')*
Psalm 8 - 12 April; 20 July; 7 Aug
Psalm 23 - 21 Oct; 25 Nov
Psalm 104 - 26 Oct
Psalm 117 - 20 April; 2 Dec
Psalm 137 - 25 Feb
Psalm 138/9 - 10,25 Feb
Pullias - Intro.
Pullman - 10 Aug
Pygmalion - 26 July

Quakers - 24 Jan, 5 March; 19 Sept; 12 Oct
Qualities *(see 'talents')*
'Quality Street' - 20 Aug
Quiet - 1 April; 12,14,27 July; 15 Dec; Vol 3 Appendix of Prayers 14
'Quo Vadis' -5 Oct
Qur'an - 19 April

Rabies - 15 July
Rabin, Yitzhak - 8 Nov
Radiation - 26 April, 6 Aug, 16 Nov
Radio - 27 March
Radioactivity *(see 'radiation')*
Radium - 16 Nov
R.A.F. - 28 Jan; 15 Sept
Railways - 3 Jan; 24 Nov
Rain - 16 Aug
Rauschenbusch, William - 16 Sept
Ravensbruck - 22 March

'Reaching the Unreached' - 23 Oct
Reagan, Presd. Ronald - 28 Jan
Reconciliation - 26 March; 9 April; 5,27 May; 1 July; Shrove Tuesday, Vol 1; 24 July; 11,13 Aug *(see 'confession', 'forgiveness', 'peace')*
Red Cross - 9 May
Redmond, Derek - 19 July
Red Square - 1 May
Reeve, Christopher - 25 Sept
Refugees - 24,27 Oct
Rembrandt - 16 May; 27 Nov
Remember - 5 Jan; 3 Aug; 27,28 Nov; 'Holy Thursday;' 'The Body and Blood of Christ'
Remembrance Day - 8,11 Nov
Renew - 31 Dec
Repent - Shrove Tuesday & Ash Wednesday of Appendix to Vol 1; 5,31 Dec *(see 'Forgiveness')*
Reports - Vol 2 Appendix of Prayers, 54
'Rerum Novarum' - 23 Aug
Respect - e.g. 16 July; 11,19 Sept; 6 Oct; 17 Nov
Responsibilities - 20 Jan; 26 April; 12,31 May
Resurrection - e.g. Easter Sunday; 18 June; 14 Sept; Vol 3 Appendix of Prayers 50-58
'Reverence for life' - 14 Jan; 18 Sept *(see also 'creation', 'wonder')*
Rheumatism - 6 March
Rice, Grantland - 27 June
Richard, Sir Cliff - 2 Sept
Richard of Chichester - 2 April
Riches - 5 Jan; 10 March; 14 July; 10 Aug; 19 Sept; Oct 29; Nov 3; 1,10,20,22 Dec; Family Fast Days, Vols 1 & 3; Vol 3 Appendix of Prayers 19,24
Ridley, Bishop Nicholas - 25 Oct
Rigel - 20 Nov
Rights - *see 'human rights' and 'responsibilities'*
Rio de Janeiro - Shrove Tuesday, Vol 1
Roads - 3 April; 5 Dec

Robert the Bruce - 7 June
Robinson, Jason - 14 Sept
Roddenberry, Gene - 4 Nov
Romans 8 - 29 June; 15 Nov; Ascension,
    Vol 2
Romans 12 - 26 Jan
Rome - 1 Jan
Romero, Oscar - 24 March; 8,9 July
Röntgen, William - 10 Feb
Roosevelt, Eleanor - 18 Nov
Rosh Hashanah - 21 Sept; 8 Oct
'ROTAS' square/cryptogram - 1 Aug
Rousseau, JJ - 20 Feb
Rugby - 14 Sept
Running - 6 May; 19 July; 25,26 Nov
Runnymede - 15 June

Sabbath - 30 March
Sacraments - see 'Baptism', 'Confirmation',
    'Reconciliation', 'Eucharist', 'Marriage',
    'Priesthood', 'Sick'
Sacred Heart - Vol 2
Sacrifice - e.g. 30 Jan; 14 Aug; 8,15 Sept;
    1 Oct
Sadat, Anwar - 19 Nov
Saddam Hussein - 13 Feb
'Saints, All' - 1 Nov
Salt - 37
Samoa - 10 Nov
Sandburg, Carl - 15 Dec
Santa Claus - 6 Dec
Satellites - 22 July
Saul - see 'Paul'
Scapegoat - 8 Oct
Schindler, Oskar - 18 Dec
Schweitzer, Dr Albert - 14 Jan; 4 Sept
Science - 4,8,9,14 Jan; 3,8,10,12 Feb;
    10,11,14,20,27 March; 18 April;
    14,18,22,31 May; 15 July; 2,6,18,26
    Aug; 11,16 Sept; 9 Oct; 6,16,20 Nov;
    4,10 Dec (see 'space')
Scotland - 30 Nov
Scott, Sir Giles Gilbert - 8,9 Feb
Scripture passages (in speech) - 28 Sept
Scrooge, Ebenezer - 17 Dec

Sculpture - 27 Sept
Sea / seafarers - see 'boat'
Seattle, Chief - 13 Oct
Second Vatican Council - 19 Jan
Second World War (see also 'Concentration
    camps','Hitler','war') - Easter Sunday,
    Vol 1; 1 Jan; 31 May; 4,6,28 June;
    6,13,18 Aug; 15 Sept; 7 Oct; 6,14,23
    Nov; 16,18,27 Dec
'Sealion, Operation' - 15 sept
Seeing - see 'blindness' and 'vision'
Segregation (see 'apartheid', 'prejudice')
Self-esteem - 22 Jan; 23 Feb; 29 April; 18
    July; Vol 2 Appendix of Prayers
Sellers, Peter - 29 Sept; 14 Oct
Semaphore - 18 June
Seneca - 22 May
Senses - 1,16 Sept; (see 'Helen Keller',
    'blindness', 'vision', 'wonder')
Seoul - 25 Nov
Serbs - 28 June; 11 July
Serenity Prayer - 11 May
Sermon on the Mount - see 'Beatitudes'
'Set-aside land' - 16 March, 11 Sept; 22
    Dec
Seuret, Georges - 16 Oct
Shackleton, Ernest - 15 Feb
Shakespeare - 6 Jan; 20 March; 23 April;
    5,21,29 May; 21 Aug
Sharing - Family Fast Day, Vol 1
Sharpeville - 21 March
Shaw, George B - 5 June; 26 July
Shaw, Percy - 3 April
Shema - 8 Aug
Shepherd - 21 Oct; 25 Nov
Ship - see 'boat'
Shoemaker-Levy Comet - 8 Jan
Shofar - 21 Sept; 8 Oct
Sickness - see 'illness' & 'Matthew 25'
Sight - see 'blindness' and 'vision'
Sign - see 'cryptogram'
'Sign of the Cross' - 14 Sept; Good Friday;
    Trinity Sunday
'Silent Night' - 24 Dec
Simeon - 2 Feb

Simon Peter - see 'Peter'
Sin - Shrove Tuesday, Vol 1 (& see 'forgiveness')
Sincere - 23 June
Sinfulness - Shrove Tuesday, Vol 1
Singapore - 23 Nov
Sioux Indians - 23 Oct
Sistine Chapel - 18 Feb
Slavery - 9 April; 24,29 July
Sleep - 4 Sept
Smallpox - 14 May
Smile - 17 June; 2,25 Sept (see 'laughter')
Smythe, FS - 24 Aug
Snail - 16 Oct
Snowdon - 10 Sept
Society of Friends - see 'Quakers'
Socrates, 1 Feb
Solomon - 4 Jan
Solstice - 21 June
Solzhenitsyn, Alexander - 28 Dec
Somme - 1 July
Sorrow - 3,6 Jan; 30 May
South Africa - 21 March; 27 April; 10 May
South Pole - 15 Feb
Space - 8,28 Jan; 9,31 March; 11,12,13,18
    April; 21,25 May; 11 June; 4,20-22,25
    July; 7,18 Aug; 3,9 Oct
Spider - 7 June
Spielberg, Steven - 11 June; 29 July; 18 Dec
Spirit - e.g. Pentecost & Trinity, Vol 2; 23
    May; 17,26 Oct; Vol 2 Appendix of
    Prayers - 68
Sport - see Archery, Athletics, Boxing,
    Cricket, Football, Olympics, Rugby,
    Running; Vol 2 Appendix of Prayers, 58
Spring - 1 March
Sputnik - 3 Oct; 3 Nov
Srebrenica - 11 July
Stamps - 10 Jan; 27 May
Stars - 31 March; 9,21 May; 20 Nov; 7,14
    Dec (see also 'Epiphany')
Star Trek - 28 Sept; 4 Nov
'Star Wars' - 2 May
Stations of the Cross - Good Friday, Vol 1
Statue - 13 March; 23 June
Stephen, St - 26 Dec

Stevenson, R.L. - 1,10,12 Nov; 25 Dec
St Helena (island) - 26 Feb
Storm - 12 Jan; 21 Aug; 8 Sept; Vol 3
    Appendix of Prayers 9,10
Story - Intro; 21 Aug
St Paul's Cathedral - 19,29 May
Strangers - see 'Matthew 25'
Strug, Kerry - 23 July
Success - 4 March; 6 April; 2,29 May; 13
    July; Vol 2 Appendix of Prayers - 7;
    Sacred Heart, Vol 2
Suffragettes - 2,14 June
Sullivan, Annie - 1 June
Sun - 9 March; Easter Sunday, Vol 1; 21 June;
    26 Aug
Sundial - 11 Aug
Superman - 25 Sept
S.V.P. - 23 Aug
Switzerland - 9 May
Sydney, Sir Philip - 22 Sept

Talents - 9,13 Jan; 9 Feb; 3 March; 6,18
    April; 6,29 May; 2,12 June; 13,30 July;
    10,15,19,20 Aug; 13 Sept; 15 Dec
Tagore, Ranindranath - 15 Dec
Tapestry - 14 Oct
Taupin, Bernie - 6 Sept
Taylor, Jeremy - 27 July
Telephone - 8 Feb, 10 March
Temple, William - Ascension, Vol 2
Ten Boom, Corrie - Sacred Heart, Vol 2; 1
    Nov; 27 Dec
Tennyson - 6 May
Teresa, Mother - 9 Feb; 4 March; 13 June;
    13 July; 27 Aug; 5,12,20 Sept
Teresa of Avila - 28 March
Teresa of Lisieux - 1 Oct; Introduction to
    the 60 prayers of the Appendix of Vol 3
Tertullian - 14 Sept; 5,15 Oct
Thanksgiving/thankfulness - e.g. 4,5 Jan;
    1,9 Feb; 23 April; 21,25 July; 4,18
    Sept; 2,31 Oct; 28 Nov; 27,31 Dec; Vol
    2 Appendix of Prayers (see 'appreciat-
    ing' and 'Eucharist')
"Think lovely thoughts" - 22 Feb

Thirst - *see 'Matthew 25'*
Thomas of Canterbury - 29 Dec
Thoreau - 5 Feb
Tiananmen Square - 27 Oct
Tidal waves - *see Tsunami*
Tightrope - 30 June
Time - 9 Jan; 29 Feb; 23 March; 1 April;
3,12,14,27 July; 9 Sept; 24 Nov; 15 Dec
'Tiny Tim' - 17 Dec
Titanic - 14 April
Tithe - 29 Oct
Together - 13 Jan; 9 Feb; 18,29 March; 6
April; 12 June; Vol 2 Appendix of
Prayers - 70
Tolpuddle - 18 March
Toothache - 6 Jan
Touch - 1,8 June; 27 Sept
'Touching hearts' - Intro.; 3 Feb; 3 April;
15 May; 10 July; 20,22 Oct; Vol 2
Appendix of Prayers - 33
Toynbee, Philip - 19 Dec
Trade Unions - 18 March
'Trading Places' - 23 Oct
Train - 3 Jan; 24 Nov
Transform - e.g. 1 Oct; 30 Nov; 19 Dec
(see also 'offering')
Transfiguration - Prayer 18 of Appendix to Vol 3
Trapeze - 27 Nov
Traynor, Jack - 3 May
Tree, Christmas - 14 Dec
Trinity - 25 Jan; Vol 2 Additional Days;
28 Sept
Trust - e.g. 4 March; 28 Aug; 1,18 Oct;
27 Nov; 31 Dec
Tsar - 17 July
Tsunami - 26 Aug
Tuberculosis - 17 May; 2 Aug; 8 Sept; 10 Nov
Turner, Joseph - 19 Dec
Tutankhamen - 16 Feb
Twain, Mark - 27 Jan; 1,21 April
Tyrol - Sacred Heart, Vol 2

Ugly - 12,19 Dec
Umbrella - 21 Jan
Underground - 11 Jan

Underhill, Evelyn - Main Intro & Intro to
Appendix of Prayers in Vol 3
Understanding - e.g. 4 Jan; 30 Sept;
25,28 Oct; 19 Nov
'United Kingdom' - 5 Nov
United Nations - 27 Feb; 25 June; 18 Sept;
6,24 Oct; 11 Dec
Unity - 18,25 Jan; 8 Feb; 5 May; 25 Oct;
9 Nov
Universe - 7 Dec
University, The Open - 30 Sept
'Unknown Warrior, The' - 11 Nov

V-1/2 weapons - 18 Aug
Vaccination - 14 May; 15 July
Valentine, St - 14 Feb; Sacred Heart, Vol 2
Valjean, Jean - 22 May
Values - e.g 9 Jan; 7 Feb; 30 May;
12,21,27 July; 30 Aug; Family Fast Day,
Vol 3; Christ the King, Vol 3
Van Breemen, Peter - Sacred Heart, Vol 2
Van Gogh, Vincent - 16 May; 3 Aug; 16 Oct
Vatican Council, Second - 18 Jan
VE Day - 8 May
Vengeance weapons - 18 Aug
Venice - 25 April
Versailles - 28 June
Vesuvius, Mount - 1,24 Aug
Vianney, John - 4 Aug
Vickers, George - 7 Sept
Victoria, Queen - 21,22 Jan; 9 June; 15 July;
3 Aug; 14 Dec
Vietnam War - Introduction; 13 Nov
Vincent de Paul, Society of - 23 Aug
Vinci, Leonardo da - 2 Sept; 15 Dec;
Maundy Thursday Vol 1
Violence - e.g. 29,30 Jan; 30 April; 13 May;
5 June; 5 Aug; 5,8 Nov *(& see 'war')*
Virgin Mary - *see 'Mary'*
Virus - 14 May
Vision - 2 Jan; 1,16,18,21 Feb; 3 March;
3,4,5 April; 2,4 May; 21 July; 30 Aug; 1
Sept; 19,21 Dec *(see also 'blindness',
'sight', 'space' & 'wonder')*
Vitality - *see 'life-giving','awareness' and 'healing'*

Vocations - 15 May; 4,12,14 Aug
Voltaire - 20 Feb
Volunteers - 29 Oct
Voting - 12 May; 14 June; Vol 2 Appendix of Prayers - 69
Voyager - 8 Jan
V-weapons - 18 Aug

Waite, Terry - 24 Jan; 18 Nov
Wales - 1 March
Wales, Princess of - 31 Aug; 6 Sept
Walker, Peter - Intro.
Wall, Berlin - 13 Aug; 9 Nov
Walsingham - 24 Sept
Wanamaker, Sam/Zoe - 21 Aug
War - 17,23,28 Jan; 4,27 Feb; 13 March; 9,30 April; 1,8,9,31 May; 4,6,28 June; 1,11 July; 6,18 Aug; 30 Oc; 9 Dect (& see "First W.W" & "Second W.W" & 'peace')
'War of the Worlds' - 30 Oct
Wassailing - 24 Dec
Water - 12 Jan; 14 April; 3,16,21 Aug; 8 Sept; Vol 3 Appendix of Prayers 6,8,9,10
Waterloo - 17 Jan; 18 June
Weakness - e.g. 14 Sept
Wealth - e.g. Family Fast Days, Vols 1 & 3 (see 'riches')
Welles, Orson - 30 Oct
Wellesley, Arthur - see 'Wellington'
Wellington - 17 Jan; 18 June; 13 Sept
Wells, HG - 30 Oct
Wembley Stadium - 24 Sept
Westminster Abbey - 9,29 July; 6 Sept; 14 Oct; 11 Nov
Whale - 2 March
Wheat - 19 Feb, 16 March
Whispering Gallery - 19 May
'White Christmas' - 6 Sept
Whitman, Walt - 26 May
Whitsun - see Pentecost
Wigan Warriors RUFC - 14 Sept
Wilberforce, William - 29 July
Wilde, Oscar - 24 May
William I, the Conqueror - 14 Oct; 20 Nov

William III, King - 13 Feb; 31 July; Holy Thursday in Volume 1
Wilson, Gordon & Marie - 8 Nov
Wilson, Harold - 30 Sept
Wilson, Bishop Leonard - 23 Nov
Wind - Pentecost, Vol 2
Wind in Willows, The - 8 March
Windows - 31 July
Winton, Nicholas - 18 Dec
Wine - 30 March; 15 July
Wisdom - e.g. 4,7,9 Jan ; 11,18 May; 4,16, 25 July; 28 Oct; 16 Nov; Vol 2 Appendix of Prayers - 16
Witness - 17 Feb; 8 July (see 'Martyr')
'Wizard of Oz' - 19 Aug
Wojtyla, Karol - 18 Dec
Wonder - 8 Jan; 10,12,16 Feb; 8,14 March; 11,12,13 April; 1 June; 3,22 July; 2 Aug; 18 Sept; 19 Dec (see also Introduction and 'appreciation', 'creation', 'space'); Vol 2 Appendix of Prayers
Word - 22 July; 22 Nov
Work - 11 Jan; 18 March; 1 May; 14 July; 23 Aug; Vol 2 Appendix of Prayers - e.g. 52
World - 29 March
World Cup - 30 July
Wreath, Advent - Appendix of Vol 3
Wren, Sir Christopher - 26 Feb
Wynne, David - 27 Sept

X-rays - 10 Feb

Year - 1,16 Jan; 9,21 Sept
Yeltsin, Boris - 17 July
Yeomen of the Guard - 5 Nov
'Yes' - 18 Sept
Yom Kippur - 8 Oct
York - 25 Oct

Zacchaeus - 23 Feb; 29 April; 11 June; Vol 3 Appendix of Prayers 34 and its Introduction
'Zakat' - 29 Oct